Cognitive Semantics
and the Polish Dative

Cognitive Linguistics Research
9

Editors
René Dirven
Ronald W. Langacker
John R. Taylor

Mouton de Gruyter
Berlin · New York

Cognitive Semantics and the Polish Dative

Ewa Dąbrowska

1997
Mouton de Gruyter
Berlin · New York

Mouton de Gruyter (formerly Mouton, The Hague)
is a Division of Walter de Gruyter & Co., Berlin.

∞ Printed on acid-free paper
which falls within
the guidelines of the ANSI
to ensure permanence and durability.

Library of Congress Cataloging-in-Publication Data

Dąbrowska, Ewa, 1963−
  Cognitive semantics and the Polish dative / Ewa Dąbrowska.
    p.   cm. − (Cognitive linguistics research ; 9)
  Includes bibliographical references and index.
  ISBN 3-11-015218-5 (cloth : alk. paper)
  1. Polish language−Case. 2. Polish language−Semantics. 3. Cognitive grammar. 4. Grammar, Comparative and general−Case. I. Title. II. Series.
  PG6221.D33   1997
  491.8′55−dc21   97-23314
                                                  CIP

Die Deutsche Bibliothek − Cataloging-in-Publication Data

Dąbrowska, Ewa:
Cognitive semantics and the Polish dative / Ewa Dąbrowska. − Berlin ; New York : Mouton de Gruyter, 1997
  (Cognitive linguistics research ; 9)
  ISBN 3-11-015218-5

© Copyright 1997 by Walter de Gruyter & Co., D-10785 Berlin
All rights reserved, including those of translation into foreign languages. No part of this book may be reproduced or transmitted in any form or by any means, electronic or mechanical, including photocopy, recording, or any information storage and retrieval system, without permission in writing from the publisher.
Printing: Gerike GmbH, Berlin
Binding: Lüderitz & Bauer, Berlin

To my parents, and to Michael

Contents

Acknowledgments ix

A note on interlinear glosses x

Chapter 1: Introduction 1

1.1. Some historical threads 2
1.1.1. Lists of "uses" 2
1.1.2. Semantic invariants 3
1.1.3. Case grammar 4

1.2. Theoretical framework and basic concepts 4
1.2.1. The network model 5
1.2.2. Conventional imagery 7
1.2.3. Action chains and grammatical relations 11
1.2.4. The participant/setting distinction and setting-subject constructions 12

1.3. Overview 14

Chapter 2: The meaning of the dative 16

2.1. The concept of personal sphere 16

2.2. The dative and the semantics of the verb 24
2.2.1. Verbs of acquisition and loss 25
2.2.2. Verbs of making available/unavailable 28
2.2.3. Verbs of helping and interference 32
2.2.4. Beneficiary datives 35
2.2.5. Verbs of ordering, obligation, and allowing 36
2.2.6. Lack of control over one's actions 37
2.2.7. Verbs of compliance and resistance 38
2.2.8. Private sphere 40
2.2.9. Sphere of awareness 41
2.2.10. Verbs of communication 47
2.2.11. Allative uses of the dative 49

2.3.	The ethic dative	55
2.3.1.	The problem	55
2.3.2.	Ethic datives and imperatives	58
2.3.3.	Ethic datives and empathy	59
2.3.4.	Ethic datives and self-determination	61
2.4.	The structure of the dative category	63
2.5.	Conclusion	68

Chapter 3: Dative and nominative experiencers — 69

3.1.	Preliminaries	71
3.1.1.	The dative patient-subject construction	71
3.1.2.	An interlude on *się* and impersonal constructions	73
3.1.3.	Folk models of the mind	77
3.2.	Perception vs. hallucination	80
3.3.	"Reasoned" convictions vs. mistakes and idiosyncratic associations	82
3.4.	"Wanting": definite intention vs. wistful longing or biological drive	83
3.5.	Attitudes: Judgement vs. natural inclination	86
3.6.	Subjective experience vs. objective properties	90
3.7.	Nominative-dative verbs	93
3.8.	Conclusion	96

Chapter 4: Dative and accusative targets — 98

4.1.	Introduction	98
4.2.	Verbs of communication	99
4.2.1.	Verbs of telling	100
4.2.2.	Call for action verbs	101
4.2.3.	Verbs of teaching	102
4.2.4.	Verbs of deception	103
4.2.5.	Verbs of verbal commendation	104
4.2.6.	Verbs of verbal aggression	105
4.2.7.	Verbs of greeting and leave-taking	108

4.2.8.	Dative vs. accusative construal of communication events: A summary	109
4.3.	Bodily experience	111
4.3.1.	The problem	111
4.3.2.	Affected body parts: Coding options	114
4.3.3.	Focus on the affected body part vs. focus on the affected person	115
4.3.4.	Dative vs. accusative construal: sublexical and explicit reference to affected body part	119
4.3.5.	Predicates of physical sensation	121
4.3.6.	Conclusion	126

Chapter 5: The dative and prepositional constructions 127

5.1.	Expressing the beneficiary: the dative and prepositional phrases with *dla* 'for'	127
5.2.	Target person, source and goal: the dative and prepositional phrases with *do* 'to' and *od* 'from'	129
5.3.	Personal sphere vs. location: the dative and prepositional phrases with *u* 'at'	132
5.4.	Dative and prepositional constructions: A summary	134
5.5.	Prepositional constructions with datives	135
5.5.1.	Prepositional constructions with *ku* 'to, towards'	136
5.5.2.	Prepositional constructions with *dzięki* 'thanks to' and *przeciw(ko)* 'against'	137
5.5.3.	Prepositional constructions with *wbrew* 'in defiance of, contrary to'	139

Chapter 6: The personal sphere in other languages 143

6.1.	The English verb *have*	143
6.2.	External NP constructions in Japanese	154
6.2.1.	The personal sphere in Japanese culture	154
6.2.2.	Japanese particles	155
6.2.3.	External NP constructions and the personal sphere	159
6.2.4.	Linguistic construal of mental experience in Japanese	160
6.2.5.	The sphere of potency	164
6.2.6.	Causatives	165
6.2.7.	Indirect passives	167

6.2.8. The honorific use of *rareru* — 170
6.2.9. Additional support: Parallels with locative constructions — 172

6.3. The personal sphere in Polish, English and Japanese — 173

6.4. A word on English ditransitives and the "dative" *ni* in Japanese — 176

Chapter 7: Conclusion — 180

7.1. Comparison with other analyses — 180
7.1.1. Wierzbicka — 180
7.1.2. Miller — 189
7.1.3. Smith — 191
7.1.4. Janda — 192
7.1.5. Rudzka-Ostyn — 195

7.2. Schemas and prototypes — 198

7.3. The status of semantic roles — 201

7.4. The importance of conventional imagery — 203

7.5. Motivation and predictability — 205

7.6. Final remarks — 206

Notes — 208

Bibliography — 227

Index — 237

Acknowledgments

I wish to thank John Taylor and Ron Langacker, who read and commented on several drafts of the manuscript and generously offered much-needed advice and encouragement. Without their guidance and support this would have been a very different book.

I am also much indebted to René Dirven and two anonymous reviewers for their helpful suggestions, and to my informants, especially my parents, Barbara Dąbrowska and Mieczysław Dąbrowski, who patiently answered innumerable questions about the Polish data at odd times of day and night. Rosa Kadokura, Mark Taniguchi and Sawako Irie helped with the Japanese data, and Neil Bermel with the Czech and Russian.

A very special thanks is due to Roman Kalisz, who first introduced me to the world of linguistics and has been my teacher and friend ever since.

Most of all, I wish to thank my husband Michael Pincombe, without whose help and support, both moral and practical, this monograph would never have seen the light of day.

A note on interlinear glosses

Interlinear glosses have been provided for all foreign language examples except where the latter are structurally identical to their English counterparts or where the grammatical details are irrelevant to the point under discussion. To keep the glosses maximally transparent, all irrelevant details (such as agreement inflections on verbs and adjectives) have been omitted, and wherever possible, morphologically complex forms are simply translated as wholes. Thus *Anna spała* 'Anna slept' would be glossed as in (i) rather than as in (ii), since the fact that the verb is feminine and third person singular is not of particular interest in a discussion of case marking, and the English translation of the verb indicates the tense.

(i)   *Anna   spała.*
        Anna:NOM slept

(ii)   *Anna   spała.*
        Anna:NOM sleep:PAST:FEM:3SG

The only exceptions to this are impersonal constructions (where the verb is translated as 'it Vs' – cf. (iii)) and where the subject left out in the original and hence only the verb can provide clues as to its identity, as in (iv) below.

(iii)   *W Anglii   zawsze pada.*
        in England:LOC always it rains
        'It always rains in England.'

(iv)   *Jeszcze spała.*
        still   she slept
        'She was still sleeping.'

Abbreviations used in interlinear glosses:

ACC	accusative
COND	conditional
COMP	complementizer
DAT	dative
EMPH	emphatic
GEN	genitive
HAB	habitual
HON	honorific
IMPF	imperfective
INST	instrumental
INTERROG	interrogative

INTR	detransitivizer
NOM	nominative
NOMIN	nominalizer
PASS	passive
PF	perfective
REFL	reflexive
TOP	topic
VOL	volitional

Chapter 1: Introduction

Case is a troublesome linguistic phenomenon. While other grammatical categories, such as number, person, or tense, can be related to aspects of the non-linguistic environment in a fairly straightforward way, it is not easy to find real-world correlates of the nominative or the dative case. Traditional grammars attempt to define cases in semantic terms by describing their "uses", but the apparent disparity and the sheer number of these can give the linguist a headache. For example, the genitive case in Polish expresses the following relationships (among others):

(1)   possession of an object: *ubranie Artura* 'Artur's clothing'

possession of a quality: *inteligencja Magdy* 'Magda's intelligence'

part-whole: *okładka książki* 'the book's cover'

contents/quantity: *filiżanka herbaty* 'a cup of tea'

spatial association: *pole bitwy* 'battle field'

temporal association: *dzień zwycięstwa* 'victory day'

subjective nominalization: *szczekanie psów* 'the barking of the dogs'

objective nominalization: *tresura psów* 'the training of dogs'

the direct object of a negated verb: *Nie czytałam tej książki* 'I haven't read that book'

partitive object: *Chcesz chleba?* 'Do you want bread?'

object of a verb designating a situation of limited duration: *Pożycz mi długopisu* 'Lend me a pen.'

Moreover, the occurrence of a particular ending is often either determined by the presence of a governing verb or preposition (for example, *słuchać* 'to listen' and *koło* 'next to' require the genitive; *pomóc* 'to help' and *dzięki* 'thanks to' require the dative; and *machać* 'to wave' and *z* 'with' the instrumental), or the case ending seems to be merely a formal exponent of a grammatical function (for example, the nominative is the case of the subject, the accusative is associated with the direct object, and the dative with the indirect object). For all these reasons, many linguists interested in case have shied away from semantics and attempted to describe the category in purely syntactic terms.[1]

This study deals with the semantics of the dative case in Polish. My main goal will be to show that it has a meaning distinct from that of the other cases and that its meaning co-determines the syntactic organization of clauses. I will also show that the decision to use a particular case hinges on how the speaker chooses to construe a particular situation for expressive purposes, which in turn depends on a host of semantic as well as pragmatic factors.

Thus, we will be exploring territory which is out of bounds for all those theories which claim that grammar is independent of semantics. The purpose of our journey of exploration will be to discover how language works, not to theorize about how it should work. This means looking at data, and we will see plenty of it. The final outcome may be surprising to those used to strictly formal accounts. A semantically-based description, as we shall see, not only covers a much wider range of phenomena, but is simpler as well. In place of the labyrinth of rules and exceptions that one is confronted with in traditional descriptions, we will find a straightforward semantic structure which will allow us to account for the occurrence of the dative in a variety of constructions, including lexically-governed datives.

We will begin our journey by looking at several traditional approaches to the study of case and considering the difficulties that they encountered. This is the subject of the next section; in the remaining parts of the chapter, I will briefly outline the basic assumptions of the theoretical framework within which this study is conducted.

1.1. Some historical threads

It is not the purpose of this introduction to provide a historical review of the study of case, as this can be found in almost any monograph dealing with this topic (see e.g. Fillmore 1968, Anderson 1971, Kempf 1978, Smith 1987, Blake 1994). However, a brief critique of the traditional approaches will provide a good point of departure for the subsequent discussion.

1.1.1. Lists of "uses"

Most of the established traditional grammars (e.g. Bartnicka-Dąbkowska, Jaworski & Sinielnikoff 1964, Benni et al. 1923, Szober 1959) provide, for each case, a list of its "uses" which are assigned labels such as "dative of interest", "of reference", "possession", "purpose", etc. The exact number of these differs from author to author, but in all accounts of this kind case categories emerge as rather arbitrary collections of disparate functions which lack internal structure or cohesion. Although authors of such descriptions occasionally hint that a particular use is related to another one, they are unable to account for the relationships in a systematic way, and hence fail to capture the psychological unity of case categories. Moreover, the same label is often associated with more than one case, and no attempt is made to explain what determines which case category will be chosen to convey a particular meaning in a specific context, or what semantic consequences a particular choice might have. For example, in Polish both dative and genitive noun phrases can designate a possessive relationship, but traditional grammars do not indicate if and how the dative of possession differs from the genitive of possession. Or, to take another example, according to Szober (1959), three cases, the genitive, the dative, and the accusative can be used to express the notions of 'direction' and 'purpose'. What Szober does not explain is why the same meaning should be signaled by three different cases or why these two uses should repeatedly be subsumed under the same category.

1.1.2. Semantic invariants

Faced with the obvious inadequacy of mere lists of uses, many linguists strove to provide a more systematic account of the semantics of case. They attempted to isolate for each case its general, invariant meaning – the common denominator of all the different contextual variants – and then to show how these general meanings enter into relationships with one another to form a system. The best known in this tradition are Jakobson's feature analysis and various versions of the localist theory.[2]

Without going into the details, I will point out the most basic shortcomings of this approach. First, the meanings postulated for each of the cases are necessarily very abstract – so abstract that one begins to wonder whether they have any semantic content at all. Jakobson (1958 [1971]) claims that the Russian dative can be defined as [+DIRECTIONAL/ASCRIPTIVE, -QUANTIFYING, +MARGINAL/PERIPHERAL]. Perhaps this is an accurate definition, but what exactly do these features mean, and how does one determine if a particular participant has them? In many instances, the proposed meanings were both *too broad and too narrow at the same time*. For example, Miller (1974) argues that the basic meaning of the dative in Russian is to express 'movement towards', either concrete (as in *He flew from Moscow to Kiev*) or abstract (*He gave me some ideas*). However, many uses of the dative are purely stative (e.g. *Petru ponjatna teorija* 'Peter (DAT) understands the theory') and thus fail to meet this characterization. On the other hand, the accusative could also be said to express an abstract movement towards the object. (See section 7.1.2 for a more detailed discussion of Miller's localist analysis.)

Another weakness of this approach is that it all but disregards the internal diversification of each case category. The various 'uses' or 'contextual variants' *are* distinct, and cannot be derived from a single abstract characterization: no general rule or 'principle of implementation' can predict that the dative can be used to signal inalienable possession in *Adam patrzył Ewie na nogi* 'Adam was looking at Ewa's legs' but not in **Adam patrzył Ewie na łokieć* 'Adam was looking at Ewa's elbow', or that the verb *przysłuchwać się* 'to listen (carefully)' requires a dative object while *słuchać* 'to listen' requires the accusative. Each 'use' or 'contextual variant' must be learned individually and specified individually in an adequate linguistic description.

Proponents of 'semantic invariants', then, while attempting to uncover the internal semantic unity of case categories, either fail to acknowledge or gloss over the existence of numerous specialized, unpredictable, quirky usages. In this respect, the abstractionist approach is the reverse of the cataloguing approach, which focuses on diversity at the expense of internal cohesion. Neither of the two approaches, however, can handle both unity *and* diversity within a category.[3]

1.1.3. Case grammar

Case grammarians attacked the problem from the opposite end. Rather than taking the actual morphological forms as the point of departure and assigning meanings to them, they began with the semantics. They postulated a set of what seemed to be sensible distinctions for languages to make (participant roles such as agent, patient, instrument, location, goal, etc.) as fundamental categories of linguistic organization and then attempted to relate these to the actual grammatical markers occurring in languages. Inevitably, it was found that "surface" structure obscured and distorted the relationships supposedly present in "deep" structure. One "deep" case could have several different "surface" realizations, and the same "surface" exponent could correspond to several "deep" cases.

Because of these difficulties, much of the later work in the case grammar tradition (e.g. Fillmore 1977, Nilsen 1972) abandoned the claim that deep cases were associated with surface markers. This, of course, begged the question of the relationship between deep and surface case; and it left case grammar on very shaky foundations, since it had never developed a satisfactory methodology even for determining how many case roles there were, let alone their semantic properties. Inevitably, very different arrays of deep cases were postulated by different linguists[4] – a serious embarrassment for a theory that claimed that these were universal concepts of fundamental importance for linguistic organization.[5] With little more than vague intuitions to support their analyses, case grammarians moved further and further away from the realm of linguistic facts and deeper and deeper into speculation.

1.2. Theoretical framework and basic concepts

This study will be conducted within the theoretical framework of cognitive linguistics (Lakoff 1987, Langacker 1987a, 1991a, 1991b, Rudzka-Ostyn 1988). One of the basic postulates of this approach to language is that grammar is inherently symbolic: its very *raison d'être* is the structuring and symbolization of conceptual content. Cognitive linguistics maintains that there are no dummies, no meaningless form words – all linguistic forms, including grammatical morphemes, are meaningful. My primary concern, therefore, will be, first, to define the meaning of the dative case and secondly, to show that the proposed semantic characterization differentiates it from other grammatical categories. First, however, I must introduce some basic conceptual tools of cognitive grammar. What follows is a very brief outline of some basic concepts which will be appealed to in later chapters. For a more systematic exposition of the framework, the reader is referred to the sources cited above (or, for a very brief introduction, see Langacker 1988).

1.2.1. The network model

Even a cursory glance at the distribution of case forms will reveal that each case category has a number of different functions. This fact, of course, is explicitly acknowledged in all descriptions which provide lists of uses for each case. The abstractionist search for the semantic invariant, on the other hand, reflects the intuition that the different uses of a case form a unified category. As I pointed out earlier, neither of these approaches could handle both the unity and the internal diversity of case categories. Cognitive linguistics, on the other hand, offers a conceptual tool which enables the linguist to address both aspects of category structure – namely, the concept of a semantic *network* (Langacker 1988, 1991a: 369ff, 1991b: 266ff). Most linguistic units, whether lexical or grammatical, are polysemous, their various senses forming a network held together by various "categorizing relationships". These include:

1. *Extension from a prototype*: a member of a category is often related to a more "established" member by some general cognitive principle, e.g. partial similarity, metaphor, metonymy, or image schema transformation (see Lakoff 1987 for an exhaustive discussion of semantic extension). For example, *warm* when used to describe someone's personality is a metaphorical extension of the temperature sense.

2. *Schematization*: the relationship between a *schema* (an abstract characterization that is fully compatible with all the members of a category or subcategory) and an expression that instantiates it. For example, the expression *dog* in the sense of 'canine' is schematic for the sense of *dog* meaning 'male canine'.

3. *Mutual similarity*: members of a category may resemble each other in some respects without one being obviously more basic than the other. For example, the game of chess shares a number of properties with checkers, but neither is a more prototypical member of the category *game*.

Figure 1 below (adapted from Langacker 1991b: 267) is a graphical representation of part of the network of senses of the lexical item *run*.[6] Dashed arrows represent extension, solid arrows represent schematization, and double headed arrows represent mutual similarity. The boxes represent the various senses of the lexeme. They are arranged in several levels representing different levels of schematization: the lowest level corresponds to local schemas (generalizations from experience), while the levels above correspond to higher-level generalizations. The heavy lines around one of the boxes symbolize the fact that it is the most deeply "entrenched" sense, i.e. the category prototype.

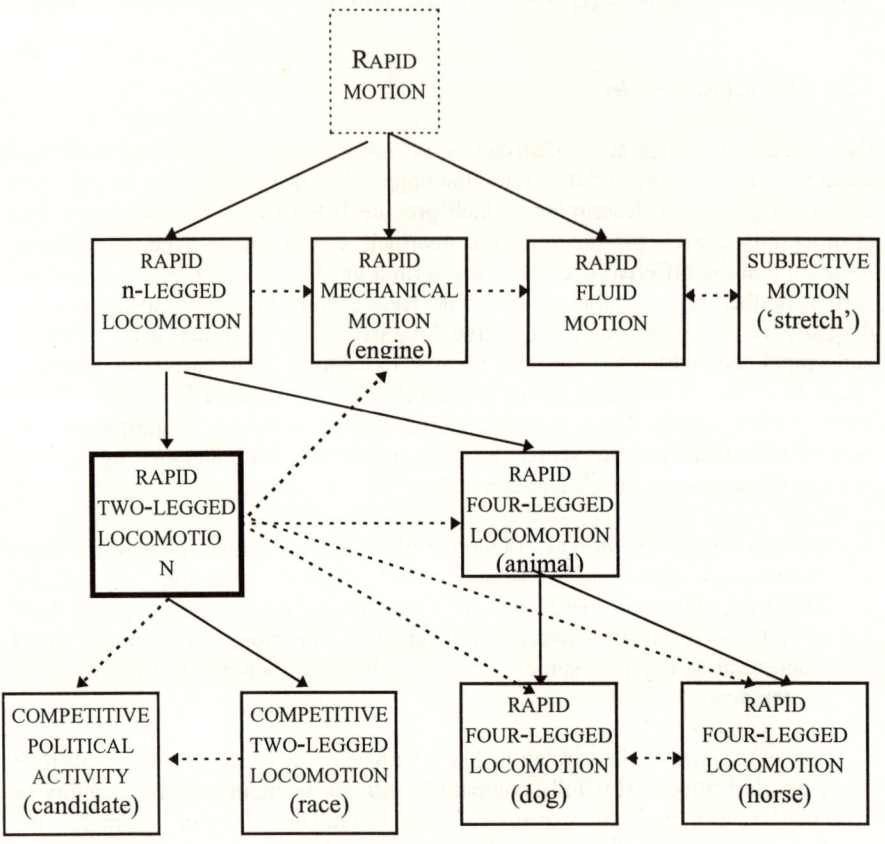

Figure 1. A fragment of the network for *run*
(Adapted from Langacker 1991b: 267)

I will assume, following Langacker, that 'rapid two-legged locomotion' is the cognitively most basic sense, or the category prototype. 'Rapid four-legged locomotion' and 'competitive political activity' are extensions of this basic sense, the former motivated by similarity to the prototype and the latter by metaphor. In a larger network, many of the extended senses will often have extensions of their own, thus forming chains of senses in which any two adjacent links are closely related, while distant links have very little or nothing in common. In our example, *run* meaning 'stretch' (as in *The road ran between the hills*) shares a number of features with the 'fluid motion' sense (e.g. *The river ran between the hills*), but is very different from the 'competitive political activity' sense.

As the category grows "outwards" through semantic extension, is also grows "upwards" through schematization. In fact, the two are part and parcel of the same process, since it is precisely the similarity embodied in the schema that makes extension possible in the first place. The higher-level schemas capture generalizations that speakers extract from the local schemas. This, however, does not mean that the more local schemas are redundant. In fact, as Langacker points out, there are good reasons to believe that it is the more specific local and intermediate-level schemas that are used in assembling new expressions and in interpreting other speakers' utterances. The higher-level schemas have "more of an organizing function than an active computational one" (Langacker 1991a: 133): they capture the common features shared by the various local schemas and thus hold the category together. Be that as it may, local schemas are necessary because the high level schemas are often too general, and would admit various non-members into the category. For example, flying is an example of 'rapid motion' (and hence it is fully compatible with the specifications of the most general schema in Figure 1), but airplanes do not run: they fly. Moreover, for many linguistic expressions it is simply impossible to extract a superschema that will be compatible with all of their senses and still specific enough to be of any use, though they may well be local schemas which capture similarities between closely related senses. In our example, 'rapid motion' subsumes neither 'competitive political activity' nor the 'stretching' sense described earlier.

I will return to the question of the role of local and global schemas later in this study. The important point to bear in mind for now is that the network model captures both the unity and the internal diversity of a category, and hence overcomes the limitations of the approaches discussed earlier. And since grammatical morphemes are, as a rule, multiply polysemous, the network model is particularly well-suited to representing the internal organization of grammatical categories.

1.2.2. Conventional imagery

Cognitive linguistics, I indicated earlier, maintains that all linguistic forms, including grammatical morphemes, are meaningful. Meaning in cognitive linguistics is held to be equivalent to conceptualization, and, crucially, it comprises not just "content" but also *imagery*, or how semantic content is *construed*. From the point of view of linguistic coding, one of the most important of all human cognitive capacities is the ability to structure, or construe, the same content in alternate ways. The following discussion will only give a very general idea of the kinds of cognitive processes involved; the interested reader should refer to Langacker 1987a, 1988, 1991a and 1991b for further details.

Perhaps the most mundane aspect of imagery is the imposition of a profile on a base. The *base* is the knowledge structure within which an expression is understood and defined; it corresponds to Fillmore's notion of *frame* (Fillmore 1975, 1978, Fillmore & Atkins 1992) and Lakoff's *idealized cognitive model* (Lakoff 1987). For example, the concept of "right triangle" is the base for the notion of *hypotenuse* (it would be impossible to explain what a hypotenuse was to someone who did not have the concept of "right triangle"); the kinship network is the base for the word *uncle;* a cognitive model of a "commercial event" is the base for *buy,* and so on. The *profile* is a particular substructure within the base that an expression designates. *Uncle* and *niece* evoke the same kinship network as their base, but they have different profiles, and hence differ in meaning. The meanings of the expressions *go, gone,* and *away* provide a more subtle example. *Go* and *gone* have the same base: the conception of one entity (which we will call the *trajector*) moving away from another entity (the *landmark*), but different profiles: *go* profiles a series of states leading to the final configuration, while *gone* profiles only the final state. On the other hand, *gone* and *away* have the same profile (they both designate the same configuration, i.e. a trajector located at some distance from the landmark), but different bases (the base of *gone* is the process profiled by *go,* while the base of *away* is simply the spatial domain). (See Langacker 1991b: 6-7 for further discussion of this example.)

As a final example of profiling, consider the expressions *investigate* and *investigation.* As far as actual semantic content is concerned, the two words are identical; but they contrast semantically because they impose different images on the same content. *Investigate* profiles a *process*, or a series of states occurring at different points in time; *investigation,* on the other hand, involves conceptual reification, or construing an event as a type of "thing". *Thing* in cognitive grammar is a technical term defined as "a region in some domain", where a region is "a set of interconnected entities". The term covers not just physical objects, but various abstract entities as well, including stretches of time, colors, and qualities. Thus, *week* designates a region in the temporal domain; the noun *blue* designates a region in color space; *beauty* designates a region in quality space, and so on. Now the component states of an event (such an investigation) include the same participants and occur at adjacent points in time. Because of these interconnections, the component states constitute an implicit region. A nominalization such as *investigation* profiles this region (and backgrounds the temporal dimension). Thus, the noun and the verb impose contrasting images on the same content: they have the same base, but different profiles.[7]

While nouns designate "things", verbs, prepositions, adjectives, and adverbs designate "relations" between two or more entities. When humans perceive relations, they tend to impose a certain perspective on the participating entities. Specifically, they tend to view one of the participants as the central element of a scene – a figure that stands out against a background of other entities. In cognitive grammar, the more salient entity is called the *trajector*, while salient elements of the background are called *landmarks*. For instance, in (2), *the Volvo* is the trajector and *the Mercedes* the landmark; in (3), the roles are reversed. These particular examples involve a spatial relationship, but the terms "trajector" and "landmark" are applicable to any kind of relation. Note that complex linguistic expressions have several levels of trajector/landmark organization. In (4), *Chris* is the trajector of *put* and *the book* its landmark; however the latter is also the trajector of *on*, while *the table* is its landmark.

(2) *The Volvo is in front of the Mercedes.*
(3) *The Mercedes is behind the Volvo.*
(4) *Chris put the book on the table.*

In most cases, some portion of the scene is inherently more salient than the rest and hence is the natural choice for the trajector. For example, a moving object is naturally perceived as the figure against a stationary background; and the active sentient initiator of an action is more likely to be construed as trajector than an inanimate and passive undergoer. This prototypical alignment is reflected in (4), where the agent is the clausal trajector, while the displaced object is the trajector of the preposition. On the other hand, in examples (2) and (3) there is no obvious asymmetry, and the choice of trajector is imposed by the conceptualizer.

Although some choices for the trajector role are cognitively more natural than others, speakers enjoy a certain amount of freedom in their choice even when the relationship in question is inherently asymmetrical. The humorous effect of (5) is due largely to the fact that the displaced object (the Scotch and soda) is construed as landmark, while what would normally have been the landmark (i.e. the "container" into which the Scotch is poured) becomes the trajector.

(5) *He was seated at the Savoy bar when he told me this, rather feverishly putting himself outside a Scotch and soda.* (P.G. Wodehouse, *The World of Mr. Mulliner*)

To take a somewhat less literary example, consider

(6) *The Volvo crashed into the Mercedes.*
(7) *The Mercedes crashed into the Volvo.*
(8) *The Volvo and the Mercedes crashed.*

All three of these sentences could be descriptions of the same event (presumably from the point of view of the driver of the Mercedes, the driver of the Volvo, and a neutral observer). Even so, they clearly differ in meaning, and the differences are due entirely to portraying one or both of the participants as the figure in the relational profile: choosing the Volvo as trajector has the effect of highlighting its causal role in the crash and downplaying the role played by the other car, and similarly for the other options.

Subtly different meanings also result when a speaker explicitly mentions an aspect of a scene which remains implicit in another description. *Triangle* and *three-sided polygon* may be extensionally equivalent, but the latter description emphasizes the fact that the object in question belongs to the class of polygons and that it has three sides. These two facts are also part of the meaning of the word *triangle*, but they remain implicit when this term is used. For a grammatical example (taken from Langacker 1991b: 13ff) of the same phenomenon consider the following two sentences:

(9) *Bill sent a walrus to Joyce.*
(10) *Bill sent Joyce a walrus.*

Both of the above examples describe a situation in which one participant (Bill) causes another participant (a walrus) to move from one location to another; the endpoint of the movement is wherever Joyce is. However, they differ in meaning because they impose slightly different images on the same content, and thus highlight different aspects of the scene. Example (9) contains an element that specifically designates the path traversed by the walrus, namely the preposition *to*. This has the effect of giving greater prominence to the path. The notion of path is also present in (10), since it is implicit in the meaning of *sent*, but it is less salient. On the other hand, the conceptualization embodied in (10) accords greater prominence to the result of Bill's action – namely, the fact that the walrus is now located in the region under Joyce's control. The possessive relationship is symbolically represented by the juxtaposition of *Joyce* and *a walrus*.

Thus, the speaker can construe the same content in different ways by imposing contrasting images, which has the effect of highlighting different aspects of the situation. It must be stressed, however, that the speaker's freedom is not absolute: it is constrained by the fact that *imagery is conventional*. That is to say, the grammar and lexicon of a language make available to the speaker a range of options, and the speaker chooses the one that best matches his communicative intentions. The options available in one language may well be different from those available in another; and often the grammar imposes a particular construal. For example, a large number of very small and similar objects can be seen as either as a (more or less) homogenous mass (and coded as a mass noun) or as a collection of separate objects (and coded as a plural count noun). Different languages often require different choices for the same category of things: witness Polish *fasola* (a mass noun) and English *beans,* English *hair* and French *cheveux,*[8] Russian *višnja* 'morellos' (a mass noun) and its Polish cognate *wiśnia* (a plural count noun). Or to take a different example: the Japanese equivalent of *John is tall* is something like 'As for John, stature is high' (*John-wa se-ga takai*). The two languages require a different choice of trajector: *John* in English, *se* 'stature' in Japanese. Both construals are logical in their own ways: strictly speaking, *John is tall* provides information about John's body, not John; on the other hand, the latter is certainly a good mental abbreviation for the former.

The existence of such inter-language differences does not entail that grammar determines, or even strongly constrains, our thought processes. Langacker repeatedly points out that the effect of imagery in structuring conceptual content is fairly superficial since any language will offer its speakers a vast array of alternative conceptualizations to choose from. Moreover, speakers are able to shift from one construal to another with remarkable ease. For example, speakers are able to construe the same entity as either a thing or a process, either a homogenous mass or a collection of objects, and so on.

1.2.3. Action chains and grammatical relations

By recognizing the role of imagery in grammar, cognitive linguistics is able to provide semantic characterizations of grammatical relations. We have seen above that the subject can be defined as the clausal trajector, i.e. the figure in the relationship profiled by the finite verb of the clause. The direct object relationship is defined against the backdrop of a cognitive structure which Langacker calls the *billiard-ball model*.

The billiard-ball model is a simplified model of reality which embodies the following beliefs: (a) the world consists of discrete objects; (b) some of these objects are capable of moving about on their own (they have their own energy), while others receive their energy from outside sources; (c) when one object hits another object, energy is transmitted to the impacted object, which may cause the latter to move and interact with another object, which in turn can interact with a third object, and so on. Such a sequence of events is called an *action chain*; it is represented graphically in Figure 2.

Figure 2. An example of an action chain

We use the billiard-ball model to think not just about physical causation, but also about various more abstract kinds of interactions, such as social manipulation. Let us assume that Figure 2 represents the following chain of events: John tells Peter to break the window; Peter picks up a stone and throws it; the stone flies through the air and hits the window; the window breaks. Here are several ways that aspects of this little drama can be encoded linguistically:

(11) a. *John told Peter to break the window.*
(11) b. *Peter threw the stone.*
(11) c. *The stone broke the window.*
(11) d. *Peter broke the window.*

The sentences in (11) profile different parts of the action chain: (11a) profiles the first link; (11b) the second link; (11c) the third, and (11d) the second and the third. In all of these sentences, the subject is consistently the *head of the profiled portion of the action chain* – that is, the participant furthest "upstream" with respect to energy flow – while the object is consistently its tail (the entity furthest "downstream"). Now the head of an action chain is cognitively more salient than the tail (it is the source of the energy for the action, and hence the more active participant), so it is normally also the clausal trajector, i.e. the subject. The qualification "normally" is necessary because not all subjects are action-chain heads. The subjects of stative predicates such as *(be) tall* are one obvious counterexample; the subjects of passive clauses are another.[9] Both of these, however, meet the definition of subject given earlier (i.e. "clausal trajector").[10] Direct objects, on the other hand, are consistently tails: the upstream participant in a passive clause is not the object.

"Tail of the profiled portion of the action chain" is not quite general enough to accommodate all direct objects: for example, it does not cover the object of perception or cognition in sentences with mental experience predicates, such as *the accident* in *Sam saw the accident*. However, the relationship between the perceiver/cognizer and the object of perception/cognition bears certain similarities to the relationship between the agent and the patient of an action: in both cases, the subject participant is more active and can legitimately be viewed as the "source" of the activity. Moreover, as we shall see in chapter 3, mental experience is often construed metaphorically as manipulation of mental objects such as ideas and memories. It is not surprising, therefore, that languages tend to extend whatever grammatical means is available for coding the patient to mark the object of mental experience as well. In order to accommodate these less prototypical cases, it is necessary to reformulate our definition of direct object. We will therefore define the direct object as "the tail of an action chain or action-chain analogue".[11]

In Polish, subjects are expressed by NPs in the nominative case, while direct objects are accusative (or, when the verb is negated, genitive). For the purposes of this study, I will assume that Langacker's characterizations of subject and object also define the meaning of these two cases. I acknowledge that this is an oversimplification, since both of these cases have functions other than to code the subject and the object: for example, the nominative is also used as an alternative for the vocative when addressing a person, and the accusative occurs as the object of some prepositions. These, however, are specialized local senses which need not concern us here.

1.2.4. The participant/setting distinction and setting-subject constructions

Another important aspect of imagery is the distinction between participants and the setting. Langacker (1987c, 1990b) argues that we organize scenes in terms of participants who interact with each other in a setting. In (12), *Donna* and *her lover* are participants, while *in the park* and *at midnight* designate aspects of the setting.

(12)   *Donna met her lover in the park at midnight.*

Typically, participants are coded as subjects and objects, while elements of the setting are specified by means of prepositional phrases.

It must be stressed that the setting/participant distinction is imposed by the conceptualizer. The world does not consist of a set of settings and a set of participants: it consists of entities which can be construed either as settings or as participants – though some objects (such as parks, cities, islands) are more likely to be construed as settings, while others (people, animals, small easily manipulable objects) are more naturally thought of as participants. However, *our park* is construed as a participant in (13), while *your stomach* in (14) is a setting.

(13)   The local government wanted to turn our park into yet another parking lot, but the residents' association managed to save it.
(14)   A tapeworm is a parasite that lives in your stomach.

Although subjects are normally participants, they need not be. In fact, Langacker argues that some grammatical constructions are best analyzed as describing the relationship between an aspect of the setting (construed as clausal trajector) and the process occurring in it. In (15) below, the garden is the setting for the swarming; and in (16) and (17), midnight and the park, respectively, are the setting in which the strange encounters occur. Such setting-subject constructions may have participant-subject analogues which are identical in content (for example, the situation in (15) could also be described by saying *Bees are swarming in the garden*), but they differ in construal, since the decision to portray the setting as the figure in the profiled relationship renders it more prominent. The difference is represented graphically in Figure 3 below. 3(a) represents the actor-subject variant, 3(b) the setting-subject; heavy lines indicate prominence.

(15)   The garden is swarming with bees.
(16)   Midnight saw another strange encounter in the park.
(17)   This park has witnessed many strange encounters.

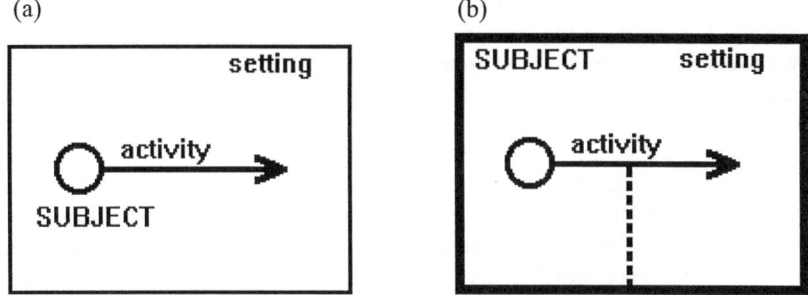

Figure 3. Participant construed as trajector (a)
and setting construed as trajector (b) (Langacker 1987c: 389)

This analysis neatly accounts for the semantics of setting-subject constructions (it is the bees, not the garden, that are doing the swarming), as well as their syntactic properties (the setting-subject is not the head of the profiled portion of the action head, so the NP following the verb cannot be its tail; hence, it is not the direct object of the verb, and the sentence does not passivize). It also explains why such usages are extremely unprototypical: settings are much less figure-worthy, so to speak, than are participants, and consequently are not normally chosen as clausal trajectors.

Langacker also suggests that the so-called "dummy subjects" are in fact abstract or highly schematic settings. He proposes that the existential *there* in (18) refers to the realm of existence (or, in some usages, to speaker/hearer awareness), while the "ambient" *it* of (19) is simply a maximally schematic setting:

(18)   *There are many good books on cognitive linguistics in our library.*
(19)   *It is very hot.*

1.3. Overview

The subject of this study is the semantics of the Polish dative case. For a cognitivist cases, just like all other linguistic categories, are meaningful. Our first task, then, will be to define the meaning of the Polish dative.

The primary function of a case inflection is to specify the role that a particular participant has in a relation (prototypically, the relation designated by the verb). A case ending, therefore, must have a relation as part of its base. Since case-inflected nouns are nominal expressions – they designate 'things' rather than 'relations' – I will assume that the profile of the case inflection itself is also nominal: that is to say, that case inflections profile (highly schematic) things. [12]

The obvious problem facing a semantically-inspired approach to case is this: participants can enter into any number of relationships, yet the number of grammatical devices available to code these relationships is highly constrained (Polish, for example, has only six cases, excluding the vocative). Hence, inevitably, the same case inflection will be used to mark participants engaged in a very wide array of different relationships. The challenge is to provide a semantic characterization that is both informative and concrete enough to provide a workable model of language use

In the pages that follow, I will argue that in spite of its apparent diversity of functions, the dative can be defined in semantic terms, and, moreover, that it makes sense for a language to subsume these seemingly heterogeneous uses under one category. I will also look at the two cases the dative most frequently contrasts with: the nominative and the accusative, and show how various semantic and pragmatic factors interact to determine the choice of case marking in specific situations. I will focus primarily on the relationship between the meaning of the case ending and the semantics of the verb in constructions which "govern" the dative, but will also discuss free datives in some detail. My approach will be the reverse of the case grammar strategy: rather than begin by postulating a set of "deep" cases, I will take the existing linguistic categories as the point of departure, and show that they are internally cohesive. (However, I will use case grammar terms such as "agent", "patient", and "experiencer". These are no more than convenient labels for certain relationships that humans perceive; I do not attribute any great theoretical significance to them.)

In the following chapter, I will survey the various "uses" of the dative case. I will propose a schematic characterization of the category which will cover most of its functions, and show how the specific uses instantiate it. I will also discuss relationships between uses and uncover local similarities that tie the category together. My second concern will be to elucidate the relationship between the verb and the dative argument in governed constructions.

The assertion that a linguistic category is meaningful is vacuous unless it can be shown to contrast semantically with other categories. Accordingly, the next two chapters will be devoted to a discussion of the contrast between the dative and the nominative to code the experiencer (Chapter 3) and the dative and the accusative to code the target of the process designated by the verb (Chapter 4). In chapter 5, I will discuss the contrast between the dative and various prepositional constructions which express similar meanings. Polish sometimes allows more than one option, and I will show that when this is the case, the choice of formal marking has semantic consequences. Usually, however, the verb requires a particular case or prepositional construction. Even then, the occurrence of the case markers is semantically motivated: the situation described by the verb, I will argue, is conventionally construed in a certain way, and I will explore the factors which motivate the lexicalization of that particular construal. In chapter 6 I will show that the concepts developed in this study are applicable to a range of data from other languages – English and Japanese. Finally, in Chapter 7 I will summarize the results of the analysis and compare my own approach with several other treatments of case conducted in similar theoretical frameworks.

Chapter 2: The meaning of the dative

2.1. The concept of personal sphere

The sentences in (20) describe a situation in which an agent (Piotr) did something to a patient (the car), which belongs to another individual (Robert). Both (20a) and (20b) assert that Piotr crashed the car; (20b) additionally specifies that Robert was affected by the event in some way – e.g. he will not be able to use the car for a while, having it repaired might cost him a lot of money, etc. Similarly, (21a) merely states that a madman killed Kowalski's wife, whereas (21b) has the additional implication that Kowalski was affected by her death. It is important to note that (21a) does not rule out this possibility; (21b), however, specifically invites such an interpretation.

(20) a. *Piotr rozbił samochód Roberta.*
Piotr:NOM crashed car:ACC Robert:GEN
'Piotr crashed Robert's car.'

(20) b. *Piotr rozbił Robertowi samochód.*
Piotr:NOM crashed Robert:DAT car:ACC
'Piotr has crashed Robert's car [and Robert was affected by this].'[13]

(21) a. *Jakiś szaleniec zamordował żonę Kowalskiego.*
some madman:NOM murdered wife:ACC Kowalski:GEN
'Some madman murdered Kowalski's wife.'

(21) b. *Jakiś szaleniec zamordował Kowalskiemu żonę.*
some madman:NOM murdered Kowalski:DAT wife:ACC
'Some madman murdered Kowalski's wife [and Kowalski was affected by this].'

I will use the term *target person* (borrowed from Wierzbicka 1988) to refer to individuals such as Robert in (20b) and Kowalski in (21b). How is this category to be defined?

Participants in a situation may be affected in a variety of ways. Objects are affected when a force is applied to them and they undergo a change of state as a result. Sentient beings, on the other hand, are also affected when their loved ones die, when their prized possessions are damaged or taken away, and when embarrassing details of their private lives are exposed to the public. To define the target person category, therefore, it is necessary to introduce the notion of *personal sphere*,[14] which comprises the persons, objects, locations, and facts sufficiently closely associated with an individual that any changes in them are likely to affect the individual as well. The target person (TP), then, is *an individual who is perceived as affected by an action, process, or state taking place within or impinging upon his personal sphere.* The dative case is the grammatical exponent of the target person role.

It should be noted that, unlike the direct participants in an event, i.e. the agent and the patient, the target person need not be present at the scene of the action, and may not experience any effects until well after the action has been completed. It would be appropriate to say (21b) even if Kowalski were happily drinking beer at a bar at the time of the murder. However, the target person must be at least potentially affectable. If the speaker knows that Kowalski drank himself to death that night, (21b) is no longer felicitous.

What exactly does the personal sphere comprise? The body is certainly one of its most central elements, since an individual is always affected when a part of his body is acted on. When one describes an action or process involving a part of the body, therefore, the 'owner' of the directly affected body part is introduced into the clause by a dative nominal (22).

(22)   *Ola   umyła Robertowi   głowę.*
       Ola:NOM washed Robert:DAT head:ACC
       'Ola washed Robert's hair.'

The clothes that one is wearing and the "air bubble" surrounding one's body are conventionally considered extensions of the body. There is ample cultural evidence for this. For example, kissing the edge of someone's robe is believed to be in some sense equivalent to kissing the person who is wearing the robe, and articles of clothing are among the most coveted items belonging to pop stars. Moreover, since one's appearance largely depends on the condition of one's clothing, there is a close link between the clothes one is wearing and one's psychological well-being as well as physical comfort. Sharing one's air bubble with another person counts as physical intimacy whether or not there is actual body contact, and the invasion of a stranger's air bubble is almost as unacceptable socially as touching the body. Moreover, any process which takes place within one's air bubble can affect the individual because the air bubble is so close to the body. It is not surprising, therefore, that one's clothing and one's air bubble are, like parts of the body, conventionally included in the personal sphere, motivating the use of the dative case in (23) and (24): for both sentences, it is obvious to both the speaker and the addressee how the individual named by the dative NP is affected by the action of the agent.

(23)   *Piotr   pochlapał Kasi   sukienkę.*
       Piotr:NOM splashed   Kasia:DAT dress:ACC
       'Piotr splashed water on Kasia's dress.'

(24)   *Kula   przeleciała chłopcu   koło ucha.*
       bullet:NOM flew   boy:DAT by   ear:GEN
       'The bullet flew right by the boy's ear.'

What is included in the personal sphere is largely a matter of shared cultural assumptions, which leave their stamp on linguistic convention. Since it is generally believed that the plight of one's relatives and the condition of one's possessions affect everyone, family members and possessions are automatically included, motivating the use of the dative in examples (20b) and (21b). Possession of an object gives the owner the right to use it; but one may also have this right without actually owning the object. Therefore, the objects that one is entitled to use or about to use are also included in one's personal sphere (25), as are objects that one is holding (26), since holding is often an indication of ownership. (The conceptual affinity of holding and ownership also has other linguistic repercussions, e.g. verbs of having frequently have secondary meanings of holding in addition to indicating actual possession. Conversely, foreign language textbooks will often feature, say, a picture of a boy holding a book with a caption like *Peter has got a book*. The learner is expected to be able to work out that the picture represents a possessive relationship.)

(25) *Piotr   naostrzył   Arturowi   ołówek.*
Piotr:NOM sharpened Artur:DAT pencil:ACC
'Piotr sharpened Artur's pencil for him./Piotr sharpened the pencil for Artur.'

(26) *Piotr wyrwał   Arturowi   nóż   z   ręki.*
Piotr pulled out Artur:DAT knife:ACC from hand:GEN
'Piotr snatched the knife out of Artur's hand.'

Humans are territorial animals that lay claim to certain spaces – their bedrooms, houses, gardens, offices, seats on the bus, etc. There are cultural norms which specify how the boundaries of one's territory are defined and marked, who can enter it and under what conditions, and so on. (see Hall 1959, 1977). Not surprisingly, one's "territory" is considered a part of one's personal sphere, motivating the use of the dative case:

(27) *Piotr   ustąpił Kasi   miejsca   w autobusie.*
Piotr:NOM yielded Kasia:DAT place:GEN in bus:LOC
'Piotr offered Kasia his seat on the bus. Piotr gave up his seat on the bus for Kasia.'

One's territory, possessions, the objects one is holding or about to use, all comprise a region of the personal sphere which I will call the *sphere of influence*. The sphere of influence can also include the people that the target person has control over (subordinates, dependants, subjects, etc.) The cultural motivation for including these individuals in one's personal sphere is quite transparent: one is often held responsible for what one's subordinates do, and one is certainly affected if they rebel against one's authority, since this will cause the personal sphere to shrink (examples (28) and (29)).

(28) Mam   straszny   bałagan   w biurze,
      I have terrible mess:ACC in office:LOC
      sekretarka   mi   zachorowała.
      secretary:NOM me:DAT got ill
      'My office is in a state of chaos: the secretary has gone and fallen ill on me.'

(29) Robotnicy   mu   zastrajkowali.
      workers:NOM him:DAT went on strike
      'The workers have gone and called a strike on him.'

Thus, parts of the target person's body, his clothes, "air bubble", possessions, the objects he is holding or about to use, his territory, relatives, and subordinates are all included in the personal sphere automatically, on the strength of what I will call *linking strategies*, or assumptions shared by all members of the community about when people are affected by actions which involve objects and other people. However, the above list of objects and persons that might be included in an individual's personal sphere is not exhaustive. In fact, no list could ever be exhaustive because the personal sphere is an open-ended category. Inclusion in it often hinges on contextual factors: for example, one's students are in one's sphere of influence only at certain times, i.e. during lectures and seminars; hence the difference in the acceptability of (30a) and (30b-c). Furthermore, inclusion in one's personal sphere is often a matter of an individual speaker's subjective assessment of the relationship between the target person and the participant directly involved in the action. Members of one's family, it was suggested above, are automatically included in the personal sphere. Other individuals might also be included if the speaker judges that the bonds between them and the target person are so strong that anything that happens to them is likely to be of primary interest to the TP. This is a reasonable assumption to make if the individual referred to is the target person's sweetheart or best friend, but not if she is merely a casual acquaintance. Thus, (31a) and (31b) are more acceptable than (31c).

(30) a. ? *Studenci   mu   śpią/ chodzą na dyskoteki.*
         students:NOM him:DAT sleep/go   on discos:ACC
         'His students sleep/go to discos.'

(30) b. *Studenci   mu   śpią na wykładach.*
         students:NOM him:DAT sleep on lectures:LOC
         'His students sleep during his lectures.'

(30) c. *Studenci   mu   uciekają z   wykładów.*
         students:NOM him:DAT run away from lectures:GEN
         'His students cut his lectures.'

(31) a. *Córka   wyjechała mu   do Ameryki.*
         daughter:NOM went away him:DAT to America:GEN
         'His daughter has gone to America.'

(31) b.   ? *Najlepszy przyjaciel   wyjechał   mu   do Ameryki.*
          best   friend:NOM went away him:DAT to America:GEN
          'His best friend has gone to America.'

(31) c.   ?? *Koleżanka   wyjechałał   mu   do Ameryki.*
          friend:NOM   went away   him:DAT to America:GEN
          'A friend of his has gone to America.'

Linking strategies are best thought of as ready-made tools for analyzing certain typical situations. Parts of the body, relatives, subordinates, etc., are included in the personal sphere as a matter of course, since it is considered self-evident that the target person is affected. Making sense of less typical situations may require more conscious effort, but the nature of the TP's affectedness will still be deducible from the context. In the final analysis, the speaker's decision to introduce the person indirectly affected by the action into the sentence by means of a dative nominal will depend on his subjective assessment of whether the addressee will be able to determine the link between the target person and the direct participant.

Let us look at a few specific examples. Ola had been reading in bed late at night, and Robert turned off the light in her room. In describing the event, one might say,

(32)   *Robert   zgasił   Oli   światło.*
        Robert:NOM turned off Ola:DAT light:ACC
        'Robert turned off the light on Ola/for Ola.'

How will the addressee interpret (32)? Since Ola is classified as a target person, the action must have taken place in her personal sphere, presumably in the room where she had been reading. Although none of the inclusion strategies discussed above are applicable to this situation, we can formulate some hypotheses about how Ola might have been affected on the basis of our knowledge of the world. Part of that knowledge is that it is impossible to read in the dark; we might thus interpret (32) as implying that Ola was unable to read as a result of Robert's action. Or we might reason as follows: People usually turn off the light before they go to sleep. To turn off the light, one must reach the switch, which may be quite far from the bed, and so Robert's turning off the light might have made it unnecessary for Ola to get out of bed. To decide between these two interpretations (or others which are also possible), one has to know whether Ola wanted the light on or off; but even without this knowledge, it is still fairly easy to construct a plausible scenario of how she might have come to be affected by Robert's action. To do this, one must assume that the action took place in Ola's personal sphere, and rely on one's encyclopedic knowledge to fill in the missing details.

The interpretation process is much more difficult in the case of sentences such as (33), which most of my informants judged as unacceptable:

(33)   ?? *Wojtek   bawił   mi   się   moim samochodem!*
       Wojtek:NOM played me:DAT INTR my   car:INST
       'Wojtek has been playing with my car [and I was affected].'

Although the car in the example apparently belongs to the speaker's personal sphere, it is not the patient of the action (hence the instrumental, rather than accusative, marking), and it is difficult to imagine how the speaker could have been affected by Wojtek's action. The sentence begins to make more sense, however, when we learn that the speaker is a little boy and the (toy) car his prized possession, and that much of the boy's pleasure in owning the car was due to the fact that he had enjoyed exclusive rights to it. Consequently, the fact that someone else played with it considerably reduced its subjective value. On this interpretation, (33) would be an infantile version of (34):

(34)   *Ten drań   uwiódł   mi   żonę!*
       this cad:NOM seduced me:DAT wife:ACC
       'This cad has seduced my wife!'

I attribute my informants' reluctance to accept (33) to their inability to make sense out of the situation without knowledge of the special context described above.

Since inclusion in the personal sphere depends on a number of subjective and contextual factors, it is not surprising that it is often a matter of degree. Consequently, partial acceptability is the rule for descriptions of actions involving the more peripheral elements. Furthermore, there is an inverse correlation between centrality in the personal sphere and the degree of affectedness of the direct participant necessary to make a sentence with a dative nominal acceptable. Peripheral elements of the personal sphere, such as various non-personal articles belonging to or used by the individual in question (e.g. a newspaper, office equipment, the place where one normally parks one's car, the fence around one's yard) must be totally affected (i.e. they must undergo a change of state or location). On the other hand, central elements (e.g. parts of the body, the clothes one is wearing, objects connected with very personal or intimate aspects of one's life, such as one's diary or bed) need only be implicated in the action in a general way. The following examples should clarify the point.

(35)   *Pies   polizał mi   rękę.*
       dog:NOM licked me:DAT hand:ACC
       'The dog has licked my hand.'

(36)   *Pies   polizał mi   bułkę.*   (Wierzbicka 1988: 402)
       dog:NOM licked me:DAT bread roll:ACC
       'The dog has licked my bread roll.'

(37)   ? *Pies   polizał mi   but.*   (Wierzbicka 1988: 402)
       dog:NOM licked me:DAT shoe:ACC
       'The dog has licked my shoe.'

(38)   ?? *Pies   polizał mi   zderzak.*
        dog:NOM licked me:DAT bumper:ACC
        'The dog has licked my [car's] bumper.'

Licking does not normally cause any change in the patient; yet (35) is acceptable because body parts are central elements of one's personal sphere and one experiences a certain sensation when one's hand is licked. One's shoe or a bread roll one is about to eat are much less central to the personal sphere. However, (36) is acceptable because a dog's licking a bread roll will for most people render it inedible; therefore, the bread roll, unlike the shoe, may be said to have undergone a change of state from edible to inedible (cf. Wierzbicka 1988). It is much more difficult, though not entirely impossible, to envisage how one might be affected when one's shoe is licked. Licking might be interpreted as a friendly gesture, or, if the shoe was spotlessly clean, it might have ruined its perfect gloss. How one might be affected if a dog licks the bumper of one's automobile is still more difficult to envisage, but, with some ingenuity, an appropriate context could certainly be invented.

(39) a.   ?? *Piotr   wszedł   Kasi   do biura.*
           Piotr:NOM   came in Kasia:DAT to office:GEN
           'Piotr came into Kasia's office.'

(39) b.   ? *Piotr   wszedł   Kasi   do sypialni.*
           Piotr:NOM came in Kasia:DAT to bedroom:GEN
           'Piotr came into Kasia's bedroom.'

(39) c.   *Piotr   wkradł   się   Kasi   do sypialni.*
           Piotr:NOM stole into INTR Kasia:DAT to bedroom:GEN
           'Piotr stole into Kasia's bedroom.'

(39) d.   *Piotr   włamał   się   Kasi   do biura.*
           Piotr:NOM broke in INTR Kasia:DAT to office:GEN
           'Piotr broke into Kasia's office.'

(40) a.   ?? *Piotr   wskoczył   Kasi   do basenu.*
           Piotr:NOM jumped in Kasia:DAT to swimming pool:GEN
           'Piotr jumped into Kasia's swimming pool.'

(40) b.   *Piotr   wskoczył   Kasi   do łóżka.*
           Piotr:NOM jumped in Kasia:DAT to bed:GEN
           'Piotr jumped into Kasia's bed.'

A location does not undergo a change of state if someone merely moves into it; accordingly, the person associated with the location would not normally be seen as affected; hence the low acceptability of (39a) and (40a). If, however, the location is a central element of one's personal sphere, such as one's bedroom or secret hideaway, then the mere act of entering it may be interpreted as an intrusion on one's privacy, and so legitimate target person coding on the NP naming the individual in question (cf. (39b); the use of the verb *wkraść się* 'to steal/sneak into', in (39c), which helps to evoke the 'breach of privacy' interpretation, enhances the acceptability of the sentence still further). Such an interpretation will also be strengthened whenever there is additional contextual evidence enabling the addressee to construct a plausible scenario of how the target person came to be affected. Thus, jumping into one's bed is readily interpreted as an invitation to have sex, or even a successful seduction; hence the full acceptability of (40b). The dative construction will also be acceptable if the entry into the location is forceful, or if anything is likely to have been damaged or demolished – cf. example (39d).

(41) a. ?? *Matka   zajrzała   Jasiowi   do gazety.*
mother:NOM looked into Johnny:DAT to newspaper:GEN
'Mother looked into Johnny's newspaper/dictionary.'

(41) b. (?) *Matka   zajrzała   Jasiowi   do szuflady.*
mother:NOM looked into Johnny:DAT to drawer:GEN
'Mother looked into Johnny's drawer.'   (Wierzbicka 1988: 412)

(41) c. *Matka   zajrzała   Jasiowi   do pamiętnika.*
mother:NOM looked into Johnny:DAT to diary:GEN
'Mother looked into Johnny's diary.'

(41) d. *Matka   zajrzała   Jasiowi   do kieszeni.*
mother:NOM looked into Johnny:DAT to pocket:GEN
'Mother looked into Johnny's pocket.'   (Wierzbicka 1988: 412)

(41) e. *Matka   zajrzała   Jasiowi   do gardła.*
mother:NOM looked into Johnny:DAT to throat:GEN
'Mother had a look at Johnny's throat.'   (Wierzbicka 1988: 412)

(42) a. **Adam   patrzył Ewie   na lampę.*
Adam:NOM looked Ewa:DAT on lamp:ACC
'Adam looked at Ewa's lamp.'

(42) b. *Adam   patrzył Ewie   na nogi.*
Adam:NOM looked Ewa:DAT on legs:ACC
'Adam looked at Ewa's legs.'   (Wierzbicka 1988: 412)

These two examples involve an extreme case in that the processes described by the verb is very distant from the causative action prototype: there is no transfer of energy, and consequently no patient (and so the target of the action is coded by a prepositional phrase). Since an object that is merely looked at is not affected, the individual to whose personal sphere it belongs cannot be affected by dint of the changes in it. Consequently, verbs of looking do not normally allow dative constructions (41a-42a). However, dative constructions are sometimes possible with very central elements of the personal sphere – such as parts of the body, particularly those not normally exposed to public view, and certain objects (e.g. one's diary or bankbook) which, when examined, might reveal facts about the owner which he might not want people to know about. In the latter case, the (potential) affectedness of the target person is obvious. With body parts, there is usually additional motivation: either the sentence has sexual overtones (in (42b), it was not Ewa's *ankles* that Adam was looking at, and the looking was no innocent gaze), or else the verb of looking occurs in idiomatic or semi-idiomatic combinations which imply the affectedness of the recipient. The expression *patrzeć komuś na ręce*, lit. 'to look someone:DAT at the hands', meaning 'to keep an eye on somebody [to prevent him from stealing]' is a good example.

It is worth noting that the sentences in (41) exhibit a gradation of acceptability depending on the centrality of the perceived object in the potential target person's personal sphere. (41e), which describes an event which involved a part of the body, uncontroversially a central element of the personal sphere, is fully acceptable. So is (41d), which Wierzbicka (1988: 412) attributes to the fact that clothing and other things worn on the body can be regarded as extensions thereof. Notice, however, that the sentence would be appropriate even if at the time of the inspection Jaś was not wearing the garment mentioned in the sentence. What justifies the use of the dative case in (41d) is not only the closeness of clothing to the body, but the fact that searching one's pockets is considered an invasion of one's privacy. The acceptability of (41c) can be explained in exactly the same way. Finally, (41b), which Wierzbicka considers ungrammatical, is perfectly acceptable if we assume that Jaś kept personal articles such as a diary or love letters in the drawer.

It should also be pointed out that, although the verb designates a purely perceptual activity, all the acceptable sentences in (41) imply some kind of interaction between the subject participant and either the target person or the object of perception which goes beyond mere visual contact. In (41e), examining Jaś's throat probably involved inserting a spatula into his mouth, or at least talking to him (*Say aaah*). It is virtually impossible to look into someone's pocket without touching the article of clothing with the pocket, and (41d) probably describes an act of rummaging in Jaś's pocket rather than merely looking into it. To look inside a drawer, one must first open it; the same is true of a diary, which might moreover be hidden away, which would make it necessary for the intruder to find it first.

2.2. The dative and the semantics of the verb

So far, I have only considered what are traditionally called "free" datives, i.e. dative NPs attached to "complete" utterances in order to specify the person indirectly affected by the process designated by the verb. The exact nature of the affectedness has to be deduced from the relationship between the dative participant and some other element of the situation, typically the patient, on the basis of the linking strategies discussed above and/or general knowledge of the world.

Traditionally opposed to "free" datives are the so-called "lexically governed" datives, i.e. those occurring with verbs which require their presence to make a grammatical or "complete" sentence. Translating this into the language of cognitive grammar, we could say that these are dative NPs which occur with verbs which designate configurations in which the schematic specification of the target person is a salient substructure – in other words, verbs which cannot be defined without making reference to the TP. For example, the very concept of giving presupposes the existence of a recipient; communication is impossible without an addressee, and so on. With these verbs, the semantic contribution of the dative ending is fully compatible with the meaning of the verb – that is to say, redundant. This, however, does not make the dative ending meaningless.

This section will be devoted to a discussion of a number of verbs which "govern" the dative. These will be grouped under headings such as "verbs of acquisition", "verbs of helping", "verbs of compliance", etc. These groupings are best thought of not as semantic classes, but rather as broad families of verbs which bear some resemblance to other members but do not necessarily share a common core of features. The groups, as we will see, are fuzzy: for example, verbs of acquisition grade off into verbs of making available, verbs of ordering overlap with verbs of communication, and so on. I do not attach a great deal of importance to these groupings: they are not a classification scheme for verbs, but a heuristic for organizing the discussion.

The purpose of the discussion is to show that the meaning of the "governed" dative is exactly the same as that of the "free" dative. Moreover, it will be seen that there is a substantial degree of overlap between the two categories, which often makes it difficult to distinguish between them.

2.2.1. *Verbs of acquisition and loss*

One large group of verbs which take dative complements comprises verbs of giving (43), handing over/sending (44) and other kinds of transfer (45), including temporary turning-over (46), as well as compensation (47) and paying back (48):

(43) *Dał/ Ofiarował jej obraz.*
he gave/he presented her:DAT picture:ACC
'He gave her a picture./He presented her with a picture.'

(44) *Wysłał/Podał jej książkę.*
he sent/he handed her:DAT book:ACC
'He sent/handed her the book.'

(45) *Sprzedał jej kilka starych rycin.*
he sold her:DAT a few old:ACC prints:ACC
'He sold her a few old prints.'

(46)   Powierzył/ Pożyczył mi   swoje narzędzia.
       he entrusted/he lent   me:DAT his   tools:ACC
       'He entrusted me with/lent me his tools.'

(47)   Wynagrodziła/ Skompensowała mu   poniesione szkody.
       she recompensed/she compensated him:DAT suffered   losses:ACC
       'She recompensed/compensated him for the losses he had suffered.'

(48)   Odwdzięczył/Odwzajemnił się   mu   za przysługę.
       he returned/ he reciprocated INTR him:DAT for favor:ACC
       'He returned/reciprocated the favor.'

All these verbs strongly evoke[15] the target person's sphere of influence, since the very concept of transfer presupposes a recipient, or a person whose sphere of influence expands as a result of the transfer. As in the examples in section 2.1, the TP is affected because something happens to another object. In the earlier examples, the object was part of the target person's personal sphere; in (43)-(46) above, the object becomes part of the personal sphere as a result of the action. The difference, of course, follows from the meaning of the verb. (47) differs from (43)-(46) only in that the reference to the transferred object (money) is sublexical. (48) could describe the conveyance of an object into the TP's sphere of influence or a more abstract kind of transaction (e.g. good deed for good deed). In the latter case, although no physical object actually enters the TP's personal sphere, it is still seen as growing as a result of the action because the agent acts in accordance with the target person's wishes. This kind of abstract expansion of the sphere of influence will be discussed in more detail further on.

One's sphere of influence expands whenever a new object enters it, so dative marking on the recipient is compatible with any event that involves acquisition, including active seizure of control over an object. However, a seizure of control is interpreted as an instantiation of the causative action prototype and the active individual will normally receive nominative marking. (See Chapter 3 for a discussion of the factors which determine the choice between the nominative and the dative construal.) On the other hand, someone who acquires a new possession effortlessly (49) or by chance (50) can be coded by a dative nominal.

(49) a.   Pieniądze   same   lazły mu   w ręce.
          money:NOM by itself crept him:DAT in hands:ACC
          'The money just kept coming his way.'

(49) b.   Znowu mi   kapnie   parę groszy   za tłumaczenia.
          again me:DAT will trickle a few pennies:GEN for translation:ACC
          'This translation job will bring in a few pennies again.'

(50) a.   Wpadła mi   w ręce   bardzo ciekawa   książka.
          fell   me:DAT in hands:ACC very   interesting book:NOM
          'I [accidentally] came across a very interesting book.'

(50) b. *Trafiło się ślepej kurze ziarno.*
   happened INTR blind hen:DAT grain:ACC
   'Even a blind man sometimes hits the mark.'

(50) c. *Napatoczył się nam strasznie śmieszny szczeniak.*
   turned up INTR us:DAT terribly funny puppy:NOM
   'We were adopted by this funny little puppy.'

Of course the recipient in (49b) might very well have worked hard to earn the money; but the effort and active involvement are treated as a separate event which remains outside the scope of predication.[16] This view of the events contrasts with the one encapsulated in (51), where the verb refers to the work and the remuneration as one event.

(51) *Ładnie zarobiłam na tłumaczeniach.*
   prettily I made money on tranlations:INST
   'I made a pretty penny on these translations.'

Just as one's sphere of influence grows when new items are added to it, it shrinks when one's possessions leave it. The person who loses control over an object is thus a kind of target person. Accordingly, verbs denoting taking away (52) and the loss or running out of something (53) typically take dative complements.

(52) a. *Zabrał/ Ukradł/ Podwędził mi okulary.*
   he took away/he stole/he pinched me:DAT glasses:ACC
   'He took away/took/took back/stole/pinched my glasses.'

(52) b. *Obcięli/ Obniżyli mi premię.*
   they cut/they lowered me:DAT bonus:ACC
   'They've cut/lowered my bonus.'

(52) c. *Zarekwirowali/ Skonfiskowali mu samochód.*
   they requisitioned/they confiscated him:DAT car:ACC
   'They have requisitioned/confiscated his car.'

(52) d. *Ola odbiła Krysi chłopaka.*
   Ola:NOM captured back Krysia:DAT boyfriend:ACC
   'Ola stole Krysia's boyfriend.'

(53) a. *Zginął mi kalendarzyk.*
   lost me:DAT diary:NOM
   'I've lost my diary.'

(53) b. Gdzieś   mi   się   zapodział portfel.
         somewhere me:DAT INTR lost   wallet:NOM
         'I've lost my wallet.'

(53) c. Zabrakło   nam   cukru.
         it ran out us:DAT sugar:GEN
         'We've run out of sugar.'

One's sphere of influence may also include people, and shrink or grow as they enter or leave it. The individual affected in this way is likewise expressed by means of a dative NP.

(54) a. Przybyło nam   studentów.
         it come us:DAT students:GEN
         'Our student numbers have increased.'

(54) b. Uciekł/ Zwiał   nam   nasz więzień.
         ran away/skedaddled us:DAT our prisoner:NOM
         'Our prisoner has run away/done a runner on us.'

Finally, a special subgroup in this category comprises verbs of exchange, which describe situations in which one object leaves the sphere of influence and another takes its place.

(55) a. Ktoś   podmienił mi   akumulator.
         someone:NOM swapped   me:DAT [car] battery:ACC
         'Someone slipped me a dud battery [for my good one].'

(55) b. Rozmieni   mi   pani   sto złotych?
         will change me:DAT madam:NOM 100 zlotys:GEN
         'Will you break this 100 zloty bill into smaller notes for me?'

(55) c. Podstawili   mu   szpicla.
         they substituted him:DAT informer:GEN
         'They have planted an informer [in his organization etc.].'

In all three cases, the verb profiles the movement of an object into or out of someone's sphere of influence. It is thus fully compatible with the meaning of the dative case.

2.2.2. Verbs of making available/unavailable

Giving and other kinds of transfer all increase the target person's sphere of influence by granting him control over new objects. One important aspect of control is *the right to use* a given object. One may also acquire this right without gaining actual possession. This would still increase one's sphere of influence, thereby motivating the use of the dative case. Thus with verbs which denote an act of giving access to an object or making something available, the person who acquires the right to use the object is expressed by means of a dative nominal.

(56) a. *Piotr   udostępnił   nam   swój księgozbiór.*
         Piotr:NOM made available us:DAT self's book collection:ACC
         'Piotr made his book collection available to us.'

(56) b. *Kowalscy   odnajmują pokój   wczasowiczom.*
         Kowalskis:NOM sublet   room:ACC holiday-makers:DAT
         'The Kowalskis sublet a room to the holiday-makers.'

(56) c. *Kasia   ustąpiła miejsca   staruszce.*
         Kasia:NOM yielded   place:GEN old woman:DAT
         'Kasia gave up her seat to an old lady.'

(56) d. *Mogę ci   tylko zaoferować mojego starego fiata.*
         I can you:DAT only to offer   my   old   Fiat:ACC
         'I can only offer you my old Fiat.'

In the above examples, the verbs themselves presuppose the existence of the person who gains the right to use the object. In other cases, the verb may evoke the TP less saliently. For example, verbs of preparing do not make direct reference to a target person. They do, however, evoke a future use, which of course entails a user. Since preparing an object for use increases the user's potency, the perpetrator of the future act is indirectly affected, and can be introduced into the sentence by means of a dative noun phrase (57a). However, it is possible to prepare an object for future use without having any particular user in mind. In this case, the utterance used to describe the event will not contain a dative NP (57b). Thus, with verbs of preparing, the reference to the TP, though still implicit in the semantic characterization of the verb, is much less salient than with verbs of giving access or making available.

(57) a. *Przygotuję/ Naszykuję   ci   wszystkie dokumenty.*
         I will prepare/I will make ready you:DAT all   documents:ACC
         'I will prepare all the documents for you.'

(57) b. *Przygotuję/ Naszykuję   wszystkie dokumenty.*
         I will prepare/I will make ready all   documents:ACC
         'I will prepare all the documents.'

(58) a. *Nazbieraliśmy wam   chrustu.*
         we gathered   you:PL:DAT dry twigs:GEN
         'We've gathered some dry twigs for you.'

(58) b. *Jutro   podłączą   nam   telefon.*
tomorrow they will connect us:DAT telephone:ACC
'They will connect our phone tomorrow.'

(58) c. *Zaraz ugotuję/ podgrzeję   ci   mięso.*
shortly I will cook/I will heat up you:DAT meat:ACC
'I will cook/heat up the meat for you right away.'

(58) d. *Piotr   uprał/ uprasował Małgosi   sukienkę.*
Piotr:NOM washed/ironed   Małgosia:DAT dress:ACC
'Piotr washed/ironed Małgosia's dress for her.'

The sentences in (58) also describe actions which render an object usable or more easily accessible, thus increasing the target person's potency. The various actions described here make it possible for the TP to build a fire, make telephone calls, eat, and wear the dress. However, the verb itself does not evoke the future action or the target person's potency. The nature of the target person's affectedness has to be deduced from the context and from encyclopedic knowledge of the world (one uses dry twigs to build a fire, a telephone must be connected to a line before it can be used, etc.) Thus, the datives in sentences in (58) are more like the "free" datives discussed in section 2.1 than the "lexically governed" datives of this section. On the other hand, if one assumes an encyclopedic view of semantics, it could be argued, for example, that, since food is cooked to make it ready for eating, the concept of cooking invokes the concept of eating and hence also the eater. Of course the conception of the eater is quite peripheral to the meaning of *gotować* 'to cook', whereas one cannot coherently describe the meaning of a verb like *udostępnić* 'to make available' without some reference to the target person. This should make clear a fact which will be discussed in more detail in the section 2.4, namely, that the sharp distinction between "lexically governed" and "free" datives is illusory: they are not two discrete and mutually exclusive classes, but rather endpoints on a continuum. When the affectedness of the TP is in profile, the verb is said to govern the dative, and the dative complement is obligatory. When its nature has to be deduced from the context, the dative is labeled "free". However, there are various intermediate cases when the verb does evoke the target person, but less saliently, and then it is difficult to decide whether or not the verb "governs" the dative. (In actual linguistic practice, it is not so much conceptual autonomy of the TP which determines whether or not a specific use will be labeled as "governed", but the frequency with which a given verb takes dative complements. Thus, although the target person is at best marginal in a semantic description of verbs of food preparation such as *gotować* 'to cook', *smażyć* 'to fry', *podgrzewać* 'to heat up,' etc., or of verbs describing the treatment of clothes such as *prać* 'to wash', *prasować* 'to iron', *skracać* 'to raise the hem', *podszyć* 'to line', etc., they are often assumed to govern the dative simply because they frequently occur in dative constructions – for example, they are subcategorized as taking dative complements in Polański 1980, 1984, 1988.) The important point is that the motivation for the use of the dative case is exactly the same in all of the sentences discussed in this section, regardless of how strongly the verb evokes the target person. In all of the sentences discussed above, the dative case is motivated to the extent that the target person's potency is altered.

Another subgroup within the larger group of verbs of making available/unavailable is verbs of making (59). The motivation for the use of the dative case is exactly the same as for its with verbs of giving: the sphere of influence grows because a new object is added to it. The difference is that, as in the examples in (58), the verb does not profile the TP's affectedness.

(59) a. *Zrobisz   mi   domek   dla lalek?*
you will make me:DAT house:ACC for dolls:GEN
'Will you make me a doll-house?'

(59) b. *Ala   uszyła mi   sukienkę.*
Ala:NOM sewed me:DAT dress:ACC
'Ala sewed a dress for me.'

(59) c. *Narysuj mi   baranka.*
draw   me:DAT lamb:ACC
'Draw a lamb for me.'

The target person is affected not only when objects become available for his use, thereby causing his sphere of influence to expand, but also when objects in it are destroyed, impaired, or made unusable, thereby causing it to shrink. Not surprisingly, therefore, verbs of destruction and impairment often take dative complements.

(60) a. *Żołnierze   zdemolowali/podpalili   mu   dom.*
soldiers;NOM demolished/ set on fire him:DAT house:ACC
'The soldiers demolished his house/set his house on fire.'

(60) b. *Uszkodziłeś/ Zniszczyłeś/Zepsułeś   mi   motor.*
you damaged/you ruined/ you broke me:DAT motorcycle:ACC
'You've damaged/ruined/broken my motorcycle.'

(60) c. *Alicja   poplamiła/zabłociła/podarła mi   spódnicę.*
Alicja:NOM stained/ soiled/ tore   me:DAT skirt:ACC
'Alice has stained/soiled/torn my skirt.'

The target person can be affected by any change in her possessions, whether or not it is instigated by an agent. Thus, the individual whose possessions are affected by a spontaneously proceeding process will also be coded by means of a dative NP. Since objects do not normally fix themselves or become available for use in and of themselves, this use is mostly restricted to verbs of impairment (61a-61b). However, (61c) is perfectly acceptable if uttered when the washing machine has completed its cycle. Of course the situation described here does require an agentive instigator, but his action is outside the scope of predication.

(61) a. Zepsuł   mi   się   samochód.
         broke down me:DAT INTR car:NOM
         'My car has broken down.'

(61) b. Kurtka   mi   się   pobrudziła.
         jacket:NOM me:DAT INTR dirtied
         'My jacket got dirty.'

(61) c. Spodnie   już   ci   się   uprały!
         trousers:NOM already you:DAT INTR washed
         'Your trousers are washed.' [said when the washing machine has completed its cycle]

2.2.3. Verbs of helping and interference

One's sphere of influence grows or shrinks as people and objects enter or leave it, and as objects become available or unavailable for use. Control over people and objects increases one's potency in that it enables one to influence the course of events and do things which one might not otherwise have been able to do. One's potency can also be affected more directly when other individuals or external conditions in general expedite or thwart one's intentions. The individual whose potency is affected in this way is also coded by a dative nominal.

Thus, among the verbs which take dative complements are those which designate actions which amplify the results of the target person's efforts, i.e. verbs of helping (62) and facilitating/enabling (63), and those which stifle them, i.e. verbs which express ideas such as interference (64), counter-action (65), and hindering/impediment (66).

(62) a. Pomożesz   mi   przenieść ten stół?
         you will help me:DAT to carry   this table:ACC
         'Will you help me carry this table?'

(62) b. Często asystował   profesorowi   przy   operacji.
         often he assisted professor:DAT at   operation:LOC
         'He often assisted the professor during the operation.'

(62) c. Służył   im   za nędzne   grosze.
         he served them:DAT for wretched pennies:ACC
         'He served them for a few wretched pennies.'

(63) a. *Twoja pomoc umożliwiła mi kontynuację*
your help:NOM made possible me:DAT continuation:ACC
studiów.
studies:GEN
'Your help has made it possible for me to carry on with my studies.'

(63) b. *Mogę ci załatwić świetną fuchę.*
I can you:DAT to arrange terrific job:ACC
'I can get you a terrific [one-off] job.'

(63) c. *Zorganizowaliśmy dzieciom zabawę noworoczną.*
we organized children:DAT New Year's party:ACC
'We organized a New Year's Eve party for the children.'

(63) d. *Zaaranżował mi kilka koncertów, ale to wszystko.*
he arranged me:DAT several concerts:ACC but that:NOM all
'He did arrange a few concerts for me, but that's all.'

(63) e. *Kierownik poszedł nam na rękę i udostępnił nam cały obiekt.*
'The superintendent obliged us (DAT) and made the whole site available to us (DAT).'

(63) f. *Bardzo mi ułatwiłeś zadanie.*
very me:DAT you facilitated task:ACC
'You've made my task much easier for me.'

(64) a. *Bardzo nam przeszkadzał.*
'He disturbed us (DAT) a great deal.'

(64) b. *Był nieznośny, do wszystkiego mi się wtrącał/ mieszał.*
he was unbearable, to everything:GEN me:DAT INTR thrust in/mixed
'He was unbearable. Everything I did, he had to stick his oar into!'

(64) c. *Bachor ciągle plątał nam się pod nogami.*
brat:NOM contantly tangled up us:DAT INTR under feet:INST
'The brat kept getting in our way/getting under our feet.'

(64) d. *Dobrze ci radzę, nie wchodź mu w drogę.*
well you:DAT I advise not get into him:DAT in way:ACC
'Here's some good advice: don't get in his way.'

(65) a. *Nie śmiał sprzeciwić się ojcu.*
'He didn't dare stand up to his father (DAT).'

(65) b. *Odważnie przeciwstawił się decyzji dyrektora.*
'Courageously he took issue with the director's decision (DAT).'

(65) c. *Dlaczego ty mi zawsze robisz na przekór?*
'Why do you always try to spite me (DAT)?'

(65) d. *Musimy przeciwdziałać zanieczyszczeniu rzek.*
'We must counteract river pollution (DAT).'

(66) a. *Uniemożliwił   mi   wyjazd.*
he precluded   me:DAT departure:ACC
'He has made it impossible for me to leave.'

(66) b. *Utrudniała   mi   zbieranie   informacji.*
she made it difficult me:DAT collection:ACC information:GEN
'She made it difficult for me to collect the data.'

(66) c. *Wszyscy rzucali jej   kłody   pod   nogi.*
all:NOM threw   her:DAT clogs:ACC under feet:ACC
'They all put spokes in her wheel.'

The target person's efforts may also be amplified or stifled by external conditions. These can be specified by a noun phrase which is very agent-like and functions as the subject, as in (67-68), or they can be left implicit, as in (69).

(67) a. *Pogoda   im   sprzyjała/dopisała.*
weather:NOM them:DAT furthered/was favorable
'The weather was favorable [to their plans].'

(67) b. *Bałagan   panujący w biurze   ułatwił/   umożliwił*
mess:NOM reigning in office:LOC made easier/made possible
im   fałszerstwo.
them:DAT forgery:ACC
'The mess in the office made it easier/made it possible for them to commit the forgery.'

(68) a. *Jego niespodziewana odmowa   pokrzyżowała jej   plany*
his unexpected   refusal:NOM crossed   her:DAT plans:ACC
'His unexpected refusal thwarted her plans.'

(68) b. *Rodzina   byłaby   mi   tylko kulą   u nogi.*
family:NOM would be me:DAT only ball:INST at foot:GEN
'A family would only be a clog at my heel.'

(68) c. *Na przeszkodzie   stanęła Pinkiemu nieznajomość*
on obstacle:LOC stood   Pinki:DAT lack of knowledge:ACC
języka.
language:GEN
'Not knowing the language turned out to be a major obstacle for Pinki.'

(69) a. *Szło   jej   dobrze/jak po maśle/jak z płatka.*
         it was going her:DAT well/ as on butter/ as from a petal
         'Everything was going well/smoothly/without a hitch (for her).'

(69) b. *Szło   jej   jak z   kamienia/ jak po grudzie.*
         it was going her:DAT as from rock:GEN/as over farrow:LOC
         'It was was uphill work for her all the time.'

(69) c. *Poszczęściło/Udało/   Powiodło   jej   się.*
         it was lucky/it was successful/it came off well her:DAT INTR
         'She was lucky./She was successful./It came off well for her.'

The sentences in (69) are unusual in that the active human participant is not the subject in spite of the fact that no other nominal competes for this role. The semantic effect of expressing the active participant by means of a dative rather than a nominative NP is to imply that the TP's success or lack of success in accomplishing his goal is due more to luck or external conditions than to her own potency. (The factors which determine whether the active participant is coded by a nominative or a dative NP will be analyzed in detail in Chapter 3.)

2.2.4. Beneficiary datives

The recipient, the person to whom something is made available or for whom something is created and the person whom the agent assists are all special cases of a more inclusive category, that of "beneficiary", or the person for whose benefit the action is performed. Beneficiaries are expressed in the dative case because the agent's actions increase their potency either by enabling them to do something or by bringing about a desirable state of affairs. In the latter case, the beneficiary's goals are met without his having to undertake any action at all.[17]

(70) a. *Krystyna   odrobiła Oli   lekcje.*
         Krystyna:NOM did   Ola:DAT homework:ACC
         'Krystyna did Ola's (DAT) homework for her.'

(70) b. *Krystyna otworzyła Oli drzwi.*
         'Krystyna opened the door for Ola (DAT).'

(70) c. *Krystyna zaniosła Oli paczkę na pocztę.*
         'Krystyna took the parcel to the post office for Ola (DAT).'

(70) d. *Krystyna zaśpiewała Oli piosenkę.*
         'Krystyna sang a song for Ola (DAT).'

These different types of beneficiaries bear close family resemblance to each other. What distinguishes those exemplified in (70) from most of the other uses considered earlier in this section is the verb itself does not evoke the target person. In this respect beneficiary datives resemble the "free" datives discussed in Section 2.1.

2.2.5. Verbs of ordering, obligation, and allowing

Another important aspect of one's potency is what I will call *self-determination*, or the freedom to do as one pleases. Human beings are subject to all sorts of obligations, prohibitions, and social pressures which often severely limit their self-determination, and hence curtail their sphere of potency, which may be said to be partially taken over by the person in authority. The nominal referring to the individual whose potency is affected in this way is also marked with the dative case. This category includes individuals who are subject to another person's orders (71) or prohibitions (72) or to general moral or social obligations (73).

(71) a. *Kazała/Poleciła mu kupić gazetę.*[18]
'She told/directed him (DAT) to buy a paper.'

(71) b. *Narzucił swoją wolę wszyskim członkom zespołu.*
'He imposed his will on all members (DAT) of the team.'

(71) c. *Związki nie będą nam dyktowały warunków.*
'We will not allow the unions to dictate the terms to us (DAT).'

(72) a. *Rodzice zabronili jej spotykać się z Piotrem.*
'Her parents forbade her (DAT) to meet Piotr.'

(72) b. *Zakazano im opuszczania hotelu.*
it was prohibited them:DAT leaving:GEN hotel:GEN
'They were prohibited from leaving the hotel.'

(73) a. *Maćkowi nie wolno chodzić po drzewach.*
Maciek:DAT not allowed to go all over trees:LOC
'Maciek isn't allowed to climb trees.'

(73) b. *Nie wypada mi prosić go o pomoc.*
not it befits me:DAT to ask him:ACC about help:ACC
'It is not appropriate for me to ask him for help.'

On the other hand, the person with authority over another may waive his claims, thus increasing the TP's potency (74), or not exercise his authority and tolerate whatever behavior the target person engages in (75). The individual whose potency is affected in this way is also expressed by means of a dative nominal.

(74) a. *Pozwolono/ Zezwolono nam wyjechać.*
　　　　it was allowed/it was permitted us:DAT to leave
　　　　'We were allowed/permitted to leave.'

(74) b. *Daj mi spróbować!*
　　　　give me:DAT to try
　　　　'Let me try!'

(75) a. *Rodzice zawsze jej pobłażali.*
　　　　'Her parents always indulged her (DAT).'

(75) b. *Popuść mu trochę cugli!*
　　　　slacken him:DAT a bit reins:GEN
　　　　'Let him off the leash a bit!'

2.2.6. Lack of control over one's actions

Another central aspect of potency is control over what one is doing, i.e. the ability to successfully carry out the action. Control over one's actions is an important agentive property, and participants who enjoy it tend to be expressed in the agent case, the nominative. On the other hand, a participant who lacks control over what he is doing departs from the nominative prototype. Loss of control counts as an infringement of the sphere of potency, thus opening the way for a dative construal. The dative case will thus replace the nominative when the most prominent participant is unable to act (76), when his action is involuntary (77), performed on impulse and against his better judgement (78), and when the participant loses control over the process he initiated, which results in an outcome which was clearly not intended (79). The contrast between the nominative and the dative in situations of reduced potency will be discussed in more detail in Chapter 3.

(76) a. *Słowa grzęzły mu w gardle.*
　　　　words:NOM got stuck him:DAT in throat:LOC
　　　　'The words just stuck in his throat.'

(76) b. *Skargi zamarły jej na ustach.*
　　　　complaints:NOM withered her:DAT on lips:LOC
　　　　'Her complaints just petered out [as she spoke them]'.

(76) c. *Głos mu się łamał.*
　　　　voice:NOM him:DAT INTR was breaking
　　　　'He faltered.'

(77) a. *Ręce mu drżały.*
　　　　hands:NOM him:DAT trembled
　　　　'His (DAT) hands were trembling.'

(77) b. Głowa   opadła mu   na piersi.
head:NOM fell   him:DAT on chest:ACC
'His head hang to his chest.'

(77) c. Oczy jej latały niespokojnie, nie mogła się skupić.
'Her (DAT) eyes were darting restlessly, she couldn't concetrate.'

(78) a. Wypsnęła/ Wyrwała mu   się   niedyskretna uwaga.
slipped out/ tore free him:DAT INTR indiscrete   comment:NOM
'He let an indiscrete comment slip out./An indiscrete comment escaped from his lips.'

(78) b. Gniewne słowa   cisnęły   jej   się na usta.
angry   words:NOM pushed forward her:DAT INTR on lips:ACC
'Angry words were trying to force their way through her lips.'

(79) a. Wylała mi   się   herbata.
spilled me:DAT INTR tea:NOM
'I spilled my tea.'

(79) b. Przypalił mi   się   kotlet.
burned   me:DAT INTR cutlet:NOM
'My cutlet has gone and burned itself.'

(79) c. Złamał mi   się   ołówek.
broke   me:DAT INTR pencil:NOM
'My pencil broke.'

2.2.7. Verbs of compliance and resistance

One's sphere of influence may include people as well as objects and will grow or shrink as people physically move into or out of it (example (54) above). However, just as one may gain the right to use an object in an act that does not involve actual physical transfer, so individuals may come under the TP's control by submitting to his demands. The individual who makes the decision appears in the nominative case and the individual whose sphere of influence grows as a result of this act of submission is expressed by a dative NP. Note that in these sentences, the subject participant's sphere of potency also changes; however, the individual who submits to another person's demands is also the head of the relevant part of the action chain, and hence is given nominative case-marking.

(80) a. Dowódca   poddał   miasto   nieprzyjacielowi.
commander:NOM surrendered city:ACC enemy:DAT
'The commander surrendered the city to the enemy.'

(80) b. *Był w niej śmiertelnie zakochany i ulegał/ustępował jej we wszystkim.*
'He was madly in love with her and he yielded to her (DAT) in every matter/indulged her (DAT) every whim.'

(80) c. *Nie damy   im   się.*
not we will give them:DAT INTR
'We won't give in to them.'

Closely related to the use exemplified in (80) are the datives in (81), where the agent's overt acknowledgment of his subordinate position reaffirms the TP's claims to control over him.

(81) a. *Podlizywał się szefowi jak tylko mógł.*
'He sucked up to the boss (DAT) whenever he could.'

(81) b. *Wszyscy mu schlebiali/kadzili/nadskakiwali.*
'Everyone flattered/adulated/fawned on him (DAT).'

(81) c. *Żołnierz zasalutował dowódcy.*
'The soldier saluted his commander (DAT).'

(81) d. *On   by   mu   z   ręki   jadł, lizus   jeden.*
he:NOM would him:DAT from hand:ACC eat toady:NOM one
'He would eat out of his (DAT) hand, the toady.'

Example (82) is somewhat unusual in that the state of affairs that it describes involves neither shrinking nor growth of the sphere of influence: the clausal trajector (*cały pion dystrybucji* 'the whole distribution department') is simply located within it. The use of the dative, though not fully predictable, is certainly motivated, since the sphere of influence is highly relevant, and it is easy to imagine how the target person may be affected by the state of affairs designated by the verb (she is responsible for it and hence will be blamed if anything goes wrong, etc.)

(82)   *Podlega   jej   cały   pion   dystrybucji.*
under-lies her:DAT whole department:NOM distribution:GEN
'She's got the whole distribution department under her.

The target person's sphere of influence also expands when another individual pledges to do something for him, since the pledger is now under an obligation to perform the action.

(83)   *Obiecał/Przyrzekł/Przysiągł nam, że załatwi wszystkie formalności związane z wyjazdem Oli.*[19]
He promised/solemnly promised/swore to us (DAT) that he was going to see to all the formalities connected with Ola's departure.'

Conversely, one's sphere of influence shrinks when other individuals refuse to comply with one's wishes (or counteract one's efforts – see example (65) above). The person whose demands are resisted or whose authority is challenged is expressed either by a dative noun phrase (84) or by a prepositional phrase with *przeciw(ko)* 'against', which also governs the dative (85).

(84) a. *Żołnierze   bohatersko opierali się/stawiali opór nieprzyjacielowi.*
    soldiers:NOM heroically resisted/put up resistance   enemy:DAT
    'The soldiers put up a heroic resistance against the enemy.'

(84) b. *Z uporem   oponował mi   we wszystkim.*
    with stubbornness:INST he objected me:DAT in everything:LOC
    'He stubbornly objected to everything I said/suggested.'

(85) a. *Cała ludność   powstała/walczyła przeciw dyktatorowi.*
    entire population:NOM stood up/fought   against dictator:DAT
    'The entire population stood up against/fought against the dictator.'

(85) b. *Odważnie   wystąpił   przeciw skorumpowanym politykom.*
    courageously he stepped out against   corrupt   politicians:DAT
    'Courageously, he spoke out against corrupt politicians.'

(85) c. *Wszyscy stanęliśmy murem   przeciw Kowalskiemu.*
    all:NOM we stood   wall:INST against   Kowalski:DAT
    'We all stood firm against Kowalski.'

2.2.8. Private sphere

I argued in section 2.1 that the invasion of one's territory or "air-bubble" motivates the use of the dative case. One's territory and "air-bubble" are just one dimension of one's *private sphere*. The private sphere also has a social dimension evident in verbs of accompanying (86), which evoke the social space surrounding the TP and indicate that the trajector is located within that space. Verbs denoting a 'breach of privacy' (87) also evoke the private sphere, since the concept of intrusion presupposes the existence of an area that is intruded into.

(86) a. *Towarzyszyła mu   bardzo atrakcyjna brunetka.*
    accompanied him:DAT very   attractive brunette:NOM
    'He was acompanied by a very attractive brunette.'

(86) b. *Czy możesz dotrzymać mi towarzystwa?*
    'Can you keep me (DAT) company?'

(86) c. *Krzysztof zawsze asystuje jej na spacerze.*
    'Krzysztof always escorts her (DAT) during her walks.'

(87) a. *Nie chciałam mu   się   narzucać.*
not I wanted him:DAT INTR to thrust upon
'I didn't want to thrust myself upon him.'

(87) b. *Napraszją   się   nam   ze   swoimi przysługami.*
they are importuning INTR us:DAT with their favors:INST
'They are making a nuisance of themselves with all their [big] favors.'

(87) c. Naprzykrzał mu się od wielu dni.   (Szymczak 1981)
'He's been bugging him (DAT) for many days.'

2.2.9. Sphere of awareness

Another region of the personal sphere is the *sphere of awareness*. The sphere of awareness can be conceived of as a region where percepts, feelings, sensations, thoughts, ideas, etc. appear and are experienced by the target person. In example (88), which describes an act of visual perception, the sphere of awareness corresponds to Wojtek's visual field:

(88)   *Wojtkowi   ukazała   się   piękna   naga   dziewczyna*
Wojtek:DAT appeared INTR beautiful naked girl:NOM
z   rozwianymi włosami.
with streaming   hair:INST
'A beautiful naked girl with streaming hair appeared to Wojtek.'

Since mental experience is often understood metaphorically in terms of vision, the same imagery is also applied to mental events of other kinds. The metaphor maps the viewer onto the experiencer, and the observed object onto the object of experience (or the experience itself). The viewer/experiencer is affected because an event or process takes place in his sphere of awareness, and is expressed by a dative NP. The imagery is particularly clear in (89), but it is also exploited for grammatical purposes in (90).

(89)   *Wojtkowi   ukazała   się   we śnie*
Wojtek:DAT appeared INTR in dream:LOC
piękna   naga   dziewczyna z   rozwianymi włosami.
beautiful naked girl:NOM   with streaming   air:INST
'A beautiful naked girl with streaming hair appeared to Wojtek in his dream.'

(90)   *Wojtkowi   śniła   się   piękna   naga   dziewczyna*
Wojtek:DAT dreamed INTR beautiful naked girl:NOM
z   rozwianymi włosami.
with streaming   hair:INST
'Wojtek dreamed of a beautiful naked girl with streaming hair.'

Of course the above formulation is merely a description of a *folk model* of mental experience, not a scientific theory. Incorporated in this model is a gross distortion of "objective reality," since it is formulated *as if* the sensations, feelings, beliefs, etc. had an independent existence outside the experiencer. This is, however, how we conceptualize mental experience. We tend to think of ideas as objects that enter and leave our minds and of emotions as waves that overwhelm us and sweep us away (see Lakoff 1987, Lakoff & Johnson 1980, Reddy 1979). The prevalence of this kind of imagery in the metaphorical expressions we use to talk about mental experience, and the difficulties that psychologists and philosophers of the mind experienced in overcoming the "homunculus" theory, both bear witness to the power of this folk model over the imagination. (For further discussion of this folk theory, see section 3.1.3.)

Experiential verbs, then, evoke the sphere of awareness, just as verbs of helping evoke the concept of a "helpee" who is engaged in some action, and verbs of resistance necessarily imply the existence of a force that is resisted. In addition to this, they evoke a mental object (for example the image of a beautiful girl with streaming hair), and they specify the mode of awareness – seeing, dreaming, imagining, remembering, etc. The mental object can be specified by means of a subordinate clause introduced by the complementizer *że* (91-92), an infinitival complement (93), or simply a nominal (94-95); in all three variants, the experiencer is expressed by a dative nominal.

(91)   *Wojtkowi   śniło   się, że   całuje*
       Wojtek:DAT it dreamed INTR that he is kissing
       piękną nagą dziewczynę z   rozwianymi włosami.
       beautiful naked girl:ACC   with streaming   hair:INST
       'Wojtek dreamed that he was kissing a beautiful naked girl with streaming hair.'

(92)   *Wydawało/Zdawało/ Przywidziało mu   się,*
       it appeared/it seemed/it hallucinated him:DAT INTR
       że ktoś   stoi   za   oknem.
       that someone:NOM stands behind window:LOC
       'It appeared/seemed to him that someone was standing outside the window./He fancied he saw someone standing outside the window.'

(93)   *Eli   chce   się   jeść.*
       Ela:DAT it wants INTR to eat
       'Ela is hungry.'

(94)   *To   nazwisko nie kojarzy   mi   się   z   żadną twarzą.*
       this name:NOM   not associates me:DAT INTR with no   face:INST
       'I don't associate this name with any face.'

(95) a. Pomyliły mu   się   daty.
        erred   him:DAT INTR dates:NOM
        'He got the dates wrong/mixed up.'

(95) b. Pomieszły/Poplątały/ Poprzestawiały mu   się   daty.
         mixed up /tangled up/rearranged   him:DAT INTR dates:NOM
         'He got the dates mixed up.'

The above account can be further extended to non-verbal experiential predicates. Examples (96)-(99) are subjectless[20] constructions in which the nature of the experience (a bodily sensation or an emotional state) is specified by an adverb or a noun, with a positive temporal profile being introduced by the copula *być* 'to be' (or *zrobić się* 'to become').

(96)   *Było   mi   gorąco/ciepło/zimno/duszno.*
        it was me:DAT hotly/warmly/coldly/stuffily
        'I was hot/warm/cold/stifled.'

(97)   *Było   mi   mdło/słabo.*
        it was me:DAT insipidly/weakly
        'I felt sick/faint.'

(98)   *Było   mi   miło/ przykro/   smutno/wesoło/ nudno/ straszno.*
        it was me:DAT nicely/disagreeably/ sadly/ happily/boringly/terribly
        'I was pleased/sorry/sad/happy/bored/scared.'

(99)   *Było   mi   żal/   wstyd.*
        it was me:DAT regret:NOM/shame:NOM
        'I was sorry/ashamed.'

Grammatically, then, they are quite different from the other constructions that have been considered earlier in this chapter. However, as in the previous examples, the person having the experience is designated by a dative NP because the relationship between the experiencer and the mental process is the same in both sets of sentences: the sensation or emotion is conceptualized as a process occurring within the experiencer's sphere of awareness.

The above analysis is supported by the fact that some of the non-verbal predicates in (96)-(99) have different but related senses which denote states of affairs existing in a setting specified by what is indisputably a locative phrase. For example, the bodily sensation predicates of (96) can also denote physical conditions (100). The experiential and the physical senses differ only with respect to the kind of setting they occur in: the sphere of awareness or a physical location.

(100)   *W pokoju   było gorąco/ciepło /zimno/duszno.*
        in room:LOC   it was hotly/ warmly/coldly/stuffily
        'It was hot/warm/cold/stuffy in the room.'

Some of the emotional predicates discussed earlier in this section also have related senses which allow the region in which the emotion takes place to be specified by means of a locative prepositional phrase. Such a construal is appropriate when the emotion is shared by many individuals in a location or when it is thought to be induced by the location itself. Examples (101)-(102) are analogous to (98) except that they describe states occurring in a different kind of setting – a physical location or a social event rather than the experiencer's sphere of awareness.

(101)   *Na imprezie   u Ani   było   nudno/ wesoło/bardzo miło.*
        at party:LOC at Ania's it was boringly/happily/very pleasant
        'Ania's party was boring/fun/very pleasant.'

(102)   *W podziemiach   było   straszno.*
        in underground:LOC it was scarily
        'It was scary underground.'

Closely related to the "sensation-in-the-sphere-of-awareness" construction exemplified in (96)-(99) is what could be called the "activity-in-the-sphere-of-awareness" construction:

(103)   *Wesoło nam   się   podróżowało po   tej pięknej   krainie.*
        happily us:DAT INTR it travelled   over this beautiful country:LOC
        'We enjoyed travelling all over this beautiful country.'

(104)   *Spało mi   się   dobrze.*
        it slept me:DAT INTR well
        'I slept well.'

(105)   *Przyjemnie nam   się   rozmawiało o   dawnych czasach.*
        pleasantly us:DAT INTR   it talked about old   times:LOC
        'It was pleasant to talk about the good old times.'

The import of (103)-(105) is that the target person experiences the activity he is engaged in as pleasant, joy-inspiring, etc. The construction differs from the previous one in that the object of experience is specified in more detail. This is reflected on the linguistic level by replacement of the maximally schematic verbal predicate *być* 'to be', by a full-fledged verb phrase which describes the process in more detail. The adverbials in the "activity-in-the-sphere-of-awareness" construction can also be typically agentive modifiers, i.e. those which specify the degree of difficulty experienced by the agent in performing the action:

(106)   *Pisze   mi   się   zawsze dość łatwo.*   (Topolińska 1984:141)
        it writes me:DAT INTR always fairly easily
        'I've always found it fairly easy to write/found writing fairly easy.'

(107) *Piotrowi pracowało się dziś bez trudu.* (ibid.)
Piotr:DAT it worked INTR today without difficulty:GEN
Piotr didn't experience any diffifulty with his work today.

The adverbial phrase must be present, however, for the construction to be grammatical, since it is the adverb that introduces the notion of sphere of awareness, thus motivating the use of the dative case (cf. the ungrammaticality of examples (108) and (109)).

(108) **Spało mi się.*
it slept me:DAT INTR

(109) **Piotrowi pracowało się.*
Piotr:DAT it worked INTR

It is worth noting that the construction with *być* 'to be', also allows the type of action to be specified periphrastically by an infinitival phrase. In this variant of the construction, the adverbs *dobrze* 'well', *przyjemnie* 'pleasantly', *smutno* 'sadly', etc. also specify how the dative participant experiences the activity she is engaged in. The construal in which the activity is represented as occurring in the agent's sphere of awareness is thus particularly well suited for expressing this kind of relationship.

(110) *Dobrze nam było wygrzewać się na słońcu.*
well us:DAT it was to bask INTR on sun:LOC
'It was nice to bask in the sun./We enjoyed basking in the sun.'

(111) *Przyjemnie nam było rozmawiać o dawnych czasach.*
pleasantly us:DAT it was to talk about old times:LOC
'It was nice to talk about the old times./We enjoyed talking about the old times.'

(112) *Smutno mi było wychodzić, kiedy wszyscy się jeszcze bawili.*
sadly me:DAT it was to leave when all:NOM INTR still enjoyed
'I was sad to [have to] leave when everyone else was still having a good time.'

(113) *Wstyd mu było prosić ją teraz o pomoc.*
shame:NOM him:DAT it was to ask her:ACC now about help:ACC
'He was ashamed to [have to] ask her for help now.'

In addition to the sensations, feelings, etc., that are currently occupying one's consciousness (notice the metaphor!), the sphere of awareness also comprises various "dormant" attitudes, ideas, beliefs, etc. – i.e. things one might believe or know about, but which one may not actually be considering at any particular moment.

(114) *Alicji odpowiadała praca w szkole.*
'Work in a school suited Alicja (DAT).'

(115) *Piotr bardzo imponował Krystynie.*
Piotr:NOM very impressed Krystyna:DAT
'Krystyna was highly impressed with Piotr.'

(116) *Markowi znudziła się praca w biurze.*
Marek:DAT bored INTR work:NOM in office:LOC
'Marek got tired of working in the office.'

(117) *Markowi ciążyły obowiązki rodzinne.*
Marek:DAT were a burden duties:NOM family
'Marek found family responsibilities a heavy burden.'

(118) *Po jakimś czasie spowszedniały/ obrzydły jej*
after some time:LOC became commonplace/palled her:DAT
te uroczyste kolacje.
these formal suppers:NOM
'After a while, the novelty of these formal suppers wore off (for her)./
After a while, she was fed up with all these formal suppers.'

Finally, there are two special subgroups of experiential predicates which take dative complements: verbs of communication, which will be discussed in the next section, and a large group of metaphorical expressions in which mental experience is described metaphorically as physical experience. These include both conventional expressions (119)-(125) and novel metaphors (126)-(127) motivated by the mind-as-body metaphor.[21]

(119) *Przyszedł mi do głowy świetny pomysł.*
came me:DAT to head:GEN terrific idea:NOM
'I got this terrific idea./A terrific idea occured to me.'

(120) *Kłębiły/ Kotłowały/Kołatały mu się w głowie*
whirled/ swirled/ banged about him:DAT INTR in head:LOC
sprzeczne myśli.
contradictory thoughts:NOM
'All sorts of contradictory thoughts were whirling/swirling/banging about in his head.'

(121) *To nazwisko obiło mi się o uszy.*
this name:NOM banged against me:DAT INTR against ears:GEN
'I have heard/come across this name before.'

(122)   *Znowu nadepnąłeś jej   na odcisk.*
        again you trod   her:DAT on corn:ACC
        'You've touched her on her weak spot again'

(123)   *Mydlił   nam   oczy   pięknymi obietnicami.*
        he soaped us:DAT eyes:ACC beautiful promises:INST
        'He pulled the wool over our eyes with his pretty promises.'

(124)   *Ta sprawa   mocno   mu   leżała na sercu.*
        this matter:NOM strongly him:DAT lay   on heart:LOC
        'This matter weighed heavily on his heart.'

(125)   *Kamień   spadł mi   z   serca!*
        rock:NOM fell off me:DAT from heart:GEN
        'It's a load off my chest!'

(126)   *Ponure myśli   płoszyły   mu   sen*
        gloomy thoughts:NOM send scampering away him:DAT sleep:ACC
        z   powiek.
        from eyelids:GEN
        'He was kept awake by gloomy thoughts.'

(127)   *Smutek   kładł   mu   się na duszę.*
        sadness:NOM lay down him:DAT INTR on soul:ACC
        'Sadness settled upon his soul.'

Since all of these expressions are understood to describe mental experience, they evoke the sphere of awareness, which motivates the use of the dative case. However, the dative ending can also be justified on the level of literal meaning, since the action is construed as affecting a central part of the personal sphere – the body.

2.2.10. Verbs of communication

Another large group of verbs which typically take dative complements is verbs of communication. This is a very inclusive group, comprising not only verbs of telling (128-132), but also a number of special subgroups such as verbs of making manifest (e.g. *wyjaśnić* 'to explain/make clear', *(wy)tłumaczyć* 'to explain', *wykazać* 'to show', *(wy)klarować* 'to make clear', *wykładać* 'to lecture', *unaocznić* 'to make evident', *wyłuszczyć* 'to set forth, to spell out'), of advice (*radzić* 'to advise', *odradzać* 'to dissuade', *służyć/wspierać radą* 'to assist with advice', *udzielać porady* 'to give [professional] advice', *perswadować* 'to persuade', *wyperswadować* 'to talk out of [doing something]', *zalecać* 'to recommend', *wybić z głowy* 'to put someone off doing something' (lit., 'to knock out of someone's head')), congratulating (*życzyć* 'to wish', *gratulować* 'to congratulate', *winszować* 'to congratulate', *składać życzenia* 'to express one's [best] wishes'), verbal aggression (*dokuczać* 'to tease, to spite', *docinać* 'to tease', *przygadywać* 'to gibe', *wymyślać* 'to abuse', *złorzeczyć* 'to vituperate, to curse' *ubliżać* 'to insult', *urągać* 'to shower abuse on someone'), flattery (*schlebiać* 'to flatter', *kadzić* 'to adulate', *podlizywać się* 'to suck up to someone', *przytakiwać* 'to flatter someone by agreeing with everything he/she says'), as well as verbs denoting artistic performance (*śpiewać* 'to sing', *grać* 'to play [a musical instrument]', *deklamować* 'to recite') and various kinds of non-verbal communication, such as verbs of showing (*pokazać* 'to show', *wskazać* 'to point out', *prezentować* 'to present', *przedstawiać* 'to introduce', *demonstrować* 'to demonstrate', *okazać* 'to show [one's ticket, papers, etc., to an official]') and greeting (*kłaniać się* 'to bow', *dygać* 'to curtsey', *salutować* 'to salute', *czapkować* 'to doff one's cap to someone').

(128) *Piotr   powiedział/wyznał/ oznajmił/powtarzał mi,*
Piotr:NOM told/   confided/declared/ repeated me:DAT
że   nie lubi Ani.
that not likes Ania:GEN
'Peter told/confided to/declared to/repeated to me that he didn't like Ania.'

(129) *Piotr   wspomniał mi   o   tym.*
Piotr:NOM mentioned me:DAT about this:LOC
'Piotr has mentioned this to me.'

(130) *Zespół   zameldował/zadeklarował dyrekcji*
team:NOM reported/   declared   management:DAT
swoją gotowość   do podjęcia   pracy.
self's readiness:ACC to taking up:GEN work:GEN
'The team informed the management of its willingness to take up work.'

(131) *Nie odpowiedział mi   na moje pytanie.*
not he answered   me:DAT on my question:ACC
'He didn't answer my question.'

(132) *Będziesz mi   podpowiadać?*
you will me:DAT to prompt
'Will you prompt me [with the correct answer]?'

Since the very concept of communication necessarily implies an addressee capable of understanding the message, verbs of communication must evoke the sphere of awareness, which motivates the use of the dative case to code the person to whom the message is communicated. Moreover, communication is usually thought of as the *transfer* of ideas (cf. Reddy 1979), so the fact that the dative is used to mark the recipient (see section 2.2.1) provides additional motivation for this use. It is worth noting that the addressee is uniformly expressed by a dative

NP regardless of the grammatical organization of the rest of the clause, that is, regardless of whether the content of the message is specified by a subordinate clause (128), a prepositional phrase (129), a direct object (130), sublexically (131), or left unspecified (132).[22]

2.2.11. Allative uses of the dative

In Protoslavonic, the primary meaning of the dative was to signal the goal towards which an object was moving (Schenker 1993: 108). In the course of the evolution of the language this use of the dative was gradually replaced by prepositional constructions (*ku* + DAT for near goals and *do* + GEN for further goals) (Kempf 1978: 92).[23] But traces of the original allative function still remain in certain structures. First, most of the prepositions that "govern" the dative may be said to be allative prepositions, since they profile either motion towards a landmark (*ku* 'towards') or motion in a direction opposite to that in which the landmark is moving (*przeciw* 'against', *wbrew* 'against, in spite of'; in the case of the latter two, the motion is abstract). It is not unreasonable to suppose that these prepositions govern the dative because the meaning of this case is compatible with their meaning (cf. section 5.5). Secondly, as pointed out by Kempf (1978:93), the allative syntax has survived in at least one construction:

(133)   *Wszyscy wyszli/wyjechali/wybiegli   mu   na spotkanie/naprzeciw.*
        all:NOM walked out/rode out/ran out him:DAT   for meeting/ opposite
        'Everyone came out/rode out/ran out to meet him.'

Third, some verbs which take dative complements are most naturally analyzed as profiling abstract motion towards the dative-marked participant. These include some of the verbs which have been dealt with above (verbs of giving, verbs of communicating), as well as two groups that do not fit the target person schema.

The first of these groups comprises experiential verbs which take dative complements denoting the *object* rather than the subject of experience. The verbs in (134) share three properties: they all describe an act of distal perception; in each case, the perception is active (the perceiver consciously directs her attention at the object of perception); and they all take the allative prefix *przy-*[24] and the detransitivizer *się*. The directionality is less obvious in (135), which also lacks the allative prefix; but even here the experiencer may be metaphorically said to direct his "mental gaze" at the object of experience, the addressee's thoughtlessness.[25]

(134)   *Przyglądała/Przypatrywała/Przysłuchiwała mu   się*
        she looked/ she observed/ she listened   him:DAT INTR
        z   zainteresowaniem.
        with interest:INST
        'She looked at/observed/listened to him with interest.'

(135)   Dziwię   się   twojej lekkomyślności.
        I am surprised INTR your   thoughtlessness:DAT
        'I'm surprised at your thoughtlessness.'

The second group includes verbs of comparison (136-142a). For each of these verbs, the dative NP specifies a standard against which the subject participant's properties or performance is measured. The nominative participant attempts to measure up to, or approximate, this standard, and the verb profiles an abstract (and subjective) motion toward this point of reference.[26] As before, some of these verbs take an allative prefix, in this case *do-* (examples (136) and (137)). The comparison can be quite straightforward, as in (136), where a characteristic of Arthur's and of Piotr's (e.g. height, knowledge) is measured on the same scale; or less direct, as in (141) and (142a). In (141) a certain amount of effort or ability is required to cope with the task: what is at stake is whether the participant designated by the nominative NP has this ability and tries hard enough. Thus the nominative participant's potency is measured against that required for the task; the abstract motion is that towards some point on the scale of potency corresponding to the amount of potency necessary for completing the task. (142a) evokes a reference point on a scale which measures the value of the results of a certain activity. The reference point is the value which normally corresponds to the amount of effort expended. The verb evokes abstract subjective motion towards this point of reference. (142b), which employs the same verb, *odpowiadać* does not describe an act of comparison, but a state of one-to-one correspondence which holds between syllables and written symbols. In this case, the conceptualizer traces a mental path from the symbols (expressed by a nominative NP) to the syllables (dative NP).

(136)   *Piotr   dorównywał Arturowi   wzrostem/   wiedzą.*
        Piotr:NOM equalled   Artur:DAT   height:INST/knowledge:INST
        'Piotr matched Artur in height/for knowledge.'

(137)   *Oni   mu   do piet   nie dorastają.*
        they:NOM him:DAT   to heels:GEN not reach in height
        'They cannot hold a candle to him.'

(138)   *Sztuka   nie sprosta   arcydziełom   przyrody.*
        art:NOM   not will match masterpieces:DAT nature:GEN
        'Art will not match up to the masterpieces of nature.' (Szymczak 1981)

(139)   *Wszyscy Filistyni   nie mogli dać rady   Samsonowi.*
        all   Philistines:NOM   not could to manage   Samson:DAT
        'All the Philistines were no match for Samson.'

(140)   *Nie ustępował   talentem   współczesnym poetom.*
        not yieleded   talent:INST   contemporary poets:DAT
        'He was just as talented as other contemporary poets.' (ibid.)

(141)   Czy   Piotr   podoła   zadaniu/ trudnościom?
        INTERROG Piotr:NOM will be equal task:DAT/difficulties:DAT
        'Will Piotr prove equal to the task/difficulties?'

(142) a. *Osiągnięte wyniki   nie odpowiadają nakładowi pracy.*
        achieved   effects:NOM not correspond   input:DAT work:GEN
        'The effects achieved do not correspond to the work put in.'

(142) b. *Znaki   pisma   sylabicznego odpowiadają*
        symbols:NOM writing:GEN syllabic   correspond
        poszczególnym   sylabom.
        individual   syllables:DAT
        'The symbols of a syllabic writing system correspond to individual syllables.' (Polański 1980)

The question that comes to mind at this juncture is how the allative use is related to the other functions of the dative case. It has already been indicated that some uses of the dative that have been subsumed under the allative schema (to mark the recipient in an act of transfer or the addressee in a communicative event) fit the allative schema as well. This suggests that if 'motion towards a goal' were characterized at an appropriate level of abstraction, then perhaps all uses of the dative case could be subsumed under this description. For example, any action that affects an object that is in the TP's personal sphere could be seen as an action directed towards the target person in some abstract metaphorical sense. Similarly, the semantic characterization of the concept of beneficiary, or of verbs which express ideas such as helping, interference, causing someone to have a mental experience, or breach of privacy, does incorporate an element of directionality, although it is not always easy to pinpoint. This could lead one to follow the localistic tradition and posit 'abstract movement towards the landmark' as the overarching schema for the dative category. This, however, would lead to two problems.

First, some uses of the dative are clearly non-directional (e.g. the sensation/action-in-the-sphere-of-awareness construction discussed in section 2.2.9, or the occurrence of dative complements with stative predicates of subordination such as *podlegać* 'to work/be under [someone's authority]' or *być posłusznym* 'to obey someone'. Secondly, the allative schema is far too general, since its specifications are also fulfilled by the accusative and by various prepositional constructions (*do* 'to' + GEN, *na* 'onto' + ACC, *dla* 'for' + GEN). The purely allative uses of the dative, in contrast, are severely restricted. For example, while *dziwić się* 'to be surprised (at)' and *przyglądać się* 'to look (at)' take dative objects, *cieszyć się* 'to be happy, to look forward to' and *zdumiewać się* 'to be amazed (at)' do not. The allative uses, therefore, require their own local schemas, and these will have to be quite specific: for example, the schema for the 'going out to meet NOM' sense exemplified in (133) will have to specify that the verb must be a verb of motion with the prefix *wy-*, and that it must be followed either by *na spotkanie* 'for meeting' or *naprzeciw* 'opposite'; the active distal perception schema will have to specify that the verb must be imperfective, have the allative prefix *przy-* and the detransitivizer *się,* and so on. (Such semi-idiomaticity is very common with the more peripheral senses of an item: see Taylor 1990.)

Therefore, I will retain the personal sphere schema as the most general formulation of the meaning of the dative case.[27] How, then, are the allative uses related to the more central personal sphere uses? To answer this question, let us first consider the meaning of the dative from a diachronic perspective. Most Slavists appear to agree that in Protoslavonic, the dative was basically an allative case. In contemporary Polish, most uses can be subsumed under the target person schema, though traces of the allative sense still remain. This means that in the course of the development from Protoslavonic to Polish, the category center shifted from the allative to the target person schema. Let us examine the semantic extensions that made this shift possible.

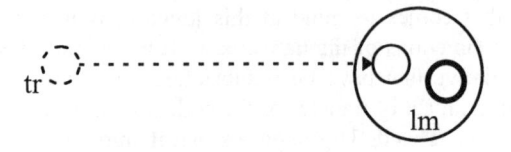

Figure 4. The goal schema

As a starting point, consider the purely spatial sense represented graphically in Figure 4. The trajector (tr) moves along a path towards the landmark (lm) until it reaches the landmark's vicinity (represented by the large circle), where it comes to rest. The dative inflection profiles the landmark of the configuration resulting from this movement.

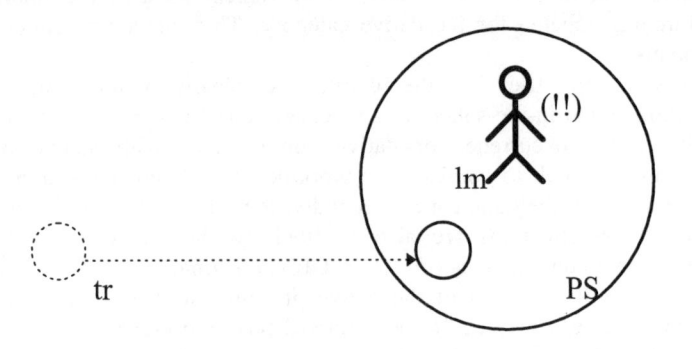

Figure 5. The recipient schema

The landmark of the configuration represented in Figure 4 can be any thing (in the technical sense), including – as a special case – a person. Now a human landmark differs from a non-human one in two relevant respects. First, it is more versatile, since it can define a region not just in physical space, but also various abstract regions such as the sphere of influence, the sphere of awareness, and the private sphere. Secondly, unlike an inanimate landmark, a human being is normally affected when an object enters the personal sphere. When we are told that, for example, an object was thrown towards a person, we can reasonably infer that the individual was affected. This specialized sense is represented in Figure 5. The large circle stands for the personal sphere; the two exclamation marks symbolize the recipient's affectedness. They are in parentheses because the inference of affectedness is not always drawn.

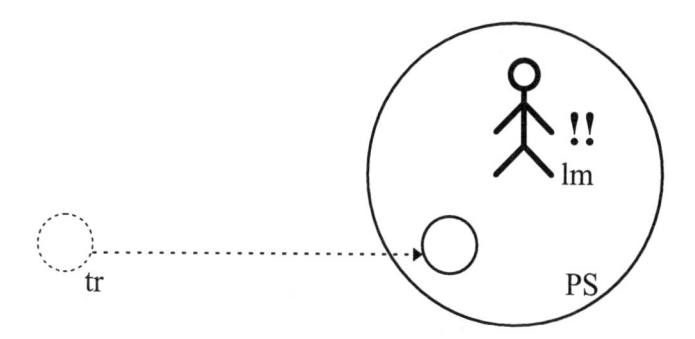

Figure 6. The affected recipient schema

When this implicature becomes conventionalized, we get the affected recipient sense, represented in Figure 6. Once conventionalized, this aspect of the meaning of the dative tends to gain in prominence, since human beings are usually more interested in how other humans are affected than in the final location of a displaced object, and hence pay more attention to this aspect of the scene. (In figure 6, this increase in prominence is represented by putting the exclamation marks in boldface.)

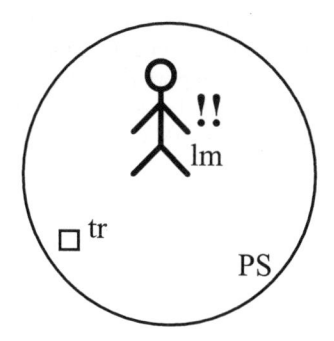

Figure 7. The target person schema

The development from the allative to the affected recipient, then, involves gradual defocusing of the path substructure and a concomitant increase in the prominence of the landmark participant's personal sphere and affectedness. Figure 7 represents the final stage of this process, in which the notion of movement towards the landmark has disappeared altogether. Notice that the trajector of this sense of the dative can be any kind of entity, including a process. (This is reflected in the diagrams by the usual convention of using a small circle to represent "things" and a small square to represent "entities".) Note too that the more abstract schema subsumes all the uses of the dative discussed in the previous sections, including the 'affected recipient' as a special case: the trajector of the dative ending might well be an action that increases the TP's potency.

What we have, therefore, is a chain of four schemas, each bearing a close resemblance to its neighbors and more distant relationship to the others. The similarities between the local schemas can be captured by higher-level schemas: the 'allative', which subsumes the local schemas which evoke the notion of movement (concrete or abstract) towards a landmark, i.e. the first three schemas in the chain, and 'target person', which subsumes 'recipient' and 'affected recipient' as special cases.

Now while the chain could in principle reflect the historical evolution of the dative category, it is more likely that at any one time most (if not all) of these schemas co-existed.[28] What changed was the category center: the recipient (i.e. human goal) in Protoslavonic, and the target person in contemporary Polish. This occurred against the backdrop of the continuous expansion of prepositional constructions, which gradually took over the more concrete spatial uses of the dative. According to Kempf (1978), this process was already well under way in Protoslavonic; and it has continued right up to the present day (cf. Buttler 1976).

Although the category center has shifted over the years, the earlier allative uses remained. What we have today is a network of senses clustered around the affected recipient schema; many of these still contain a path substructure as part of their semantic make-up, but in most of the local schemas it is rather attenuated. The target person superschema captures the common core shared by all category members except the purely allative uses discussed at the beginning of this subsection. The allative thus emerges as a fairly peripheral sense, related to the other values of the dative (e.g. recipient, addressee, beneficiary) by family resemblance. This conclusion is supported by the fact that this use seems to be restricted to the dozen or so verbs discussed in this section,[29] and, unlike the other uses of the dative, it is not extendable to novel situations.

2.3. The ethic dative

2.3.1. The problem

Traditional grammars often mention a special use of dative personal pronouns, the "ethic" dative, exemplified in (143) and (144):

(143)   *Tylko mi   nie hałasuj!*
        just me:DAT not make noise
        'Don't you make any noise!'

(144)   *Chodzę sobie   po   mieście.*
        I walk REFL:DAT all around town:LOC
        'I just walk all around town.'

The semantic contribution of the dative pronoun in the above sentences is anything but obvious; in fact, it is often considered entirely meaningless: "[the meaning of the ethic dative (*dativus ethicus*)] is so vague that it fades away completely, and its use becomes superfluous... Leaving out the ethic dative would do no harm whatsoever to the completeness of the thought expressed by the sentence" (Szober 1959: 352, my translation).

However, when we compare pairs of sentences with and without these supposedly meaningless pronouns, we find that they do differ in meaning, although the differences are sometimes quite elusive.

(145) a.   *Nie używaj tej szminki.*
           not use   this lipstick:GEN
           'Don't use this lipstick.'

(145) b.   *Nie używaj mi   tej szminki.*
           not use   me:DAT this lipstick:GEN
           'Don't you use this lipstick [or else!]'[30]

(145a) could be offered as friendly advice (*Don't use that lipstick. It doesn't look good on you.*), whereas the second sentence can only be a categorical prohibition (*Don't you use that lipstick! A respectable girl of your age should dress modestly and use no make-up!*).[31]

(146) a.   *Proszę zamykać za   sobą   drzwi.*
           please to close behind REFL:INST door:ACC
           'Please close the door behind you.'

(146) b.   *Proszę mi   zamykać za   sobą   drzwi.*
           please me:DAT to close behind REFL:INST door:ACC
           'Close that door behind you!'

(146a) is a request and (146b) a rather abrupt command; moreover, (146b) suggests that the speaker is irritated. Utterances containing ethic datives are often perceived as less polite than those without them. (In (146b) the polite *proszę* 'please', clashes with the brusque command.) This becomes particularly clear in utterances addressed to individuals of higher social status than the speaker. A junior member of faculty could say to a professor,

(147) *Panie profesorze,   proszę nie używać dziś   drukarki,*
       Sir   professor:VOC please not to use   today printer:GEN
       jest uszkodzona.
       it is out of order
       'Please do not use the printer today, professor: it's out of order.'

but not

(148) *Panie profesorze,   proszę mi   nie używać dziś   drukarki,*
       sir   professor:VOC please me:DAT not to use   today printer:GEN
       jest uszkodzona.
       it is out of order
       'Please don't you dare use that printer today, professor, it's out of order.'

An imperative clause can express a command, a request, advice, etc.; adding a first person dative pronoun seems to preclude the possibility of interpreting it as a request or advice. In all of the above examples, the clauses with the ethic datives are commands with overtones of impatience, irritation, lack of respect, or even a veiled threat. On the other hand, in some cases the very same dative pronoun has very different connotations. A mother who says to her child

(149) *Tylko mi   nie choruj.*
       just me:DAT not be ill
       '[Now be a good girl and] don't get ill.'

or

(150) *Nie płacz mi   już.*
       not cry   me:DAT already
       '*Please* don't cry. [It's breaking my heart.]'

expresses empathy rather than irritation. The ethic dative, therefore, communicates that the mother identifies with the child's feelings.

Ethic datives also pose a distributional problem for the linguist. One can explain the occurrence of a dative nominal with nouns such as *dać* 'to give' or *ufać* 'to trust' in terms of the valence properties of the verb. On the other hand, it should be possible for the supposedly meaningless dative pronoun to occur in any clause, which would justify a separate treatment of the two types of dative nominals in linguistic description. This, however, is not the case:

(151) a. *Wszyscy mu   śpią.
        all:NOM   him:DAT sleep

(151) b. ? Sąsiedzi   mu   hałasują.
         neighbors:NOM him:DAT are noisy

(151) c. *Jola   jej   siedziała.
         Jola:NOM her:DAT was sitting

The unacceptability of the sentences in (151) cannot be accounted for in terms of the combinatorial properties of the verbs because other sentences with the very same verbs are entirely acceptable:

(152) a. Studenci   mu   śpią na wykładach.
         students:NOM him:DAT sleep on lectures:LOC
         'His students sleep during his lectures.'

(152) b. Dzieci   sąsiadów   hałasują   mu
         children:NOM neighbors:GEN make noise him:DAT
         pod   oknami.
         under windows: LOC
         'The neighbors' children are making a lot of noise right under his windows.'

(152) c. Siedź mi   spokojnie.
         sit   me:DAT quietly
         'You sit here quietly [or else!].'

By manipulating the other parts of the sentence one can obtain various degrees of acceptability:

(153) a. *Wszyscy im   śpią.
         all:NOM   them:DAT sleep

(153) b. ? Dzieci   im   śpią.
         children:NOM them:DAT sleep

(153) c. (?) Dzieci   już   im   śpią.
         children:NOM already them:DAT sleep
         'Their children are already asleep [so they are going to have some peace].'

(153) d. Moja mała   ostatnio bardzo źle mi   sypia.
         my   little girl:NOM lately   very   badly me:DAT sleeps:HAB
         'My little girl has been sleeping very badly recently [so I haven't been getting too much sleep either].'

58 *The meaning of the dative*

To summarize: sentences with "ethic" datives differ in meaning from sentences without them. However, it is by no means obvious why adding the dative pronoun has the peculiar semantic consequences described above. The meaning of a sentence with an "ethic" dative is certainly not the sum of the meanings of the pronoun and the rest of the sentence. Moreover, it does not appear easy to specify which sentences with ethic datives are grammatical and which are not.

2.3.2. Ethic datives and imperatives

Most of the ethic datives cited as examples in the literature occur in imperatives or in infinitival clauses used as commands:

(154) a. *Nie udawaj mi   idioty.*
         not pretend me:DAT idiot:GEN
         'Don't play the idiot with me.'

(154) b. *Siedź mi   spokojnie.*
         sit   me:DAT quietly
         'You sit here quietly [or else!]'

(154) c. *Nie wyglądać mi   przez okno!*
         not to look out me:DAT through window:ACC
         'Don't look out that window [or else!]'

The basic function of the imperative mood is to express commands. For a sentence to be used felicitously as a command, the following conditions must be met:
1. The speaker wants the addressee to perform a future act A;
2. The speaker has the authority to make the addressee do A;
3. The speaker believes the addressee can do A; and
4. The speaker believes that the addressee will not do A in the normal course of events of his own accord (Searle 1969 [1984]: 66).

There are two (mutually non-exclusive) reasons why the speaker may want the addressee to do A: either the action itself or its results are beneficial for the speaker or the speaker wants to assert his power over the addressee. In the former case, the utterance will contain a "dative of benefit":

(155) *Zrób mi kanapkę.*
       'Fix me (DAT) a sandwich.'

and in the latter case, an "ethic" dative:

(156) *Siedź mi   spokojnie.*
       sit   me:DAT quietly
       'You sit here quietly [or else!]'

It is no coincidence that most sentences with the ethic dative are commands. Commands presuppose that the speaker has the authority to make the addressee do what he is told to do – in other words, they presuppose that the addressee is within the speaker's sphere of influence. This condition is the link which triggers off one of the sphere-of-influence interpretation strategies for the dative. In all the examples in (154) the agent (i.e. the addressee of the command) is within the speaker's sphere of influence, and the sphere of influence will either expand or shrink depending on whether the agent carries out the command or not. The speaker is thus a target person and is coded by a dative pronoun.

Therefore, it is the use of the imperative mode *to express a command* that sanctions the use of the dative pronoun. At this point it should be clear why an imperative clause with an ethic dative is interpreted as a command and not as a request or advice, although these are possible values of the imperative mode. Neither a request nor an act of giving advice presupposes that the speaker has the authority to direct the actions of the addressee; consequently, the addressee's failure to comply with the request or the advice will not result in a shrinking of the speaker's sphere of influence. If (145b) or (146b) were to be interpreted as either of these, nothing would motivate the presence of the dative pronoun. Thus, unless there is something else in the utterance or in the context to motivate a different interpretation, the dative pronoun forces the command interpretation of the imperative.

We can now explain the special connotations of the imperative with an ethic dative. Sentences such as (145b), (146b) and (154a-c) not only presuppose that the addressee is in the speaker's sphere of influence, but they *explicitly code* this as well. Since it is considered impolite to assert one's authority openly, imperative clauses with ethic datives are judged to be less polite than those without them. Moreover, one does not usually need to assert one's authority unless it is being challenged or disregarded (or one feels it is disregarded). Since any infringement of an individual's sphere of influence is likely to arouse feelings such as impatience or irritation, these feelings are often attributed to speakers who add the first-person ethic dative pronoun to a simple imperative clause.

2.3.3. Ethic datives and empathy

Examples (157-159) below illustrate a different use of the ethic dative, which I will call the empathic use.

(157)   *Tylko mi   nie choruj!*
            just   me:DAT not be ill
            '[Now be a good girl and] don't get ill.'

(158)   *Tylko mi   się   nie skalecz.*
            just   me:DAT INTR not cut
            'Just don't get yourself cut. [This would really make mamma sad!]'

(159) No nie płacz mi   już.
       oh not cry   me:DAT already
       '*Please* don't cry now [It's breaking my heart].'

The effect of the use of the dative pronoun in these sentences is not to assert the speaker's influence over the addressee. Sentences (157-159), though imperative in form, are not commands, since they fail to meet the felicity conditions on commands (in (157), carrying out the command or request is beyond the addressee's control, and in (158), it fully coincides with the addressee's will). The dative pronoun in these sentences softens the abruptness of the command: thus its effect is opposite to that of the uses we have considered so far. Moreover, unlike the sentences in the preceding section, (157-159) have perfectly acceptable non-imperative analogues:

(160) Dziecko   mi   choruje.
       child:NOM me:DAT is ill
       'My child is ill.'

(161) Moje maleństwo   mi   się   skaleczyło.
       my little baby:NOM me:DAT INTR cut
       'My little baby has cut herself.'

(162) Serce   mi   się   kraje jak ona   mi   tak płacze.
       heart:NOM me:DAT INTR slices as she:NOM me:DAT so cries
       'It's wringing my heart to hear her cry so.'

The empathic use of the dative pronoun is possible only when the relationship between the nominative and the dative participant is so close that the dative participant shares all the emotions of the nominative participant. The archetype of this kind of relationship is that between a mother and her young child; the relationship between lovers would also be a good example. The close emotional link motivates the use of the dative case, since the dative participant is seen as affected by anything that happens to the nominative participant: the latter is in the former's sphere of empathy, another subregion of the personal sphere. The main difference between this use of the dative case and lexically governed and non-pronominal free datives is that in this case, information about inclusion in the personal sphere is not stated explicitly in the sentence, but must be deduced from the context.[32]

2.3.4. Ethic datives and self-determination

Still another variant of the ethic dative construction is exemplified in (163-164)

(163)   *Ojciec   mu   kazał siedzieć w domu   i   się   uczyć,*
        father:NOM him:DAT told to sit   at home:LOC and INTR to teach
        a   on   sobie   chodzi na dyskoteki.
        and he:NOM REFL:DAT goes   on discos:ACC
        'His father told him to stay at home and study, so what does he do? – he goes to discos.'

(164)   *Ty   tu   sobie   piwo   pijesz, z   dziewczynami*
        you:NOM here REFL:DAT beer:ACC drink with girls:INST
        flirtujesz, a   ja   pracuję za dwóch,   tak?
        flirt   and I:NOM work   for two:GEN   yes?
        'So here you are drinking your beer and flirting with girls, and I am supposed to do the work for both of us, huh?'

Here the "ethic dative" is the reflexive pronoun *sobie*. If we extend the analysis developed in 2.3.2 to cover these sentences, we must conclude that they assert that the nominative participant engages in an action because he is in his own sphere of influence – i.e. because he does exactly what he wants to do. Though of course such an assertion is perfectly coherent, it seems somewhat strange that this should be explicitly coded, since the fact that the agent's involvement in the action is volitional is certainly the normal expectation. The semantic contribution of *sobie* would thus appear negligible, apparently corroborating the traditional claim that it is meaningless.

I will presently show that although the effect of the use of *sobie* is to assert that the agent is in his own sphere of influence, it does not follow that the pronoun is meaningless. For one thing, even if the effect of the use of the pronoun is nothing more than the assertion of the agent's volitionality, this does have semantic consequences, since the *sobie*-less sentence is open to the interpretation that the agent's action was non-volitional. Thus, (165b), in contrast to (165a), is contradictory.

(165) a. *Chodził sobie   na dyskoteki   i   pił   piwo,*
         he went REFL:DAT on discos:ACC and he drank beer:ACC
         bo   miał   ochotę.
         because had   desire:ACC
         'He [willfully] went to discos and drank beer because he felt like it.'

(165) b. ?? *Chodził sobie   na dyskoteki   i   pił   piwo,*
         he went REFL:DAT   on discos:GEN and he drank beer:ACC
         bo   mu   ojciec   kazał.
         because him:DAT father:NOM told

'He [willfully] went to discos and drank beer because his father told him to.'

Moreover, the insertion of the reflexive pronoun does more than merely indicate that the agent's action is volitional, as the sentences with *sobie* invariably have special implications. The import of (163) and (164) is that the agent does not do what is required or expected of him, but indulges his own whims: in other words, he breaks out of someone else's sphere of influence and into his own, so to speak. In (166a) and (167a), the explicit reference to the fact that the agent is in his own sphere of influence implies that the motivation for performing the action is entirely internal: the agent engages in the action merely for the pleasure of performing it, and with no other end in mind. Consequently, *sobie* cannot be used when the action is performed with a specific external end – hence the ungrammaticality of the (b) sentences.

(166) a. *Śpiewam sobie,   bo   mam   ochotę.*
I sing   REFL:DAT because I have desire:ACC
'I'm singing because I feel like it/for my own pleasere.'

(166) b. **Śpiewam sobie,   bo   chcę   uśpić   dziecko.*
I sing   REFL:DAT because I want to lull to sleep baby:ACC
'I sing for my own pleasure because I want to lull the baby to sleep.'

(167) a. *Dzieci   biegały   sobie   po   podwórku.*
children:NOM were running REFL:DAT all over yard:LOC
'The children were running all over the yard [because they felt like it].'

(167) b. **Dzieci   biegały   sobie,   żeby   się   nie*
children:NOM were running REFL:DAT in order to INTR not
spóźnić   do szkoły.
to be late to school:GEN
'The children were running [because they felt like it] so as not to be late for school.'

Sometimes the assertion that the action occurs within the agent's sphere of influence has the effect of suggesting that it does not impinge on any other individual's personal sphere. Thus, (168),

(168)   *Siedział   sobie   w kącie   i czytał   książkę.*
he was sitting REFL:DAT in corner:LOC and was reading book:ACC
'He was [quietly] sitting in a corner reading a book.'

could be used to set the scene for a description of unprovoked aggression:

(169) Siedział   sobie   w kącie   i   czytał   książkę.
       he was sitting REFL:DAT in corner:LOC and was reading book:ACC
       Nagle   zaatakował go   jakiś pijany wyrostek.
       suddenly attacked   him:ACC some drunk young bully:NOM
       'He was [quietly] sitting in a corner reading a book. Suddenly he was attacked by some drunk young bully.'

Thus, the function of *sobie* in all of the above sentences is to assert that the agent is in his own sphere of influence at the time of the action. Contextual factors will trigger off one of the specific interpretations discussed above. When reference is made to the agent's obligations or another individual's authority, assertion of self-determination results in the 'defiance' reading. Otherwise, asserting that the agent is in his own sphere of influence has the effect of implying that his motivation is entirely internal – in other words, that the action is undertaken just for the pleasure of performing it. If the action is also harmless, the sentence with *sobie* is open to the interpretation that the agent is doing what he has a right to do and is not bothering anyone else.

Finally, let us see how the "ethic" *sobie* affects the meaning of imperative clauses.

(170) A   siedź sobie   w domu   i   nic   nie rób.
       and sit   REFL:DAT at home:LOC and nothing:ACC not do
       'OK, stay at home doing nothing – see if I care!'

Although (170) is imperative in form, it is not an order or even a request, but a *waiver*: by explicitly asserting that the addressee is in his own sphere of influence, the speaker acknowledges his (the addressee's) self-determination, and possibly also lack of empathy with the addressee. (170) would only be appropriate if the addressee wanted to stay at home and had insisted on that right. Compare this to (171), where the speaker asserts that the addressee is in her (the speaker's) sphere of influence:

(171) Siedź mi   w domu   i   nic   nie rób.
       sit   me:DAT at home:LOC and nothing:ACC not do
       'Stay at home like I tell you and don't do anything.'

(171) is a stern command which suggests that the addressee does not want to stay at home. Hence, the addition of the dative pronouns *mi* and *sobie* clearly leads to different interpretations of the sentence; they are thus anything but meaningless.

2.4. The structure of the dative category

The primary aim of this chapter was to show that the Polish dative case is an internally cohesive category. It was demonstrated that the vast majority of the "uses" of the dative instantiate the category schema, which specifies that the landmark participant (expressed by the nominal which carries the dative ending) is affected by an action or process occurring in his personal sphere. The one use that does not fit the category schema – the allative – bears family resemblance to a number of other uses. We have seen that the distinction between datives in transitive and in intransitive constructions is spurious: what motivates the use of the dative case are the consequences of the process for the target person, and the consequences of losing a wallet are not very different from those of having it stolen. We also noted that there are many local similarities and a great deal of overlap between the various "uses". As far as the semantics of the dative case is concerned, it is irrelevant whether the target person is a recipient in an act of giving or an individual to whom an object is made available. In the same vein, making an object available to the target person and preparing it for the TP's use have essentially the same effect on his potency, and preparing an object for the TP's use is one of many things that an agent can do to an object within the TP's sphere of influence. What all of these uses have in common is a prominent reference to the target person's potency. Potency is an important aspect of the personal sphere which also lies behind several other uses of the dative case: those which relate to the ability to do as one pleases (what I have referred to as "self determination," section 2.2.5), control over one's own actions (section 2.2.6) and control over other participants (section 2.2.5 and 2.3.2).

The relationships between the various aspects of the personal sphere are summarized in Figure 8, which also makes explicit the areas of overlap between the five "sub-spheres".

Although this chapter has observed the traditional distinction between "free" and "governed" datives for expository purposes, it should by now be quite clear that no sharp dichotomy of this kind can be maintained. A nominal complement is "governed" when its schematic representation figures as a prominent substructure in the semantic representation of the verb. However, prominence is a matter of degree, and consequently what we have is a continuum of various degrees of "governedness" rather than two mutually exclusive categories. For example, verbs such as *dać* 'to give' and *dostarczyć* 'to deliver' profile the movement of the patient into the recipient's sphere of influence, and thus strongly evoke the recipient (a special kind of target person): the verb may be said to "govern" a dative complement. Verbs such as *sprzedać* 'to sell' and *płacić* 'to pay' profile the interconnections between participants in another kind of event: the former profiles the relationship between the seller and the goods, and the latter, between the buyer and money. However, both evoke the 'commercial transaction' frame, which has the recipient as one of its central participants (see Fillmore & Atkins 1992, also Fillmore 1975, 1978); consequently, the recipient also features quite prominently in their semantic representations. Although both verbs take dative complements, they do not "govern" the dative in the same sense that *dać* and *dostarczyć* do, since the target person can be left unspecified. Finally, verbs such as *rzucić* 'to throw' and *przynieść* 'to bring' profile the path traversed by the patient, and thus evoke the Source-Path-Goal schema. The goal can be elaborated either by a locative phrase, as in (172a), or by a recipient NP, in (172b). The semantic representation of this part of the schema must be general enough to accommodate both variants. Thus although the semantic representation of the verb does include a part that is compatible with the meaning of the dative, the verb does not saliently evoke the notion of target person; hence, it can hardly be said to "govern" the dative. On the other hand, the dative complement in (172b) is not exactly "free" either.

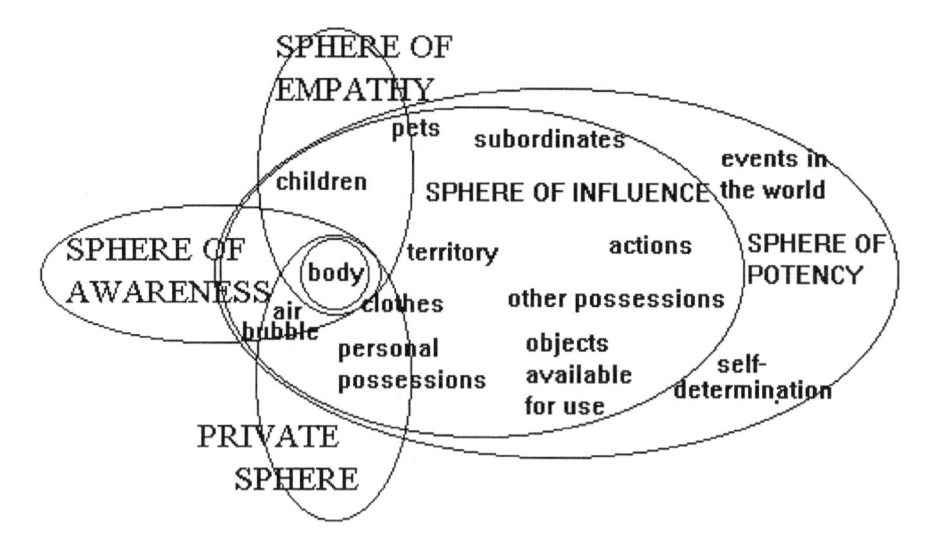

Figure 8. A map of the personal sphere

(172) a. *Piotr   rzucił/przyniósł piłkę   do piaskownicy.*
          Piotr:NOM threw/brought   ball:ACC to sandbox:GEN
          'Piotr threw/brought the ball to the sandbox.'

(172) b. *Piotr   rzucił/przyniósł piłkę   Alicji.*
          Piotr:NOM threw/brought   ball:ACC Alice:DAT
          'Piotr threw/brought the ball to Alice.'

In traditional approaches, the sharp dichotomy between "free" and "governed" datives is often blurred by introducing the notion of "optional" dative complements. The rationale for this move becomes apparent when one acknowledges that the degree of prominence of a given substructure in the semantic representation of the verb roughly corresponds to the degree of likelihood of the occurrence of the complement which elaborates that substructure. In other words, the more prominent the target person is in the semantic representation of the verb, the more likely it is to be overtly expressed. If the target person is in profile, it must be overtly expressed and may be described as an obligatory complement; if the TP is a salient substructure which is not in profile, the corresponding nominal can be described as an optional dative complement; in all other cases, the TP will be expressed by a "free" dative.

The important point is that the distinction between "free" and "governed" datives has nothing to do with the semantics of the case itself. The motivation for the use of the dative case is the same in (173a) and in (173b): in both cases, the nominative participant is in the dative participant's sphere of influence.

(173) a. *Studenci sprzeciwiali/podporządkowali mu się.*
'The students (NOM) opposed/obeyed him (DAT).'

(173) b. *Studenci   mu   spali na wykładach.*
students:NOM him:DAT slept on lectures:LOC
'His students slept during his lectures.'

There is an important difference, however, in the way that sentences with free and governed datives are processed, specifically, in the way that the meaning of the dative NP is integrated with other elements to arrive at a coherent interpretation of the sentence in context. In the case of the governed dative, the blueprint for integrating the dative nominal with the rest of the sentence is provided in the semantic representation of the verb itself. For example, the semantic representation of *śnić się* 'to dream of', must make schematic reference to a participant endowed with a sphere of awareness. This participant is equated with the participant designated by the nominal with the dative ending. In a similar fashion, the verbs in (173a) evoke the TP's sphere of influence, and the target person corresponds to the referent of the dative nominal.

In a sentence with the "free" dative, the blueprint for the integration is usually provided by one of the linking strategies discussed in Section 2.1. The dative ending initiates the integration process by evoking the target person's personal sphere; the addressee's task is to identify some entity mentioned in the sentence (usually the patient, or, if there is no patient, a location or an agent) as belonging to the TP's personal sphere and to determine how the target person might be affected by an action which affects this entity. The addressee must thus determine if either the subject or the object nominals could possibly refer to a family member, a subordinate, a part of the body, a possession or object used, or someone's territory; if this is so, he assumes that this is in fact the case. If the relevant noun is relational, the linking process is fairly straightforward, since the relationship is assumed to hold between the dative participant and the individual named by the relational noun. For example, in (174-176) it is assumed that the individuals referred to are the target person's daughter, secretary, and students.

(174)   *Córka   dobrze mu   się   uczyła.*
daughter:NOM well   him:DAT INTR teach
'His daughter did well at school.'

(175) Sekretarka   mu   zachorowała.
       secretary:NOM him:DAT got ill
       'His secretary got ill.'

(176) Studenci   mu   śpią na wykładach.
       students:NOM him:DAT sleep on lectures:LOC
       'His students sleep during his lectures.'

If the noun is not relational, its referent can be included in the target person's personal sphere on the basis of knowledge of the real world or by assumption. For example, the addressee may know that Alicja in (177) is the TP's daughter and hence the interpretation of that sentence will pose no problems. In (178), the addressee could know that the car referred to belonged to Robert, or perhaps that he had the right to or was about to use it. If she does not know this for a fact, she will probably assume it to be the case, since only then will the sentence be interpretable. The next two examples are interpretable only if one assumes that the addressee of the command is in the target person's sphere of influence (179) or that the TP empathizes with him (180).

(177) Alicja   dobrze mu   się   uczyła.
       Alicja:NOM well   him:DAT INTR teach
       'That Alice of his was a good student.'

(178) Piotr   rozbił   Robertowi   samochód.
       Piotr:NOM crashed Robert:DAT car:ACC
       'Piotr crashed Robert's car.'

(179) Siedź mi   spokojnie.
       sit   me:DAT quietly
       'You sit here quietly [or else!].'

(180) Nie płacz mi   już.
       not cry   me:DAT already
       '*Please* don't cry.'

In some cases, the sentence element which triggers off the appropriate linking strategy is a locative prepositional phrase rather than the subject or object nominal. The object of the preposition is typically a part of the body, and is assumed to belong to the dative participant; the prepositional phrase defines a region near the body part, thus making possible the application of the "air-bubble" strategy (181).

(181) Kula   przeleciała chłopcu   koło ucha.
       bullet:NOM flew   boy:DAT near ear:GEN
       'The bullet flew right by the boy's ear.'

Once the element in the personal sphere has been identified, the addressee formulates a hypothesis about the way the target person might be affected by the process involving that part of his personal sphere. To do this he must draw on his knowledge of the world and of how humans react to events and states in the world. The hypothesis (or the set of hypotheses) is part of the interpretation of the utterance in context.

2.5. Conclusion

We have seen that, in spite of all the differences in the way free and governed datives are processed, they share a common meaning: the dative noun refers to an individual affected by a process or state which obtains in some part of his personal sphere, be it the sphere of potency, the sphere of empathy, the sphere of awareness, or the private sphere. (The only use of the dative which does not fit this general formulation is the allative – see section 2.2.11.)

The above definition, however, raises a problem. Although it captures what all the different "uses" of the dative case (except the allative) have in common, it fails to account for the actual distribution of dative nominals. It has been suggested that mental experience verbs evoke the sphere of awareness, which explains why they take dative complements. However, the experiencer is often expressed by a nominative rather than a dative nominal. Therefore, to maintain the claim that the choice of case-marking is semantically motivated, we must explain (1) why the nominative case can also be used in this function, and (2) what determines which case is actually used in a specific situation. Similarly, an individual affected by another person's actions can be designated by a dative *or* an accusative nominal, and the above definition of the dative case does not make explicit the mechanisms underlying the choice. In the next two chapters, therefore, I will discuss the factors which determine the choice between the nominative and the dative marking of the experiencer and between the accusative and the dative marking of the target of the action.[33]

Chapter 3: Dative and nominative experiencers

We have seen in Chapter 2 (section 2.2.9) that the dative case is often used with verbs of experience to mark the experiencer. I suggested that what motivates this usage is the fact that the personal sphere comprises the sphere of awareness – a mental region where mental processes take place and are observed by the experiencer. However, as I pointed out in the concluding section of the chapter, experiencers can also be expressed by means of nominative noun phrases.

(182)   *Krysia myśli/uważa/podejrzewa, że księżyc jest zrobiony z żółtego sera.*
'Krysia (NOM) thinks/believes/suspects that the moon is made of cheese.'

(183)   *Robert kocha/uwielbia Annę.*
'Robert (NOM) loves/adores Anna (ACC).'

The nominative, we saw in chapter 1, is the case associated with the clausal trajector – the figure in the relationship profiled by the main verb. It is not difficult to see that experiencers are very "figure-worthy": they tend to be active and potent (i.e. they are the source of energy for the process designated by the verb); moreover, they are sentient and typically human – and since our attention is naturally attracted to the human participants, we perceive humans as figures.

The prominence-based figure-ground distinction is a basic feature of conceptual organization. When we look at a scene we see a figure against a background; similarly, when we think about a scene we tend to focus our attention on one part of it and conceive of the remaining aspects in relation to this focal point.[34] At the linguistic level, this translates into singling out one salient substructure of the scene as subject. As a first approximation, then, we can say that when the situation to be described involves only one participant, as in (182), the nominal naming this participant becomes the subject by default. If this participant also has experiencer characteristics (i.e. is endowed with a sphere of awareness), they are not overtly signaled in the sentence, since a nominal cannot be both nominative and dative at the same time. When there are two participants, as in (183), the more prominent one becomes the subject. In this particular example, Robert is clearly the more salient of the two: he engages in a mental activity, while Anna is merely its (possibly unwitting) object. Thus Robert becomes the subject, and as a result his experiencer characteristics are suppressed. However, when there is a more prominent participant to assume the subject role – for example an agent – the experiencer's special properties can be explicitly signaled by a dative ending, as in (184).

(184)   *Anna dokucza Robertowi.*
'Anna (NOM) is teasing Robert (DAT).'

The decision to highlight or to suppress experiencer characteristics is actually much more complex than it may appear from the above examples. This is seen most clearly in the following examples, in which apparently synonymous or near-synonymous verbs differ in their "subject selection properties":

(185) a. *Ania lubi to zdjęcie.*
Ania:NOM likes this picture:ACC
'Ania likes this picture.'

(185) b. *Ani podoba się to zdjęcie.*
Ania:DAT pleases INTR this picture:NOM
'Ania likes this picture./This picture is pleasing to Ania.'

(186) a. *Ania podziwiała Piotra.*
Ania:NOM admired Piotr:ACC
'Ania admired Piotr.'

(186) b. *Ani imponuje Piotr.*
Ania:DAT impressed Piotr:NOM
'Piotr impressed Ania./Ania was impressed by Piotr.'

(187) a. *Piotr przypuszcza, że Ania pojechała do Krakowa.*
'Piotr (NOM) reckons that Ania has gone to Cracow.'

(187) b. *Piotrowi wydaje się, że Ania pojechała do Krakowa.*
'It seems to Piotr (DAT) that Ania has gone to Cracow.'

(188) a. *Jurek zapomniał jej nazwiska.*
'Jurek (NOM) forgot her name (GEN).'

(188) b. *Jurkowi uciekło/ wyleciało z głowy jej nazwisko.*
Jurek:DAT escaped/flew out from head:GEN her name:NOM
'Her name has slipped Jurek's memory.'

Moreover, some verbs allow the person having the mental experience to occur either in the nominative or the dative case, sometimes with no obvious difference in meaning.

(189) a. *Artur chce spać.*
'Artur (NOM) wants to sleep.'

(189) b. *Arturowi chce się spać.*
Artur:DAT it wants INTR sleep
'Artur wants to sleep/feels sleepy.'

In traditional case theory, such examples were considered proof that subject selection is an arbitrary property of verbs. In this chapter, I will show that the choice between nominative and dative marking is motivated by semantic factors.

3.1. Preliminaries

3.1.1. The dative patient-subject construction

Let us consider the linguistic options available in Polish to code an event in which one participant brings about a change of state in another participant. The default option is the standard transitive sentence in which the nominative NP corresponds to the agent of the action and the accusative NP corresponds to the patient. A common variant is the passive clause, in which the patient NP is accorded the highest degree of prominence and the nonstandard subject selection is signaled by passive morphology on the verb. Still another possibility is the dative patient-subject (DPS) construction exemplified in the (b) sentences below.[35] This construction is unusual in that it allows both the patient and the instigator of the action to appear in the same clause with the patient in subject position and no passive morphology on the verb. In this subsection, I will examine the factors which determine whether the instigator is expressed by a nominative NP, as in the standard transitive clause, or a dative NP, as in the dative patient-subject construction.

(190) a. *Piotr   pobrudził kurtkę.*
Piotr:NOM made dirty jacket:ACC
'Piotr got his jacket dirty.'

(190) b. *Piotrowi pobrudziła się   kurtka.*
Piotr:DAT made dirty INTR jacket:NOM
'Piotr's jacket got dirty.'

(191) a. *Magda przypaliła rybę.*
'Magda (NOM) burned the fish (ACC).'

(191) b. *Magdzie   przypaliła się   ryba.*
Magda:DAT burned   INTR fish:NOM
'[Magda was cooking the fish and] the fish burned; Magda was affected.'

(192) a. *Ola stłukła okulary.*
'Ola (NOM) broke the glasses/her glasses (ACC).'

(192) b. *Oli   stłukły się   okulary.*
          Ola:DAT broke   INTR glasses:NOM
          'Ola's glasses got broken.'

Although both the standard transitive construction and the dative patient-subject construction can be used to describe the same situation, the (a) and (b) sentences above differ in meaning. In the (a) sentences, the change in the patient may or may not have been intended; in the (b) sentences, the result is clearly *not* intended. The (b) sentences imply that the change in the patient occurred as a result of a process which, though it had been instigated by the dative participant, proceeded spontaneously, i.e. the human participant expended no further effort beyond the initial energy input and was not in control of the process. The (a) sentences, in contrast, though not incompatible with this interpretation, strongly suggest that the nominative participant was fully in control of the action and expended effort towards its completion. In other words, the (a) sentences stress the active participant's responsibility for the change of state in the patient, whereas the (b) sentences absolve him or her from the blame by emphasizing the spontaneous unfolding of events. Finally, the (b) sentences imply that the human participant was affected by the result of the action, whereas the (a) sentences have no such implications. For example, (190a) simply states that a jacket became dirty as a result of something Piotr did; in (190b) it was clearly Piotr's jacket rather than any other jacket and he is affected in that, for example, he will not be able to wear it tomorrow.

The special semantic properties of the DPS construction are clearly related to its formal properties. The instigator of a process is inherently more prominent than the patient and is consequently the neutral choice for the subject. The choice of the patient for the clausal trajector has the effect of maximally backgrounding the active participant's causal role. After the initial energy input, the process assumes a dynamism of its own, and events unfold without the instigator's involvement. The clause with a patient subject profiles the events following the spark-off point. In other words, the sentence is not about what the instigator does but about events that occur without his volition, control, or energy input. The agent is pushed outside the scope of predication, making the patient the only direct participant. Since the clause no longer profiles the transfer of energy from the agent to the patient, the verb can no longer be transitive: hence the detransitivizing particle *się*.[36] Because the verb is no longer transitive, (190b-192b) are grammatical even when only one nominal, that designating the core participant, is present:

(193)   *Kurtka pobrudziła się.*
        'The jacket (NOM) got dirty.'

(194)   *Ryba przypaliła się.*
        'The fish (NOM) burned.'

(195)   *Okulary stłukły się.*
        'The glasses (NOM) broke.'

The dative nominal introduces another participant and signals that the process designated by the verb impinges on his or her personal sphere. Under the relevant interpretation of (190b-192b), it is the target person's sphere of potency which is affected: it shrinks as the action gets out of control. However, the same sentence pattern can be used to describe a situation in which the dative participant is not agentively involved at all, not even as a hapless instigator, but is affected because some object belonging to his personal sphere undergoes a change of state. For example, (190b) could describe a situation in which Piotr was not causally involved in the process at all, but was simply affected by the result: for example, his jacket might have become dirty because someone pushed him into a puddle. Similarly, the noun *ryba* in (191b) could refer to the fish Magda was frying (the 'unlucky agent' interpretation: she was affected because she lost control) or to the fish that Magda was about to eat (the 'unlucky experiencer' interpretation: she will have to go without dinner tonight). The ambiguity (vagueness?) arises because the dative does not specify which region of the personal sphere is involved.

To summarize: the contrast between the standard transitive construction and the dative patient-subject construction is a contrast of imagery: the former profiles the transfer of energy from the agent to the patient, whereas the latter describes a spontaneously proceeding change of state in the patient which takes place within the personal sphere of another participant. By choosing one construction or the other, the speaker highlights different characteristics of the active participant. The nominative allows the speaker to stress his agent-like properties: the fact that he provides the energy necessary for the accomplishment of the result, and that he wants to accomplish the result and is in control of the process which makes it possible. The dative case, on the other hand, will be used when the speaker wants to focus on the affectedness of the sentient participant, the fact that his involvement was non-volitional, or on the fact that he was not in control of the action.

3.1.2. An interlude on się and impersonal constructions

Many of the dative constructions discussed in this chapter contain the clitic *się*, which I have glossed as a detransitivizer. Since this is a rather unconventional analysis – traditionally, *się* is regarded as a reflexive pronoun – it requires some justification.

Although the particle is frequently used to indicate that the agent and patient are the same individual, as in (196), it also has a number of other functions, some of which are illustrated below.

REFLEXIVE:
(196)   *Chłopiec myje się.*
        boy:NOM washes INTR
        'The boy is washing.'

RECIPROCAL:
(197) *Chłopcy biją się.*
'The boys are fighting.'

PATIENT-SUBJECT
(198) *Woda gotuje się.*
'The water is boiling.'

EXPERIENCER
(199) *Mama martwi się (twoim postępowaniem).*
'Mother is worried (by your behavior).'

(200) *Mama boi się (wilków).*
'Mother is afraid (of wolves).'

IMPERSONAL:
(201) a. *Tu się nie pali.*
here INTR not it smokes
'One doesn't smoke here.'

(201) b. *Białe wino pije się schłodzone.*
white wine:ACC it drinks INTR chilled
'White wine is drunk chilled.'

In (196)-(198), what would normally have been a transitive verb becomes intransitive: the detransitivizing function of *się* is therefore quite apparent in these sentences. Note that the verb is intransitive not just in the syntactic sense of not allowing a direct object, but also semantically: the action is no longer construed as the transfer of energy from an agent to a patient, but as a process centered around the trajector (which has both agentive and patientive properties – cf. Schenker 1985, 1986). The semantic contribution of *się* is to narrow down the verb's profile by defocusing one of the participants, thus turning a two-participant event into a one-man act. This obliterates the distinction between the head and the tail of the action chain, making the whole concept of action chain irrelevant.[37]

The effect of this narrowing of the verb's profile is best seen by comparing *się* reflexives such as (196) with sentences containing the independent reflexive pronoun *siebie* (202). In (202), the reflexive action is construed as initiated by an agent and directed at a patient. The agent and patient roles are filled by the same person, but they remain distinct; their distinctness is symbolized by the independent status of the pronoun. In contrast, (196) features only one participant engaged in a grooming action. It is in the nature of such actions that the subject is affected, and hence has both agent- and patient-like properties; but the two roles have become coalesced into one "middle" role. The fact that there is no patient participant is symbolized by the clitic status of *się;* furthermore, because the agent and patient roles are no longer distinct, *się* – unlike *siebie* – cannot be conjoined with patient NPs (cf. example (203) below).

(202)   *Chłopiec   myje   siebie.*
        boy:NOM washes REFL:ACC
        'The boy is washing himself.'

(203) a. *Chłopiec umył   najpierw siebie,   a   potem siostrę.*
          boy:NOM washed first   REFL:ACC and later sister:ACC
          'The boy first washed himself, and then his sister.'

(203) b. **Chłopiec   najpierw się   umył,   a   potem siostrę.*
          boy:NOM   first   INTR washed and later sister:ACC

The one-man (or rather one-woman) nature of the event is even more clear in (199): the subject participant here is not a masochist who causes herself to go into a mental state and then suffers its result; she simply has an emotional experience in which the cause and the result are rolled into one.

(200) differs from the earlier examples in that it contains an intrinsic reflexive: the verb *bać* occurs only in combination with the particle *się*, and does not have a transitive analogue. However, (200) resembles (199) in that engaging in mental experience and being affected by it are inseparable; thus, coding with *się* seems quite appropriate. I suggest that it is no coincidence that the overwhelming majority of intrinsically reflexive verbs are verbs of mental experience: this is clearly attributable to the fact that the experiencer role combines agent and patient properties,[38] and hence is highly compatible with *się*.

Finally, the sentences in (201) differ from all of the earlier examples in that they do not contain a nominative noun for the verb to agree with; hence, the verb occurs in the default impersonal form, the third person singular. It is not clear how such sentences should be analyzed. Traditionally, they are regarded as subjectless constructions; in GB, they are claimed to have null subjects. In a cognitive framework, they could be analyzed as setting-subject (cf. section 1.2.4) – but since they do not always contain a nominal corresponding to the schematic setting, this does not seem a very promising approach. An alternative approach would be to treat them as profiling a relationship between a diffuse (and hence unspecified) trajector and a setting-landmark (which can also be implicit). The issue is extremely controversial and I do not propose to resolve it here.[39] However, perhaps we can glean some hints about the nature of a more satisfactory solution by comparing the impersonal sentences in (201) with the archetypal impersonal construction: weather expressions.

We think of events as interactions between independently existing participants or processes affecting independently existing participants. Meteorological phenomena, however, are not particularly amenable to such a construal. Take an occurrence such as a spell of rainy weather. The object that rains does not occur independently of the process of raining: a spell of rainy weather, therefore, is most naturally conceptualized simply as a diffuse state or force contained in a setting:

(204) a. *Znowu padało.*
  again   it was falling
  'It was raining again.'

(204) b. *Było   pochmurno.*
  it was cloudily
  'It was cloudy.'

This is not to say that a Participant + Process conceptualization is not possible with meteorological phenomena: it clearly is, as evidenced by the existence of (205), which uses the same verb (*padać* 'to fall') as (204a) to describe the same occurrence. The difference is that in (205), the verb has a subject (the noun *deszcz* 'rain') and is inflected to agree with it. The point is that such a view of events is *imposed by the conceptualizer* on a content that does not obviously lend itself to such a construal.

(205) *Padał   deszcz.*
  was falling rain:NOM
  'It was raining.'

Other typical uses of subjectless constructions are to refer to permission and obligation, as in (206-207), and to established practice, as in (201) above. Intuitively, the process designated by the verb in these constructions is a disembodied "being" or "becoming" rather than "doing". It is possible, therefore, that these constructions embody a construal in which moral and social forces are viewed as something resembling meteorological phenomena – a process in which the actor is diffuse and inseparable from the event itself.

(206) *Nie wolno/ Nie można   tak postępować.*
  not allowed/not possible so   to act
  'One cannot act like that.'

(207) *Trzeba   walczyć o   swoje prawa.*
  necessary to fight about self's rights:ACC
  'One must fight for one's rights.'

Be that as it may, it seems clear that the semantic contribution of *się* in sentences such as (201) is to maximally background one of the participants evoked by the verb – the agent of the action. This function is related to the detransitivizing use described earlier: in both cases, *się* narrows down the verb's profile by defocusing one of the participants, thus obliterating the idea of action chain. It is in this sense, then, that the resulting construction is "intransitive": it longer designates the transfer of energy from an agent to a patient.

3.1.3. Folk models of the mind

It will be useful to begin our discussion of how people talk about mental experience with some comments about how they conceptualize it. I have argued elsewhere (Dąbrowska 1994b) that there are two mutually incompatible folk theories of the mind, and that these map directly onto the grammatical categories of nominative and dative.

In the first theory, which I will call the *craftsman model*, mental experience is construed as a kind of action that the experiencer engages in – a manipulation of mental objects like ideas or images. We can infer its existence from the systematic polysemy of expressions normally used to talk about the physical manipulation of objects. The verbs in (208) are all used metaphorically to describe mental actions.

(208) a. *Chciałabym trochę podszlifować francuski.*
'I would like to *polish up* my French a bit.'

(208) b. *W mig złapał, o co mi chodzi.*
'He immediately *caught* my drift.'

(208) c. *W ten sposób będziesz mogła wyrobić sobie własny pogląd.*
'This will allow you to *make up* your own mind.'

(208) d. *Gliwiński podważa/obala tę tezę w swoim artykule.*
'Gliwiński undermines (lit. *levers*)/refutes (lit. *knocks over*) this claim in his article.'

(208) e. *Asia pierwsza rozwiązała zadanie i znalazła odpowiedź.*
'Asia was the first to solve (lit. *untie*) the problem and *find* the answer.'

In the craftsman model, understanding is seen as grasping ideas (which are construed as objects), creative thinking involves shaping raw material, judgement is weighing up ideas, remembering is retrieving memories from a mental store, and so on. (See Jäkel 1995 for a detailed discussion.)

The second theory, the *mental arena model*, was briefly alluded to in section 2.2.9. It capitalizes on the fact that the mind is conceptualized as a container for ideas (cf. Lakoff & Johnson 1980) and portrays remembering, thinking, etc., as spontaneous processes occurring in the "mental arena" – the experiencer's sphere of awareness. The experiencer is merely a passive observer of events unfolding in the arena, and the events themselves are construed as existing independently of the observer:

(209) a. *Różne możliwości kłębiły się Ani w głowie.*
various possibilities:NOM were whirling INTR Ania:DAT in head:LOC
'Various possibilities were whirling around in Ania's head.'

(209) b. *Magdzie   przyszedł do głowy   lepszy tytuł.*
Magda:DAT   came   to head:GEN   better   title:NOM
'A better title occured to Magda.'

(209) c. *Jego słowa   wryły   się   chłopcu   głęboko w pamięć.*
his   words:NOM engraved INTR boy:DAT deeply   in memory:ACC
'His words left a deep imprint in the boy's memory.'

(209) d. *Jurkowi   uciekło/ wyleciało   z   głowy   jego nazwisko.*
Jurek:DAT escaped/flew out   from   head:GEN his   name:NOM
'His name slipped right out of Jurek's mind.'

(209) e. *Sróbuję jej   to   wybić   z   głowy.*
I will try her:DAT it:ACC knock out from head:GEN
'I will try to talk her out of doing it.'

Perhaps the best evidence for the robustness of this folk theory comes from popular books on psychology and the philosophy of mind, which often warn their readers against this naive view. Consider the drawing below, taken from Jackendoff 1993:

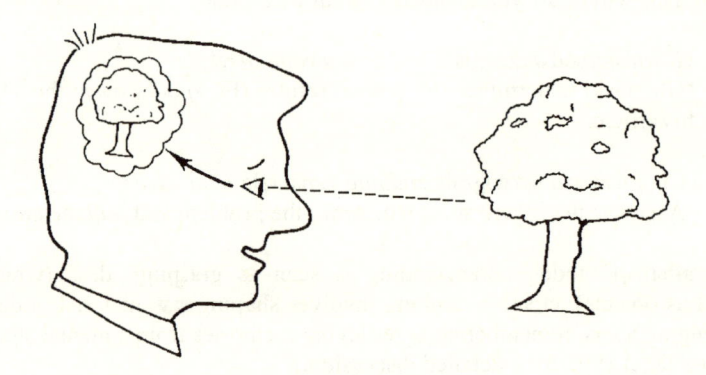

Figure 9: The way we think about Harry seeing a tree (Jackendoff 1993: 171)

Jackendoff points out that people think of vision as producing images inside the head and then explains that this view cannot be right, since it presupposes the existence of a little person (a homunculus) who looks at the images;[40] if the theory were true, this little person would also have a homunculus inside *his* head and so on. To drive the point home, he offers this drawing (both captions come from Jackendoff's book):

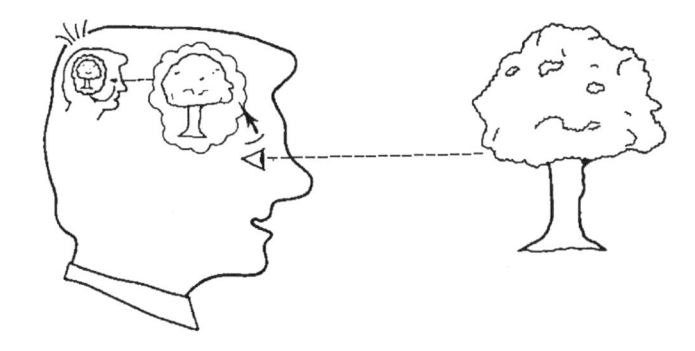

Figure 10: Who looks at the image of a tree inside Harry's head?
(Jackendoff 1993: 172)

Clearly, Jackendoff (and other writers of similar texts) would not need to explain the logical problems with the mental arena model if it weren't such a well-established folk theory of the mind.

Jackendoff's discussion deals with the folk theory of vision, but the model is applicable to other mental processes as well, since these are often thought of metaphorically as seeing. *He has seen a lot of action* means 'He has experienced a lot of action', not that he merely perceived it visually; and many visual expressions are used metaphorically to talk about understanding (cf. *I see, insight, point of view, I've got the picture*; see also Lakoff & Johnson 1980 and Jäkel 1995). I would venture to speculate that we find the "understanding is seeing" metaphor so intuitively appealing precisely because it fits in so nicely with the mental arena model and the idea that mental experience is merely the observation of independently occurring events which is implicit in it.

The two folk theories – the craftsman model and the mental arena model – highlight different characteristics of the experiencer. When mental experience is construed as an action, the experiencer becomes a kind of agent: an active participant who aims at a certain result and expends effort to achieve it – and, not surprisingly, the corresponding nominal is given a case prototypically associated with agents, the nominative. When thoughts and feelings are conceptualized as processes occurring in the experiencer's sphere of awareness, the experiencer is represented as essentially passive and setting-like,[41] and is given dative case marking.

It should be pointed out, however, that the nominative construal of the experiencer (the performer of mental actions) is generally easier to accommodate to other grammatical requirements than is the dative construal (the setting for a mental process). Experiencers are inherently more figure-worthy than the objects of experience: they are concrete participants rather than abstract concepts, and, moreover, they are human and active. Because of this asymmetry, nominative coding of the experiencer is the default option, whereas the dative requires special motivation.

3.2. Perception vs. hallucination

In section 2.2.9 I argued that verbs of perception evoke the sphere of awareness and that perception can be construed as a process occurring in this sphere. But perception is also an inherently asymmetric relationship. The perceiver is more active than the perceived object, endowed with consciousness, has at least some control over the process, and sometimes expends effort to sustain it – in other words, the perceiver is inherently more figure-worthy than the perceived object. Consequently, the perceiver is normally chosen as the clausal trajector and given nominative marking.

(210) *Michał widział/zauważył/zaobserwował, że Anna gra w tenisa.*
'Michał (NOM) saw/noticed/observed that Anna was playing tennis.'

(211) *Michał słyszał płacz dzieci.*
'Michał (NOM) heard some children crying.'

(212) *Michał poczuł, że ktoś go ciągnie za rękaw.*
'Michał (NOM) felt somebody tug at his sleeve.'

The dative construal would be motivated to the extent that it was important to downplay the perceiver's agent-like properties and to focus on the process within the sphere of awareness rather than on the real-world relationship between the perceiver and the perceived object. There is a class of perception events that fits this description very well – namely, illusions and hallucinations. An individual who experiences a hallucination sees or hears something that is not "out there" in the real world. What we have, then, is not a relationship between two objectively existing entities, but a process which is entirely subjective, which occurs only in the perceiver's sphere of awareness. Moreover, the person who falls prey to hallucinations has no control over the experience and is seen as entirely passive – a victim of strange forces rather than an agent-like explorer. In the case of hallucinations and illusions, therefore, there is much more to motivate the dative construal, and the experiencer is in fact expressed by a dative nominal (examples (213-218)). (Of course ordinary perception does have a subjective element, but it also has an objective aspect: the relationship between the perceiver and the perceived object – and it is this "public" aspect which is exploited for coding purposes. The objective relationship is absent in hallucinations.)

(213) *Michałowi wydawało się, że Anna gra w tenisa.*
Michał:DAT it seemed INTR that Anna:NOM play in tennis:ACC
'It seemed to Michał that Anna was playing tennis.'

(214) *Michałowi przywidziało się, że Anna gra w tenisa.*
Michał:DAT it appeared INTR that Anna:NOM play in tennis:ACC
'Michał imagined that he saw Anna playing tennis.'

(215) *Michałowi śniło się, że Anna gra w tenisa.*
Michał:DAT it dreamed INTR that Anna:NOM play in tennis:ACC
'Michał dreamed that Anna was playing tennis.'

(216) *Michałowi dwoiło się w oczach.*
Michał:DAT it doubled INTR in eyes:LOC
'Michał saw double.'

(217) *Michałowi zrobiło się ciemno przed oczami.*
Michał:DAT it became INTR dark in front of eyes:INST
'Everything went black before Michał's eyes.'

(218) *Michałowi szumiało/dudniło/ dzwoniło w uszach.*
Michał:DAT it buzzed/it rumbled/it rang in ears:LOC
'Michał's ears were buzzing/rumbling/ringing.'

In all of the above sentences the experiencer is clearly the most prominent entity by any objective criteria; nevertheless he is not chosen as the clausal trajector. There is no other participant to take over that role, so the sentence remains subjectless – that is to say, it does not contain a subject nominal, although one could argue that it does contain a trajector (the embedded clause in (213)-(215) and the locative expression in (216)-(218)).[42] Thus the highly unusual construal results in a marked construction. It must be stressed that although this conceptual skewing is motivated by the factors discussed above, it is certainly not predictable from the content to be expressed. The construal itself is part of the semantics of the verb: it comes with the content as part of the same conceptual package.

(219) *Michałowi ukazała się przedziwna scena.*
Michał:DAT appeared INTR very strange scene:NOM
'A strange scene unfolded itself before Michał's eyes.'

Example (219) is similar to (213)-(218) in that it downplays the agent-like properties of the perceiver and highlights the inner subjective nature of the experience; however, in contrast to the earlier examples, the object of experience is really there, and is perceived, rather than merely imagined, by the human participant. Moreover, unlike (213)-(218), example (219) has a subject nominal. The dative construal is possible because the event is not conceptualized as perception, but as *coming into view*: the scene is construed as an entity moving into Michał's field of vision, which gives it the prominence necessary to be coded as subject. Michał's visual field is construed as the location the scene moves into, which motivates the dative inflection on the corresponding nominal.

3.3. "Reasoned" convictions vs. mistakes and idiosyncratic associations

In the preceding section, I argued that hallucinations and illusions are highly compatible with the dative construal because they are subjective experiences – that is to say, processes which occur only in the target person's sphere of awareness and have no objective correlates in the external environment. It might seem that this is also true of thinking, believing, etc., which are internal mental processes as well. We could therefore expect thinkers and holders of beliefs to be expressed by means of nominative noun phrases. This, however, is not the case:

(220) Ola *wie/przypuszcza/podejrzewa/myśli/uważa/wierzy/rozumie*, że Ania była dobrą uczennicą.
'Ola (NOM) knows/reckons/suspects/thinks/is of the opinion/believes/ understands that Ania was a good student.'

The reasons for this become apparent when we consider the folk theory of the mind which is the backdrop against which linguistic construal of thinking processes takes place. In this theory, facts and premises are objects which *exist independently of any mind* (cf. Reddy 1979); moreover, they are *public* (available to anyone who has access to them) and the thinking process itself is construed metaphorically as physical manipulation (208), seeing (221), or movement from premise to conclusion (222).

(221) *Nie* widzę *innego rozwiązania, jak odesłać mu ten dokument.*
'I can see no other solution than sending the document back to him.'

(222) *Wychodząc z błędnego założenia nie można dojść*
coming out from erroneous assumption:GEN not is possible to come
do właściwych wniosków.
to correct conclusions:GEN
'If you start out with erroneous assumptions, you cannot hope to reach correct conclusions.'

All of this strongly supports the nominative construal. Moreover, metaphorical models put aside, the person who reasons or holds a conviction (and our convictions, we like to believe, are products of reasoning processes) is active, conscious, and has at least some control over the process – in other words, he or she is a highly prominent participant. Since the nominative construal is the default choice in any case, there being no other participant competing for the subject role, the fact that the experiencer is the subject of (220) is anything but arbitrary.

On the other hand, linguistic convention requires the dative construal when the target person makes a mistake (223-224) or when the speaker wishes to emphasize the subjective nature of the mental activity (225-226). Mistakes, like hallucinations, occur when the experiencer sees something that exists only in his personal sphere rather than in the "external" reality of "objective" facts. Moreover, like hallucinations, mistakes occur in situations of reduced control. The motivation for the dative construal of mistakes, therefore, is analogous to that outlined in the previous section. Individual idiosyncratic associations and "gut feelings" (as opposed to "reasoned" conclusions based on publicly verifiable facts) are very similar in this respect. In examples (225) and (226), the subjective nature of the experience is a central aspect of the semantics of the verb, and is consequently more likely to be reflected in its syntactic properties.

(223)   *Oli wydaje się, że Ania była dobrą uczennicą.*
        'It seems to Ola (DAT) that Ania was a good student.'

(224)   *Oli coś się pomyliło/pomieszało/pozajączkowało.*
        'Ola (DAT) was mistaken/got it all mixed up/got it all wrong.'

(225)   *Ania jawiła się Oli jako dobra uczennica.*
        'To Ola (DAT), Ania appeared to be a good student.'

(226)   *Dzieci kojarzyły się Oli z brudnymi pieluchami.*
        'Ola (DAT) associated children with dirty diapers.'

Notice, however, that the verb in (226), *kojarzyć* 'to associate', can also occur with a nominative experiencer (227); under this construal, however, the verb describes conscious mental manipulation of information:

(227)   *Ola skojarzyła te dwa fakty i wysnuła odpowiednie wnioski.*
        'Ola (NOM) associated (put together) these two facts and drew the appropriate conclusions.'

It should be stressed that, as in the previous section, the dative construal, though highly motivated, is not predictable from the semantic content to be expressed. In fact, *pomylić się* 'to make a mistake', can take a nominative experiencer (228). On the other hand, it is the dative pattern which is extended to newly-coined words such as *pozajączkować się* 'to get something wrong' – cf. example (224).

(228)   *Ola pomyliła się.*
        'Ola (NOM) made a mistake.'

3.4. "Wanting": definite intention vs. wistful longing or biological drive

Wanting, like perception and thinking, can be given either a nominative or a dative construal. The choice depends on the specific meaning of the verb. Predicates which express a definite desire, intention, determination, or resolution take nominative experiencers:

(229)   *Ten człowiek chce/pragnie/pożąda/łaknie sławy.*
        'This man (NOM) wants/desires/covets/craves fame.'

(230)   *Ten człowiek zamierza/planuje objąć władzę.*
        'This man (NOM) intends/plans to seize power.'

(231)   *Ten człowiek dąży/prze do objęcia władzy.*
        'This man (NOM) strives to seize power/is pushing for power.'

(232)   *Piotr stara się /ubiega się o to stanowisko.*
        'Piotr (NOM) is trying/angling for that job.'

This is highly motivated, since the nominative is the default choice, and, moreover, emphasizing volitionality and control enhances the prominence of the experiencer. It should also be noted that the situations described in (231-232) involve effort and probably action, thus making the nominative participant very agent-like.

The dative construal, on the other hand, will be suitable when the speaker wishes to suppress the active, agent-like properties of the experiencer and portray him as a passive receiver of impulses which originate elsewhere. Thus, the dative construction will be used to describe cravings which spring from instinct and physiological drives, i.e. experience which is non-volitional and not subject to conscious control. In this case, the complement of the verb of wanting will typically be a verb which describes the satisfaction of a bodily need, a physiological process such as excretion, or a behavioral correlate of an emotional reaction (e.g. laughing or crying). The verb *chcieć* 'to want', is a good illustration of the contrast because it allows both a nominative and a dative construal, and the resulting sentences differ in meaning. For example, (233a), where the experiencer is nominative, means that Magda made up her mind that she is going to eat, whereas (233b), with a dative experiencer, means that she feels a craving for food. The bodily sensations in (233b) are beyond the experiencer's control: one cannot decide to feel hungry, and no effort of the will is going to cause the feeling to go away.

(233) a. *Magda chce jeść.*
          'Magda (NOM) wants to eat.'

(233) b. *Magdzie   chce   się   jeść.*
          Magda:DAT it wants INTR to eat
          'Magda is hungry.'

(234) a. *Magda chce pić/spać.*
          'Magda (NOM) wants to drink/sleep.'

(234) b. *Magdzie chce się pić/spać.*
'Magda (DAT) is thirsty/sleepy.'

The contrast becomes particularly clear when the complement verb describes an involuntary physiological reaction. In this case, the nominative construal is inappropriate:

(235) a. ?? *Magda chce rzygać/płakać.*
'Magda (NOM) wants to vomit/cry. [It is her desire to vomit/cry.]'

(235) b. *Magdzie chce się rzygać/płakać.*
'Magda (DAT) feels sick/feels tears welling up inside her.'

Conversely, the desire to engage in an activity such as work or composing a poem is normally the result of a conscious decision. Hence, the nominative construal is more appropriate: example (236b), though not exactly ungrammatical, is decidedly odd without a special context.[43]

(236) a. *Magda chce pracować/pisać wiersze/oglądać telewizję.*
'Magda (NOM) wants to work/write poetry/watch television.'

(236) b. (?) *Magdzie chce się pracować/pisać wiersze/oglądać telewizję.*
'Magda (DAT) wants to work/write poetry/watch television.'

The dative construction is also used to describe sudden impulses (as opposed to conscious resolves) and indefinite yearnings or wistful longings (as opposed to clear desires which are likely to lead to action):

(237) a. *Magda postanowiła, że (nie) będzie pracować.*
'Magda (DAT) made up her mind (not) to work.'

(237) b. *Magdzie zachciało/ odechciało się pracować.*
Magda:DAT it became inclined/it became disinclined INTR to work
'Magda felt a (sudden) urge to work/(suddenly) lost her inclination to work.'

(238) a. *Piotr marzy o stanowisku kierownika działu.*
'Piotr (NOM) dreams of (getting) the position of department manager.'

(238) b. *Piotrowi marzy się stanowisko kierownika działu.*
Piotr:DAT dreams INTR position:NOM manager:GEN department:GEN
'Piotr has this fantasy about becoming department manager.'

(237a) suggests that Magda has reasons for feeling the way she does and that she is going to do something (either take up or give up a job), whereas (237b) emphasizes the unconscious nature of her motivation and implies that it is unreasonable. *Marzyć* 'to dream', is compatible with either construal, but the choice of the dative marking in (238b) suggests that the dreamer is not likely to take any action to get the position he wants.

3.5. Attitudes: Judgement vs. natural inclination

Generally speaking, verbs which designate attitudes take nominative experiencers:

(239)   *Ania zawsze podziwiała/ceniła/szanowała/lubiła/kochała/uwielbiała/ lekceważyła/nienawidziła takich ludzi.*
'Ania (NOM) has always admired/esteemed/respected/liked/loved/ adored/disdained/hated such people.'

This is hardly surprising, since the experiencer is inherently more prominent than the object of experience. Moreover, attitudes are usually a result of an assessment or evaluation, a judgement against one's system of values, or at least we like to believe they are. Consequently, the person doing the evaluation is naturally perceived as agent-like.

The dative construal is used with predicates which describe a *natural inclination* as opposed to an attitude that was formed on the basis of a conscious judgement or evaluation:

(240)   *Ta dziewczyna od razu trafiła mu do gustu/przypadła mu do serca.*
'The girl (NOM) immediately took his (DAT) fancy/won his (DAT) sympathy.'

(241)   *Ten jego płaczliwy głos strasznie działa mi na nerwy.*
'This whimpering voice (NOM) of his really gets on my (DAT) nerves.'

This effect is due to two factors. The dative marking on the experiencer downplays the cognitive component of the attitude. At the same time, the fact that the object of experience is expressed by a nominative nominal gives it special prominence, inviting the interpretation that it has a greater effect on the quality of the experience than the experiencer. The attitude is construed as arising spontaneously, a natural consequence of the properties of the object of experience: the experiencer likes an object because it is likable or dislikes it because it is unpleasant.

The following contrasting examples will help to bring out the difference:

(242) a.   *Ania podziwiała Piotra.*
'Ania (NOM) admired Piotr (ACC).'

(242) b.   *Piotr imponował Ani.*
'Piotr (NOM) impressed Ania (DAT).'

(242a) indicates that Ania was impressed with Piotr because she admired certain qualities that he was endowed with: the nominative highlights Ania's active assessment, a weighing of the positive qualities. In (242b), Piotr is the subject, which brings out *his* agent-like qualities: Ania was impressed with the things he *did*. The dative marking downplays the cognitive factor in the appraisal: Ania's admiration is more of a blind teenager-type devotion. The difference is even more clear when the object of admiration is inanimate, in which case *podziwiać* 'to admire', is the only appropriate lexical choice:

(243) a. *Ania podziwiała wspaniałą antyczną rzeźbę.*
        'Ania (NOM) admired the magnificent ancient sculpture (ACC).'

(243) b. **Wspaniała antyczna rzeźba imponowała Ani.*
        'The magnificent ancient sculpture (NOM) impressed Ania (DAT).'

Another illustration of the contrast is provided by the verbs *lubić* 'to like' and *podobać się* 'to be pleasing':

(244) a. *Ania lubi tę sukienkę.*
        'Ania (NOM) likes this dress.'

(244) b. *Ani   podoba   się   ta   sukienka.*
        Ania:DAT is pleasing INTR this dress:NOM
        'Ania likes this dress./Ania finds this dress pretty.'

(245) a. *Robert lubi Alicję.*
        'Robert (NOM) likes Alicja (ACC).'

(245) b. *Alicja   podoba   się   Robertowi.*
        Alicja:NOM is pleasing INTR Robert:DAT
        'Robert likes Alicja.'

As in the previous example, Ania's attitude is seen as depending primarily on properties of the object of experience in (244b) and on properties of Ania herself in (244a). Thus, in (244b) Ania might like the dress because it is "pretty". Of course "prettiness" is not an *objective* property, but there is something *in the dress* that appeals to her. In (244a), Ania's feelings do not take their source in any intrinsic properties of the dress, but rather in certain facts about Ania herself: for example, she might like the dress because she believes she looks attractive in it, or because it reminds her of her holidays in Spain. Similarly, in (245a), Robert may like Alicja for any number of personal reasons; (245b), on the other hand, strongly suggests that he finds her physically attractive.

When used to describe a liking for food, *lubić* contrasts with *smakować* 'to be tasty', which takes dative experiencers:

(246) a. *Lubisz winogrona?*
you like grapes:ACC
'Do you like grapes?'

(246) b. *Smakują ci (te) winogrona?*
are tasty you:DAT (these) grapes:NOM
'Do you like (these) grapes?'

(247) *Chociaż Ania specjalnie nie lubi naleśników, te, które zrobiła Joanna bardzo jej smakowały.*
'Although Ania (NOM) doesn't particularly like pancakes (GEN), she (DAT) found those (NOM) that Joanna made very tasty.'

Lubić, which takes nominative experiencers, denotes a liking for a particular *type of food*, whereas *smakować* 'to find tasty', which requires a dative experiencer, places much greater emphasis on the taste qualities of the *particular serving*: this is why (247) is not contradictory. Notice also that (246a) is a question one might ask before the grapes are served, but (246b) is appropriate only if the experiencer is actually eating the grapes. These differences are perfectly consistent with the semantics of the dative and the nominative. Although *lubić* does invoke the sphere of awareness, the experiencer must be the subject because it is much more prominent than the object of experience: not only is he human, but also a *specific* person rather than a *type* of thing; and, most importantly, *lubić* specifies the property of a person (a preference for a particular kind of food). *Smakować*, on the other hand, attributes certain taste qualities to an object, which makes the latter the most prominent participant. Notice that *smakować* can also be used as a simple intransitive verb (248), where it simply means 'to have a particular taste'. Introducing the experiencer by means of a dative nominal has the effect of locating these taste qualities within someone's sphere of awareness.

(248) *Ten ser smakuje jak trociny.*
'This cheese (NOM) tastes like sawdust.'

It is also worth noting that when the verb profiles a change of taste preferences – in other words, when it describes an acquired taste rather than a natural inclination – the event may be given a nominative construal. Thus, the verb in (249), *zasmakować*, normally takes nominative experiencers[44] in spite of the fact that *smakować* 'to taste' – without the prefix *za-*, which introduces the idea of change – requires the dative (cf. example (246b)).

(249) *Magda zasmakowała w awokado.*
'Magda (NOM) developed a taste for avocado.'

Most other verbs which describe a change in the experiencer's attitude, as when the experiencer learns to appreciate something, or adapts to a new environment, also require a nominative construal. This is because change naturally attracts attention and therefore the changing participant is the natural choice for the clausal trajector when there is no agent. Moreover, getting used to a new environment or learning new things usually requires at least some effort, so the experiencer also has some agentive characteristics.

(250) *Ola szybko przyzwyczaiła się/przywykła/wdrożyła się do ciężkiej pracy.*
'Ola (NOM) quickly got used to the hard work.'

(251) *Ola szybko odzwyczaiła się/odwykła od ciężkiej pracy.*
'Ola (NOM) quickly became unused to hard work.'

(252) *Po jakimś czasie dzieci przystosowały się do nowego otoczenia.*
'After a while the children (NOM) adjusted to the new environment.'

(253) *Chłopiec szybko zaaklimatyzował się w nowej szkole.*
'The boy (NOM) quickly acclimatized to the new school.'

(254) *Po paru miesiącach wszyscy zadomowiliśmy się w nowym mieszkaniu.*
'After a few months we all (NOM) felt at home in the new apartment.'

(255) *Kasia otrzaskała się trochę z marketingiem.*
'[As a result of practical experience] Kasia (NOM) acquired a patchy knowledge of marketing.'

(256) *Andrzej osłuchał się trochę z angielskim.*
'Andrzej (NOM) picked up a little English [as a result of hearing it spoken around him].'

One exception to the above generalization is the idiom *wejść w krew* (lit., 'enter the bloodstream'):

(257) *Punktualność   weszła Markowi   w krew.*
punctuality:NOM went in Marek:DAT in blood:ACC
'Punctuality has become second nature with Marek.'

The expression is based on a metaphor in which the new habit is depicted as a substance that seeps into the experiencer's bloodstream. On the metaphorical level, it is the habit, not the experiencer, which is active, and hence a natural choice for the clausal trajector. The body metaphor provides a foundation for the dative construal, parts of the body being central elements of the personal sphere (see section 2.1). But the dative construal is also motivated by some non-metaphorical aspects of the meaning of the expression. *Wejść w krew* describes a habit that one acquires effortlessly, almost unawares, and which causes one to act almost in spite of oneself. Marek is punctual not because he plans to or wants to, but because he cannot help but be punctual. The dative construal matches these implications perfectly, since it maximally backgrounds effort and volitionality, and portrays the experiencer as essentially inactive.

There is also a systematic exception to the general rule formulated above – verbs of satiety/jadedness, which take dative experiencers as well:

(258) *Obrzydły/   Spowszedniały mi   jego dowcipy*
       became odious/palled   me:DAT his   jokes:NOM
       'I'm fed up with his jokes./His jokes have palled on me.'

(259) *Znudził jej   się   adorator.*
       bored her:DAT INTR admirer:NOM
       'She is tired of/bored with her admirer.'

(260) *Wszystkim opatrzyła   już   się   ta   sukienka.*
       all:DAT   saw aroun   already INTR this dress:NOM
       'This dress has palled on everyone.'

This, too, is semantically motivated. The change in the way the experiencer perceives the object of experience in (258)-(260) is not a result of something that would normally be described as learning behavior. In fact, the change is not due to any characteristic feature of the experiencer, but to the obtrusive ubiquity of the object of experience: satiety is a perfectly natural reaction to being bombarded with the same or similar stimuli over a substantial period of time. In other words, it is the object of experience which is construed as the *active cause* of the reaction, and the experience is perceived as something almost like a bodily reaction to a stimulus.

3.6. Subjective experience vs. objective properties

In section 2.2.9 I pointed out that bodily sensations are often construed as processes occurring in the sphere of awareness.

(261) a. *Ani   jest zimno/ciepło/gorąco.*
         Ania:DAT it is   coldly/warmly/hotly
         'Ania is cold/warm/hot.'

(262) a. *Ani   jest słabo.*
         Ania:DAT it is weakly
         'Ania feels faint.'

(263) a. *Ani   jest mdło/niedobrze.*
         Ania:DAT it is   insipidly/unwell
         'Ania feels sick.'

(264) a. *Ani   jest niewygodnie.*
Ania:DAT it is uncomfortably
'Ania is uncomfortable.'

It is interesting to observe that these predicates also have variants which take nominative arguments:[45]

(261) b. *Ania jest zimna/ciepła/gorąca.*
'Ania (NOM) is cold/warm/hot. [Her body feels cold, etc.]'

(262) b. *Ania jest słaba.*
'Ania (NOM) is weak.'

(263) b. *Ania jest mdła/niedobra.*
'Ania (NOM) is insipid/not tasty.'

(264) b. *Ania jest niewygodna.*
'Ania (NOM) is uncomfortable [e.g. to sit on].'

The above sentences, however, differ in meaning from the (a) sentences. They describe *objective properties* of the individual named by the subject noun rather than the sensations that he or she experiences. (261b) comments on the temperature of Ania's body, or, on the metaphorical interpretation, makes a statement about her personality; (262b) is a statement about her muscle power or her will power; (263b) is rather unusual, but it would be appropriate if said by a cannibal to describe the gustatory qualities of a meal prepared from Ania; (264b) might be said by someone who is sitting on Ania or perhaps by a tapeworm which is not satisfied with its accommodation. All of these are facts that can be established objectively rather than processes that only occur in the experiencer's sphere of awareness.

I also observed in section 2.2.9 that a few basic emotions, such as sadness, happiness, general well-being, and uneasiness, are conventionally given the dative construal:

(265) a. *Ani   jest wesoło/smutno.*
Ania:DAT it is happily/sadly
'Ania is happy/sad.'

(266) a. *Ani   jest miło/ przyjemnie/głupio/ dobrze.*
Ania:DAT it is nicely/pleasantly/ stupidly/well
'Ania feels delighted/pleased/stupid/well.'

(267) a. *Ani   jest straszno/nudno.*
Ania:DAT it is terribly /dully
'Ania is scared/bored.'

These, too, have analogues with nominative experiencers (265b-267b) and again the nominative and the dative constructions differ in meaning. (266b) provides information about the kind of person that Ania is rather than her internal state. (267b) describes the feelings she evokes in other people rather than feelings she experiences herself. The distinction between (265a) and (265b) is more elusive, since they both describe Ania's emotions. (265b) focuses on the external signs of the emotion: facial expression and objectively ascertainable behaviors such as laughing or crying, exuberant hyperactivity or a quiet retreat into a corner. (265a), on the other hand, focuses on Ania's inner experience. (265b) could also mean that Ania is a happy (or sad) kind of person, rather than that she is experiencing a particular emotion; (265a) is not open to this interpretation.

(265) b. *Ania jest wesoła/smutna.*
'Ania (NOM) is happy/sad.'

(266) b. *Ania jest miła/przyjemna/głupia/dobra.*
'Ania (NOM) is nice/pleasant/stupid/good.'

(267) b. *Ania jest straszna/nudna.*
'Ania (NOM) is terrible/boring.'

Thus, there is a systematic contrast between the nominative and the dative construal: the dative sentences focus on the experiencer's internal state and emphasize the subjective nature of the experience, whereas the nominative sentences describe objectively ascertainable properties and states. Now it is clear that the dative construction is, grammatically speaking, extraordinary, since it does not contain a nominative subject. It is a matter of some debate whether this and other so-called "subjectless constructions" are genuinely trajectorless, or whether they simply have highly unprototypical non-nominative trajectors (cf. the discussion in section 3.1.2). I do not propose to resolve the debate here, and merely note that the dative constructions are highly marked: they present a very skewed view of the situation, since what is undoubtedly the most prominent participant (in fact the only participant) is not chosen as the trajector. On the other hand, the special implications of the dative sentences are fully compatible with the increased prominence of the personal sphere accorded by explicit reference to it by means of the dative ending. The fact that Polish grammar allows the dative to come on the stage means that a contrast becomes available which enables speakers to convey finer nuances of meaning, and thus increases the overall expressiveness of the language. Of course this comes at a price: it also makes the grammar somewhat less logical, more inconsistent. The grammatical properties of the bodily sensation and emotional predicates discussed above are unusual, and certainly not predictable from their semantics, if semantics is taken in the narrow sense of "content" as opposed to "content plus construal". It is a matter of conventional imagery, and must be learned. However, humans seem to have no great difficulty in learning to construe situations in a particular way, as required by the grammar of their language. It must be stressed, moreover, that "conventional" does not mean "arbitrary": given the semantics of the dative case, it makes sense to use it to emphasize the subjective aspects of mental experience.

3.7. Nominative-dative verbs

Many of the examples discussed in this chapter were borderline cases: the participants had properties of both the nominative and the dative prototype, and hence both forms were motivated. However, a participant cannot be coded as half nominative, half dative: grammatical markers are discrete, even if the situations that they are used to describe are not. Consequently, any decision that is made will be somewhat arbitrary.

In this section, I consider another solution to this coding problem, one which accommodates both of the conflicting motivations. This is accomplished by marking one of the categories (nominative) on the noun and expressing membership in the other by means of a reflexive pronoun. It is the obvious solution in situations where the human participant can be plausibly construed as both instigator of the process and passive experiencer of the result. Recall is easily seen as a special case of reminding – reminding oneself: the situation described in (269) is parallel to that in (268) except that Leszek plays a two-part role in the latter.

(268) *Leszek   przypomniał Arkowi   jej nazwisko.*
       Leszek:NOM reminded   Arek:DAT her name:ACC
       'Leszek reminded Arek of her name.'

(269) *Leszek   przypomniał sobie   jej nazwisko.*
       Leszek:NOM reminded   REFL:DAT her name:ACC
       'Leszek remembered her name.'

It is worth noting at this point that *przypomnieć* can also occur in the DPS construction:

(270) *Leszkowi   przypomniało się   jej nazwisko.*
       Leszek:DAT it reminded   INTR her name:NOM
       'Leszek remembered her name./Her name came back to Leszek.'

The above sentence differs in meaning from (269) in that it is the object of experience, rather than the experiencer, that is construed as an agent-like entity and accorded the special prominence associated with subjecthood. This semantic difference has several syntactic repercussions. For example, only the variant with *sobie* allows agent-focus modifiers such as *z trudem* 'with difficulty', *bez trudu* 'without difficulty', *z łatwością* 'with ease'.

(271) a. Leszek   z   trudem   przypomniał sobie
        Leszek:NOM with difficulty:INST reminded   REFL:DAT
        jej adres.
        her address:ACC
        'Leszek remembered her name with difficulty.'

(271) b. *Leszkowi   z   trudem   przypomniał się jej adres.
        Leszek:DAT with difficulty:INST remembered INTR her adress:NOM

Also, *przypomnieć sobie*, but not *przypomnieć się*, can function as the complement of a verb phrase which profiles effort or volitionality:

(272) a. Leszek   nie mógł przypomnieć sobie   jej adresu.
        Leszek:NOM not could to remind   REFL:DAT her address:GEN
        'Leszek couldn't remember her address.'

(272) b. *Leszkowi   nie mógł przypomnieć się   jej adres.
        Leszek:DAT not could to remind   INTR her address:NOM

(273) a. Leszek   próbował przypomnieć sobie   jej adres.
        Leszek:NOM tried   to remind   REFL:DAT her address:ACC
        'Leszek tried to remember her address.'

(273) b. *Leszkowi   próbował przypomnieć się   jej adres.
        Leszek:DAT tried   to remember INTR   her address:NOM

This is just the difference that we would expect, given the fact that although both the experiencer subject and the object-of-experience subject resemble the agent, they resemble it in different ways. The object of experience is like the agent in that it is seen as playing a causal role in the process, but being inanimate, it cannot experience difficulty or attempt to accomplish something. The experiencer, on the other hand, resembles the agent to the extent that his involvement in the action is volitional and he has control over the execution of the mental process.

The nominative + dative coding strategy is sometimes resorted to even when the very nature of the process is such that both the instigator and the experiencer are necessarily the same person, and the verb does not have a ditransitive analogue. A good example would be the verb *wyobrazić sobie* 'to imagine', and its synonyms *przedstawić sobie (w myśli)* 'to represent to oneself (in one's mind)', *imaginować sobie* 'to imagine [literary]'.

(274)   Piotr   próbował wyobrazić sobie   takie urządzenie.
        Piotr:NOM tried   represent REFL:DAT such apparatus:ACC
        'Piotr tried to imagine such an apparatus.'

Imagining is a purely subjective process, and its subjective nature is an important part of the meaning of the verb; hence the dative. On the other hand, unlike a hallucination, it is a volitional process that the experiencer has control over; hence the nominative. The experiencer's dual role (invoker of image and subjective observer) is symbolized by two nominals, each with a different case marking.

Verbs such as *uświadomić sobie, uzmysłowić sobie, uprzytomnić sobie, zdać sobie sprawę* 'to realize, become aware of, waken up to something' also focus on purely internal, subjective processes, but since the processes involve effort and growing control (better grasp of the truth), it would be inappropriate to express the experiencer by a dative noun phrase. Therefore, the compromise nominative-dative construal is adopted (275). (These verbs can also be used in ordinary ditransitive constructions (276), where they mean 'to communicate X to', but such are much less common than the *sobie* uses. They do, however, help to motivate the nominative-dative construal.)

(275) *Piotr   uświadomił sobie,   że Marta   jest chora.*
       Piotr:NOM made aware REFL:DAT that Marta:NOM is   sick
       'Piotr realized that Marta was sick.'

(276) *Leszek   uświadomił Piotrowi, że Marta jest chora.*
       Leszek:NOM made aware Piotr:DAT that Marta is   sick
       'Leszek informed Piotr that Marta was sick.'

We have seen in section 3.3 that verbs of misjudgement are particularly amenable to a dative construal, since they specify that a state of affairs exists only in the experiencer's sphere of awareness. The nominative-dative construal will be appropriate when the experiencer arrives at his or her erroneous conclusion after conscious deliberation:

(277) *Jan   ubzdurał/   ubrdał/uroił   sobie,*
       Jan:NOM got it into head/fancied/fantasized REFL:DAT
       że   jest wielkim poetą.
       that he is great   poet:INST
       'Jan took it into his head that he was a great poet/fancied himself a great poet.'

Finally, let us consider two typically nominative verbs, *(po)myśleć* 'to think' and *postanowić* 'to decide'. The nominative construal, it was argued in sections 3.3 and 3.4, is motivated by the strong cognitive and, in the case of the latter, volitional component of the meaning of these verbs, as well as the general tendency to choose the most prominent participant as the clausal trajector. The special focus on the sphere of awareness which results from adding the dative pronoun *sobie* produces the implication that the thought or decision was private, i.e. that the experiencer did not communicate it to others.

(278) Piotr pomyślał sobie, że on by tak nie postąpił.
Piotr:NOM thought REFL:DAT that he:NOM COND so not acted
'Piotr thought that he would not have acted like that [but he didn't communicate this to anyone].'

(279) Marta postanowiła sobie, że nie będzie dokuczała
Marta:NOM decided REFL:DAT that not she will tease
innym.
others:DAT
'Marta decided that she would not tease other people [but she didn't tell anyone about her decision].'

3.8. Conclusion

In this chapter, I analyzed the factors which determine whether the experiencer is expressed by a nominative or a dative nominal. The sphere of awareness, I argued, is part of the semantic structure of all mental-experience predicates. Whether it is explicitly mentioned or remains implicit is determined by its prominence vis-à-vis the prominence of other aspects of the scene, including the experiencer himself, and by general rules of grammatical organization.

Since each clause normally has a subject, and subjects are nominative in Polish, when the situation described involves only one participant, the participant is normally expressed by a nominative noun phrase, and the sphere of awareness remains implicit.

When there are two participants – an experiencer and an object of experience – the more prominent one gets the nominative coding. Experiencers are inherently more figure-worthy than objects of experience since they are active (they are the source of energy for the mental process and they often expend effort to sustain it), they are aware of the process, their involvement in it is often volitional, and they generally exercise at least some control over it; finally, they are human, and humans are typically more interested in other humans than in non-human participants.

The less figure-worthy the experiencer is, the more likely it is to be expressed by a dative nominal. Dative experiencers are passive or re-active rather than active; they are not in control of the mental process; and their involvement in it is non-volitional. These properties are not enough to motivate the dative construal in and of themselves, but they will tip the balance when they interact with other factors. If the other participant (the object of experience) is clearly delineated, concrete, and can be construed as having a causal role in the process described by the verb, then it is the object of experience which becomes the clausal trajector, allowing the experiencer to take the dative ending. This is what motivates the dative construal in the dative patient-subject construction and with predicates of satiety and natural inclination.

Another factor which motivates a dative construal is high prominence of the sphere of awareness. The sphere of awareness is particularly salient when the object of the experience has no independent existence outside of it (and hence cannot be construed as playing a causal role) – that is to say, when the experience is purely subjective. This kind of experience is more naturally conceptualized as a process within the experiencer's sphere of awareness than a relationship between the experiencer and an object of experience. Examples include bodily sensations, physiological drives, and hallucinations.

Cultural beliefs also play an important role in determining the construal conventionally associated with certain types of events. Western thought traditionally distinguishes the rational, conscious self from its irrational, intuitive complement. The conscious, rational self is the part of us that thinks, evaluates, makes decisions, and plans actions. It is the active part, the part that is in control of what we do. The irrational aspect of our mental life, on the other hand, is the dark side, the id. It is often thought of as an area swarming with unreasonable beliefs, unconscious desires, and evil impulses. It is the part that is responsible for hallucinations, mistakes, instinct, and biological drives, as well as intuition and spontaneity.

The rational, conceptual aspect of the mind is the one that we identify with; the irrational, affective aspect is one we would like to dissociate ourselves from.[46] We tend to think of ourselves as active rather than passive, conscious rather than lacking consciousness, rational rather than irrational, capable of relating to the objective world and seeing things that are really "out there". This has important consequences for the grammatical organization of utterances used to describe mental experience. Mental objects which are believed to originate in the rational, conceptual part of the mind are believed to be products of the self, and the experiencer is expressed by a nominative noun phrase. Irrational, intuitive experience, on the other hand, is seen as something that originates outside the self and is merely observed by the rational ego. Since the dative construal presupposes the mental arena theory of mental experience with its homunculus-observer, it is perfectly compatible with this part of the folk theory. Consequently, individuals who experience feelings and impulses which are believed to originate outside the rational, conscious self are expressed by dative noun phrases.

The folk theory of mind described above helps to explain some interesting correlations between cultural values and the choice of either the nominative or the dative construal. I observed earlier that mistakes and illusions are typically given the dative construal. This is because we believe that the conscious rational self perceives the world as it is and reasons correctly; false beliefs, therefore, must originate elsewhere. Biological drives are also construed as originating outside the self. The reason for this is that our culture has taught us to distrust impulses from the flesh. They are considered evil and we tend to dissociate ourselves from them. Accordingly, they are given the dative construal. Conversely, mental states and activities which are highly valued in our culture – knowledge, correct reasoning, higher values such as the desire to write poetry – are generally conceptualized according to the nominative scenario.

Chapter 4: Dative and accusative targets

4.1. Introduction

In this chapter I examine the contrast between the dative and the accusative, and argue that, like the contrast between the dative and the nominative, it reflects different ways of organizing the situation for expressive purposes. It will be useful, therefore, to begin with a brief description of the semantics of the accusative case.

Prototypically, the accusative case is used to mark the patient of the action, i.e. a participant that is manipulated by the agent in the course of the action and undergoes a physical change of state as a result (280). This basic sense is extended to cover a very wide range of situations. For example, the accusative case can be used to designate an entity that is acted on by the agent, but does not undergo a change of state, as in example (281), a participant that is affected non-physically (282), or any person or object that is the passive target of the agent's action (283).

(280) a. *Kasia naprawiła lodówkę.*
'Kasia (NOM) fixed the fridge (ACC).'

(280) b. *Kasia zjadła banana.*
'Kasia (NOM) ate a banana (ACC).'

(281) a. *Magda przeczytała książkę.*
'Magda (NOM) read a book (ACC).'

(281) b. *Magda pocałowała Maćka.*
'Magda (NOM) kissed Maciek (ACC).'

(282) a. *Beata awansowała Roberta.*
'Beata (NOM) promoted Robert (ACC).'

(282) b. *Sędzia skazał oszusta na cztery lata więzienia.*
'The judge (NOM) sentenced the con man (ACC) to four years in prison.'

(283) a. *Jola zobaczyła zieloną sukienkę.*
'Jola (NOM) saw a green dress (ACC).'

(283) b. *Jola wybrała/kupiła tę zieloną sukienkę.*
'Jola (NOM) chose/bought this green dress (ACC).'

Thus, although the prototypical sense of the accusative case is very different indeed from the target person prototype, the more peripheral uses seem to cover more or less the same ground as some uses of the dative. Specifically, if an agent's action causes a certain emotional state in another participant, that participant is certainly affected, which motivates the use of the accusative case. On the other hand, the non-active participant experiences an emotion, and emotions, I argued earlier, are conceptualized as processes occurring in the sphere of awareness; this, in turn, motivates the use of the dative case. The choice of case category, I will argue in this chapter, depends on whether the verb profiles the agent's action and the target's affectedness as a single act of causation or whether the agent's action is seen as sparking off an autonomous process in another participant's sphere of awareness. In the case of verbs such as *ucieszyć* 'to please, delight', *rozweselić* 'to cheer up', *rozśmieszyć* 'to amuse, make laugh', *rozbawić* 'to amuse', *zasmucić* 'to make sad', *przygnębić* 'to depress, deject', *rozgoryczyć* 'to embitter', *rozżalić* 'to aggrieve, dispirit', *zmartwić* 'to worry', *zakłopotać* 'to nonplus, perplex', *strapić* 'to distress, afflict', *rozczarować* 'to disappoint', *zawstydzić* 'to embarass', *onieśmielić* 'to daunt, overawe', etc., the agent's actions and the target's affectedness are clearly one and the same event, and hence all of these verbs govern the accusative.[47] Other verbs profile only the first part of this chain of causation, and hence the affected person is given dative case marking. The difference is once again a matter of construal, though some types of events more amenable to the dative construal than others.

One type of action which naturally lends itself to the dative construal is communication. In the case of communication events, it is fairly easy to dissociate the action itself (e.g. the production of speech sounds) from the effects it produces on the addressee (e.g. feelings of sadness or disappointment). The following section is devoted to a discussion of the factors which motivate the choice construal with verbs of communication. The second part of the chapter will be devoted to another area of partial overlap of the dative and the accusative, namely, actions directed at only a *part* of the non-active participant's body. Since body parts are central elements of the personal sphere, such processes are open to both construals.

4.2. Verbs of communication

I will discuss seven classes of verbs which can be subsumed under the category of "verbs of communication": verbs of telling, teaching, deception, greeting and leave-taking, commendation, verbal aggression, and what I will refer to as "call for action verbs". The distinction between dative and accusative verbs cuts across these semantic classes, but, as we will see, the groupings that result from this division form semantically natural subclasses.

4.2.1. Verbs of telling

Michael Reddy (1979) argues that communication in our culture is understood metaphorically in terms of what he calls the *conduit metaphor*. The conduit metaphor represents communication as an act of sending: the speaker *puts a message into words* and *sends it* along a conduit to the *addressee*, who removes it from its packaging and puts it in his head, as it were. This construal matches the semantics of the dative case perfectly: the addressee of an act of communication is seen as analogous to the receiver in an act of transfer, the only difference being that the relevant region of the personal sphere is the sphere of awareness rather than the sphere of influence. Thus, the dative construal is the obvious template for organizing communication events for expressive purposes, and nearly all verbs which designate an act of telling allow dative addressees:

(284)   *Piotr mówił/powiedział Oli o wyjeździe Artura.*
        'Piotr was telling/told Ola (DAT) about Artur's departure.'

(285)   *Piotr oświadczył/oznajmił Oli, że Artur wyjechał.*
        'Piotr advised Ola (DAT) that Artur had left.'

Other predicates belonging to this group include *komunikować* 'to communicate', *zapowiedzieć* 'to announce', *zwiastować* 'to annunciate', *sygnalizować* 'to signal', *meldować* 'to report', *anonsować* 'to announce [a visitor]', *obwieścić* 'to announce, proclaim', *wspomnieć* 'to metion', *napisać* 'to write'.[48]

However, two verbs, *zawiadomić/powiadomić* 'to advise, notify' and *poinformować* 'to inform', though very similar in meaning to the above predicates, take accusative objects:

(286)   *Ola zawiadomiła/poinformowała dyrektora, że Artur wyjechał.*
        'Ola advised/informed the director (ACC) that Artur had left.'

This grammatical difference is due to the way these verbs construe the same content. *Zawiadomić* and *poinformować* treat the communication event as an act which brings about a change of state in the addressee: the addressee is caused to know something. The enunciation of the message and the addressee's affectedness are a single indivisible event; the sphere of awareness, though implicit in the very concept of communication, is maximally backgrounded. This is best seen by considering the ways in which an act of communication can fail to go through.

The sentences in (287) both describe such unsuccessful acts of communication, but they differ in meaning. (287a), which contains the accusative-governing *zawiadomić* 'to advise, notify', can only mean that the speaker could not contact the intended addressee; (287b), with the dative verb, could also mean that the speaker didn't succeed in communicating the message because she couldn't bring herself to break the news or because the addressee wasn't listening or didn't understand its implications. With the accusative verb, once communication is established, the message automatically goes through and the expected changes in the addressee take place.

(287) a. *Próbowałam go zawiadomić, że firma poniosła straty, ale nie udało mi się.*
'I tried to inform him (ACC) that the company had suffered losses, but I didn't succeed.'

(287) b. *Próbowałam mu powiedzieć, że firma poniosła straty, ale nie udało mi się.*
'I tried to tell him (DAT) that the company had suffered losses, but I didn't succeed.'

As a corollary to this, with a verb governing the accusative, the addressee's role in the communication event is passive and patient-like: he is merely caused to know. If he refuses to cooperate, this can only be by preventing communication in the first place: this is the only interpretation possible for (288a). In contrast, the most likely interpretation of (288b), which contains a dative-governing verb and a dative addressee, is that the addressee either refused to take the message on board or expressed disagreement.

(288) a. *Nie dał się poinformować/zawiadomić, że firma poniosła straty.*
'He wouldn't let anyone inform/notify him that the company had suffered losses.'

(288) b. *Nie dał sobie oznajmić/powiedzieć, że firma poniosła straty.*
'He wouldn't let anyone advise/tell him that the company had suffered losses.'

4.2.2. Call for action verbs

This group includes five subclasses: verbs of tempting/encouraging (*kusić* 'to tempt', *nęcić* 'to entice', *zachęcać* 'to encourage', *namawiać* 'to egg on', *nakłaniać* 'to induce'), verbs of urging (*prosić* 'to ask', *błagać* 'to beg', *molestować* 'to pester', *zaklinać* 'to entreat'), verbs of inciting to revolt/aggression (*buntować* 'to incite to revolt', *podburzać* 'to rouse, stir up', *judzić* 'to sow dissension', *szczuć* 'to bait'), of summoning (*wezwać* 'to summon', *wołać/przywołać/zawołać* 'to call', *wywołać* 'to call out', *zaprosić* 'to invite'), and asking (i.e. calling for an answer: *pytać* 'to ask', *indagować* 'to inquire', *interpelować* 'to interpellate', *egzaminować* 'to give an oral examination'). They differ from the preceding verbs in that they all profile attempts to provoke an externally observable reaction; consequently they require an accusative construal.

It is interesting to compare one of these subgroups, verbs of urging, with verbs of ordering (*kazać* 'to tell', *rozkazać* 'to order', *polecić* 'to direct'), which only allow dative objects:

(289)   *Anna kazała/rozkazała/poleciła Robertowi, żeby pojechał do Szczecina.*
'Anna told/ordered/directed Robert (DAT) to go to Szczecin.'

(290)   *Anna prosiła/błagała/zaklinała Roberta, żeby pojechał do Szczecina.*
'Anna asked/begged/implored Robert (ACC) to go to Szczecin.'

Verbs of ordering, unlike those in the other group, strongly evoke the addressee's potency: one can give orders only to individuals who are within one's sphere of influence. It is the potency relationship which makes it possible for Ania to influence Robert's behavior and, as we have seen in section 2.2.5, the infringement of the potency of the target person motivates the dative construal. It should be noted that *błagać* 'to beg' also presupposes a potency relationship between the speaker and the addressee – the opposite one: in (290), Robert is more potent than Ania. Still, it is Ania who is trying to get him to do something. Therefore, the potency relationship is independent of the action profiled by the verb (Ania's attempt to influence Robert's behavior).

4.2.3. Verbs of teaching

Verbs of teaching can be subdivided into two groups: verbs of making manifest (*tłumaczyć/wyjaśniać* 'to explain', *klarować* 'to make clear', *udowadniać* 'to prove', *wykazywać* 'to demonstrate, prove', *unaoczniać* 'to make manifest', *wyłuszczać* 'to set forth, expound', *wskazywać* 'to point out', *pokazywać* 'to show', *demonstrować* 'to demonstrate', *przedstawiać* 'to introduce'), and verbs of training (*uczyć* 'to teach', *kształcić* 'to educate', *szkolić* 'to instruct', *instruować* 'to give instructions', *wychowywać* 'to bring up, educate', *oświecać* 'to enlighten', *cywilizować* 'to civilize', *zaznajamiać* 'to acquaint', *zapoznawać* 'to brief', *ćwiczyć/trenować* 'to coach', *musztrować* 'to drill', *tresować* 'to train'). Verbs belonging to the first group take dative objects (291-292), whereas those belonging to the second take accusative objects (293-294):

(291)   *Małgosia wytłumaczyła/wyjaśniła mi pierwsze prawo termodynamiki.*
'Małgosia explained the first law of thermodynamics to me (DAT).'

(292)   *Małgosia wykazała/udowodniła mi, że nie mam racji.*
'Małgosia demonstrated/proved to me (DAT) that I was wrong.'

(293)   *Małgosia nauczyła mnie fizyki.*
'Małgosia taught me (ACC) physics.'

(294)   *Małgosia zapoznała/zaznajomiła mnie z najnowszymi osiągnięciami biologii molekularnej.*
'Małgosia acquainted me with/briefed me (ACC) on the newest discoveries in molecular biology.'

The distinctive syntactic behavior of the two subgroups is also semantically motivated. The dative verbs all profile the process of making clear, proving, etc.; the addressee's affectedness is implicated rather than asserted. Thus, although (295) presupposes that the agent has already explained to or shown the dative participant how to open the lock, the sentence is not contradictory since a person who has been shown how to do something has not necessarily learned anything from the demonstration. On the other hand, the next example, with the accusative-governing *nauczyć* 'to teach', is contradictory since the perfective form of the verb indicates that the addressee already knows how to open the lock.[49]

(295)   *Czy mógłbyś mi jeszcze raz wytłumaczyć/pokazać, jak się otwiera ten zamek?*
'Could you explain to/show (PF) me (DAT) how to open that lock one more time?'

(296)   *Czy mógłbyś mnie jeszcze raz nauczyć, jak się otwiera ten zamek?*
'Could you teach (PF) me (ACC) how to open that lock one more time?'

The autonomous nature of the process of making manifest is particularly clear with the verbs *wyjaśnić*, which literally means 'to make clear', *udowodnić* 'to prove', and *wykazać* 'to demonstrate, prove' which designate a process which does not even require the existence of an addressee. (You can prove that the earth is round without anybody knowing it: a proof is a proof even when no one has seen it.)

Verbs of training, on the other hand, specifically assert that the addressee learns something as a result of the process. Moreover, the action designated by the verb generally produces externally observable behaviors as well as changes in the addressee's knowledge (the trainee may have to demonstrate her knowledge, or - imitate the behavior taught), and the training process may involve physical action on the trainee's body (e.g. helping him to perform the activity taught, corporal punishment).

4.2.4. Verbs of deception

This class also includes both verbs which govern the dative and those which govern the accusative. The dative verbs (*kłamać* 'to lie', *łgać* 'to fib', *bajać/bajdurzyć* 'to tell nonsensical lies', *blagować* 'to tell tall tales, to bluff') profile just the first stage of the typical lying scenario: the delivery of a false message. The sphere of awareness is relevant in that the addressee must be able to understand the message and must be at least potentially deceivable: one cannot lie to a table or a new-born baby. However, the dative verbs do not imply that the addressee actually believes the speaker's words or is affected in any way.

The accusative verbs (*okłamać* 'to deceive', *oszukać* 'to cheat', *kantować/oszachrować/ocyganić/oszwabić* 'to swindle', *okpić* 'to dupe, trick', *nabrać* 'to hoodwink, make a fool of', *wykiwać* 'to pull a fast one on', *zwodzić* 'to lead somebody astray, to mislead', *łudzić* 'to deceive, to delude [with false hopes]') focus primarily on the effects that the untruthful message produces on the addressee. They imply that the addressee believes the speaker, acts on his words, and suffers some unpleasant consequences as a result – e.g. loses money, accepts a defective product, or is made to look silly. The effect of the action on the addressee is externally verifiable, which further motivates the use of the accusative.

The only exception to the above generalizations is the verb *bujać* 'to tell fibs' (lit. 'to rock or swing'), which, like the dative verbs, profiles the act of lying itself rather than its effects, and yet governs the accusative case. It seems that this apparently idiosyncratic property is inherited from the basic physical action sense of the verb, which predictably takes the accusative case.

4.2.5. Verbs of verbal commendation

This class can also be subdivided into two contrasting groups, verbs of flattery (*schlebiać* 'to flatter', *kadzić* 'to adulate', *podlizywać się* 'to suck up to', *basować* 'to fawn', *przytakiwać* 'to flatter someone by agreeing with everything he/she says', *klaskać* 'to clap [in applause]'), which take dative objects, and verbs of praise (*chwalić* 'to praise', *sławić* 'to celebrate, glorify', *oklaskiwać* 'to applaud [by clapping]'), which take accusative objects. As before, the different syntactic behavior of the two groups is a reflection of underlying semantic differences, though these are of a slightly different nature than those discussed earlier. Verbs of flattery can be used felicitously only when the target person is present when the speaker makes the flattering remark, and thus is potentially affectable; however, the verb itself does not actually profile any affectedness on the part of the addressee. Verbs of praise, on the other hand, do not describe an attempt to provoke an emotional reaction in the addressee or to win his favor. In fact, the addressee's reactions are quite irrelevant. The object of praise need not be present at the scene of the action, need not know about it, and need not even be human. The verbs describe a 'public' relationship between two participants, the commender and the commended, and therefore take accusative objects.

Before we pass on to the next group of verbs, it will be worthwhile to consider an interesting pair from this class: *klaskać* 'to clap [in applause]', which takes dative objects, and *oklaskiwać* 'to applaud [by clapping]', which governs the accusative. The latter verb is derived from *klaskać* by adding the perfectivizing prefix *o-* and the imperfectivizing suffix *-iwać*; the resulting formation is, like *klaskać*, imperfective. Since they are both derived from the same root, they seem to contradict the claim that the choice of dative or accusative object is semantically motivated. It should be observed, however, that the two verbs are not synonymous. *Oklaskiwać* is used to describe a situation in which an audience expresses its favorable appraisal of the target's performance by clapping (297). *Klaskać*, on the other hand, describes a situation in which the audience engages in behavior which conventionally indicates acclaim; the verb, however, does not specify that the agent actually commends the addressee's actions (298). In fact, the use of a form that does not specifically indicate favorable appraisal strongly suggests that the audience did not find the addressee's performance praiseworthy and applauded him insincerely – perhaps because they were afraid not to, or because they wanted to please him. It is interesting to note that *klaskać* can also be used in an extended sense to denote any kind of insincere applause, not necessarily expressed by clapping. Thus, *klaskać* is not a verb of evaluation; the target's personal sphere, however, is highly relevant.

(297)   *Zebrani długo oklaskiwali mówcę.*
        'The audience applauded the speaker (ACC) for a long time.'

(298)   *Nic mądrego nie powiedział, a mimo to mu klaskali.*
        'He didn't say anything worthwhile, but they applauded him (DAT) anyway.'

4.2.6. Verbs of verbal aggression

This class can be subdivided into three groups: verbs of teasing, which govern the dative case; verbs of reprimanding, which govern the accusative, and verbs of verbal abuse, some of which take accusative objects, and some dative.

The contrast between verbs of teasing on the one hand and verbs of reprimanding on the other is analogous to that discussed in the preceding section. Verbs of teasing (*dokuczać* 'to tease, to spite', *docinać* 'to tease', *przygadywać/dogadywać/dojeżdżać* 'to gibe') denote a verbal act performed with the sole purpose of provoking a certain emotional reaction in the addressee (as opposed to an evaluation of the addressee or his actions); the verb does not specify whether the addressee was actually affected. The addressee's sphere of awareness is highly prominent; moreover, the addressee must be present at the scene of the action, and must at least be able to understand the teasing remark.

Verbs of reprimanding (*ganić* 'to admonish', *karcić* 'to upbraid', *strofować* 'to remonstrate', *besztać* 'to take to task', *łajać* 'to chide', *skrzyczeć* 'to scold', *gromić* 'to objurgate, castigate', *upomnieć* 'to reprimand', *ofuknąć* 'to tell off'), on the other hand, describe events in which a speaker expresses disapproval of the addressee's actions in order to influence his future behavior. Although the sphere of awareness is relevant (the addressee must understand the criticism, and the reprimand will affect his future behavior only if it provokes an emotional reaction such as compunction), it is not in profile: the verb does not specify what emotion, if any, the speaker's words provoke, so it will have been used felicitously whether the addressee felt compunction or fear or resentment or remained indifferent. The verb focuses on the "public" aspect of the event: the evaluation of the addressee's actions and its possible effects on his future behavior. Therefore, the addressee is expressed by an accusative noun phrase.

The last of the three groups, verbs of abuse, includes verbs which govern the dative as well as those which govern the accusative. The dative verbs (*ubliżać/urągać/wymyślać* 'to revile, abuse' *złorzeczyć* 'to vituperate, curse', *bluźnić* 'to blaspheme, curse') designate the hurling of verbal insults at a target, with the main focus on the actual delivery of the message rather than the effects it produces. This is reflected in their aspectual properties. *Złorzeczyć, urągać,* and *bluźnić* lack perfective forms; *ubliżyć,* the perfective form of *ubliżać,* indicates that the action was non-iterative, not that the intended effect has been accomplished; and *zwymyślać,* the perfective form of *wymyślać,* governs the accusative (see below). Since the verbs do not specify that the target was affected in any way, there is little to motivate the use of the accusative. On the other hand, the sphere of awareness is a prominent substructure in their semantic representation, since the addressee must be at least potentially affectable. (The dative object must be a person or an attribute of a person, or, in the case of *bluźnić* 'to blaspheme', God.)

Accusative verbs of abuse fall into two subgroups. The first includes verbs of insulting: *obrażać* 'to insult', *znieważać* 'to affront', *upokarzać/poniżać* 'to humiliate, abase'. All of these verbs highlight the effect that the agent's action produces on the target, and they all have perfective forms. The effect is externally relevant rather than purely internal: the agent's action has important social consequences since the target's honor or reputation are affected. Furthermore, the target may have to respond to the agent's provocation: for example, the code of honor may oblige him to avenge the insult. It is also worth noting that the events designated by these verbs are not specifically verbal (one can also insult non-verbally); moreover, with two of the verbs, *obrażać* and *znieważać,* the target need not be human or even present at the scene of the action (299-300). Both of these facts are indicative of the relatively low relevance of the sphere of awareness.

(299) *Telewizja podobno obraża wartości chrzescijańskie.*
'They say that television offends Christian values (ACC).'

(300) *Twoje słowa znieważają pamięć zmarłych.*
'Your words profane the memory (ACC) of the dead.'

The very same factors determine the choice of case marking of the objects of verbs of denigration, the other subgroup of accusative verbs of abuse, and they are, if anything, even more pronounced. This group includes verbs like *obmawiać/obgadywać* 'to backbite', *obsmarowywać* 'to throw mud at, heap dirt upon', *oczerniać* 'denigrate, malign', *zniesławiać* 'to slander, defame', *szkalować/spotwarzać* 'to slander, calumniate, traduce', *kląć* 'to curse, execrate', *winić* 'to blame', *oskarżać* 'to accuse', and *pomawiać* 'to impute [terrible deeds] to'. What these verbs profile is the social effects of the action, namely, the damage that the speaker's words do to the target's reputation (and, in the judiciary sense of *oskarżać,* also the changes in his legal status). The relevance of the sphere of awareness, on the other hand, is minimal. The target of the abuse is not the addressee in the communication event designated by the verb, need not be present or know of the censure leveled at him, and his emotional reactions are outside the scope of predication.

It is worth noting that the effects of denigration are analogous to the effects of defiling or desecrating, except that for the latter, the sphere of awareness is entirely irrelevant since they involve targets which are inanimate, and therefore not endowed with a sphere of awareness. Verbs of defiling/desecrating (e.g.

bezcześcić, profanować, kalać 'to profane, desecrate, defile',) all govern the accusative case; it should come as no surprise, therefore, that verbs of denigration share their syntactic properties. It should also be noted that verbs which designate the tarnishing of someone's reputation without specifying whether this is accomplished verbally or non-verbally (e.g. *(s)kompromitować* 'to disgrace', *zdyskredytować* 'to discredit', *ośmieszyć* 'to ridicule') also govern the accusative case.

The public dimension is also very prominent when the target's social or legal status changes as a result of a verbal act, for example when a person is excommunicated, anathematized, or formally accused of a crime. Hence, *wykląć* 'to excommunicate', *przekląć* 'to curse, anathematize' and *oskarżać* 'to accuse' also govern the accusative.

To summarize: accusative verbs of abuse differ those which govern the dative case in that they focus on the externally assessable results of the agent's action; the target's emotional experiences are only marginally relevant. The dative verbs, on the other hand, highlight the sphere of awareness.

Three verbs, however – *zwymyślać, (ze)lżyć* 'to revile, abuse', and *wyzywać/wyzwać* 'to call names' – do not seem to fit this pattern. They all designate the hurling of verbal abuse, which makes them semantically very similar to dative verbs such as *złorzeczyć* 'to vituperate' and *urągać* 'to abuse'. In spite of this, they govern the accusative case. They are thus exceptions to the generalizations formulated above, though in each case there is some residual motivation for their behavior.

Wyz(y)wać (od najgorszych/od durniów/od idiotów) 'to call (the worst names/a blockhead/an idiot)' is morphologically related to other forms with which the accusative is highly motivated. These include call-for-action verbs such as *wezwać* 'to appeal to', *pozwać* 'to summon (to appear in court)', *przyzwać* 'to call (for someone)' and the other sense of *wyzwać* 'to challenge (to a duel)', as well as verbs of name-giving such as *zwać* 'to call', *nazwać* 'to name', and *przezwać* 'to give a nickname'.[50] Furthermore, it should be noted that *wyzwać* differs in meaning from the dative verbs of abuse in that it designates a particular kind of insult – name calling. This aspect of its meaning, of course, strengthens the analogical pressure of the naming verbs and hence the motivation for the use of the accusative case.

Lżyć 'to revile', is a rare word, one to be found only in fairly literary texts. Although today it means 'to hurl insults at a target' originally it meant 'to compromise the target's reputation' (Brückner 1957 glosses it as *hańbić* 'to disgrace, dishonor'), which provides a historical explanation for its syntactic alignment with verbs of denigration. It is still occasionally used in this older sense, as in the following example from *Gazeta Wyborcza* (a liberal newspaper):

(301)   *Nie lżymy wartości chrześcijanskich.*
        'We do not revile Christian values (ACC).'

Moreover, the syntactic pattern seems to have become unsettled. Although middle-aged and older speakers all use the accusative case with this verb, many younger speakers prefer the dative.

The last of the exceptional verbs is *zwymyślać*, which takes accusative objects only when it occurs in the perfective form. (Its imperfective counterpart, as we have seen above, governs the dative.) Although this is clearly an idiosyncratic property of the verb, it is worth noting that the perfective aspect, with its focus on the completion of the action, also makes the effects of the action more salient, and thus more compatible with the accusative construal. It is significant in this connection that all three of the exceptional verbs of verbal abuse, but none of the "regular" ones which govern the dative, have perfective forms.

4.2.7. Verbs of greeting and leave-taking

In the previous section, it was argued that the change of the target's social status brought about by an insult or censure provides the motivation for the accusative construal. The accusative case is also used to signal the target in a variety of other social acts, such as the conferral or divestment of a role or title (with verbs such as *mianować* 'to nominate', *ogłosić* 'to proclaim (king etc.)', *zatrudnić* 'to hire', *angażować* 'to employ', *awansować* 'to promote', *doktoryzować* 'to give a doctorate', *zwolnić* 'to fire', *zredukować* 'to lay off', *wylać* 'to give the sack', *odprawić* 'to dismiss, give the golden handshake', *emerytować* 'to retire', *zdymisjonować* 'to discharge', *zdetronizować* 'to dethrone') or the conferral of membership in a group (*przyjąć* 'to admit [a new member]', *adoptować, usynowić* 'to adopt [a son]', *poślubić* 'to marry', *zaprosić* 'to invite', *gościć, podejmować* 'to entertain [guests]'), as well an act of recognition of the target's status or - membership in a group. Verbs of greeting and leave-taking belong to the latter category, since they designate an act of symbolic acknowledgment of group membership. One might therefore expect them to govern the accusative case. This prediction is borne out in some cases (302) but not in others (303-305):

(302) *Robert pozdrowił/przywitał/pożegnał Artura.*
'Robert greeted/said hello/said good-bye to Artur (ACC).'

(303) *Poddani kłaniali się/czapkowali/hołdowali księciu.*
'The subjects bowed/doffed their caps/paid homage to the prince (DAT).'

(304) *Żołnierz zasalutował/zameldował się dowódcy.*
'The soldier saluted/reported to the commander (DAT).'

(305) *Dziewczyna dygnęła gościom i schroniła się w kuchni.*
'The girl curtseyed to the guests (DAT) and took shelter in the kitchen.'

On closer scrutiny, the apparently erratic behavior of the verbs in examples (302-305) turns out to be consistent with their semantics. It should first be noted that the actions designated by dative-governing verbs such as *kłaniać się* 'to bow, greet', *czapkować* 'to doff one's cap to', *hołdować* 'to pay homage to', *salutować* 'to salute', *meldować się* 'to report to [one's commanding officer]', and *dygać* 'to curtsey', involve more than just a simple greeting. Each of these acts is also an acknowledgment of the addressee's higher status. In other words, for the verb to be used felicitously, the greeter must be within the addressee's sphere of influence. This may not be immediately apparent in the case of *kłaniać się*, which can denote the socially inferior person's opening turn in the greeting sequence as well as the superior's response. However, in its primary sense the verb clearly designates the initial greeting: thus, (306a), where the superior person initiates the greeting, describes a very unusual situation. In contrast to this, there is nothing extraordinary about the situation described in (306b), in which *ukłonić się* is replaced with *pozdrowić*, which, like other accusative-governing verbs does not specify the relative status of the two individuals involved.

(306) a. *Dyrektor szkoły ukłonił się chłopcu.*
    'The principal bowed to (greeted) the boy (DAT).'

(306) b. *Dyrektor szkoły pozdrowił chłopca.*
    'The principal greeted the boy (ACC).'

It is also worth noting that Polish has another verb, *odkłonić się* 'to bow back, to return a greeting', which specifically designates the superior's response. The existence of fairly elaborate rules which specify who initiates the greeting in what situation is further evidence that the relative social status of the interacting individuals is very important.

Thus, verbs such as *czapkować, salutować,* and *dygać* strongly evoke the sphere of influence, which motivates the dative construal. In contrast, the accusative verbs in (302) all designate greetings among equals, or at least they do not specify the relative social status of the participants; hence, they are more compatible with the accusative construal.

4.2.8. Dative vs. accusative construal of communication events: A summary

It was noted at the beginning of this section that all communication predicates evoke the sphere of awareness. Hence, all communication predicates are potentially construable according to the dative scenario, though other factors may overshadow this aspect of their semantics, thereby forcing an accusative construal.

Among the factors which motivate the accusative construal are decreased relevance of the sphere of awareness and emphasis on the effects of the action. The sphere of awareness is minimally relevant when the action designated by the verb can also be achieved by non-verbal means or when it is successfully accomplished even if the target does not hear or understand the message; it is irrelevant when the target is incapable of understanding the message – for example, when it is not human.[51] The effects of the agent's action are likely to be emphasized if they are externally ascertainable, for example, if the addressee performs the action he is urged or encouraged to do, or if he begins to use newly acquired skills, suffers losses, or if his reputation is either tarnished or enhanced.

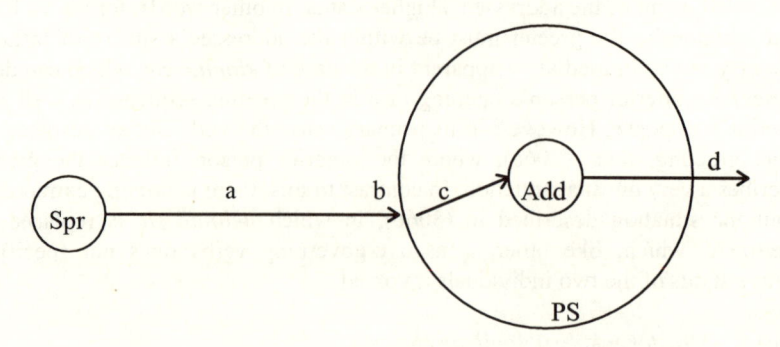

Figure 11. A communication event: base representation

Thus, the accusative and the dative construal highlight different aspects of an event. The difference is summarized schematically below. Figure 11 depicts a base event chain which is open to both construals: for example, the agent says something [a], the words reach the target's personal sphere [b] and set off a process within the personal sphere [c] which in turn causes an externally perceptible reaction [d]. The dative case, it was argued in chapter 2, evokes the target's personal sphere as part of its semantic structure; therefore, the dative construal will be more appropriate when the speaker's communicative intention is to focus primarily on the initial parts of the chain (stages a, b, and possibly c), and in particular, on the moment of penetration into the personal sphere. The agent's actions might well have effects which 'spill' beyond the personal sphere, but these are not explicitly mentioned. This kind of profile is represented schematically in Figure 12.

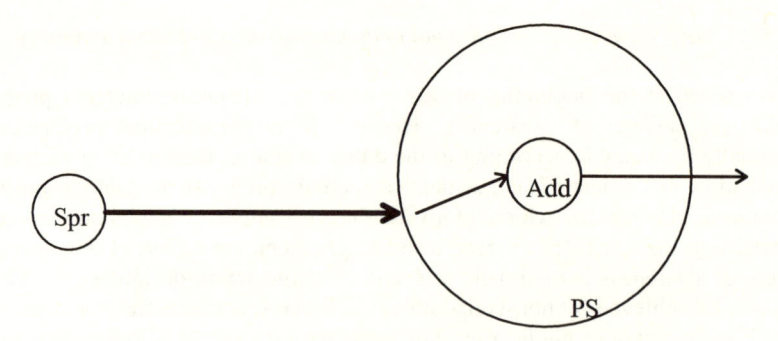

Figure 12. A communication event: dative construal

The accusative construal, on the other hand, is more compatible with a focus on the action as a whole and particularly on the final effects. The passive participant may be endowed with a personal sphere, but this is entirely incidental. This kind of profile is represented in Figure 13. Since the choice of a particular verb entails a choice of profile, the choice of either the dative or accusative case follows as a natural consequence.

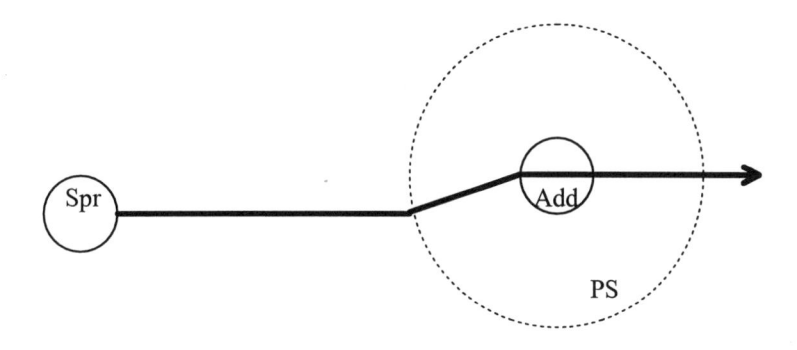

Figure 13. A communication event: accusative construal

4.3. Bodily experience[52]

4.3.1. The problem

Another area of partial overlap between the uses of the dative and the accusative are expressions describing physical actions which affect only a part of the target's body. A person whose hand or arm is acted on by the agent is certainly directly affected by the action, which motivates the use of the accusative case. On the other hand, parts of the body are central elements of the personal sphere (see section 2.1), and hence any process which they participate in can be given a dative construal. Thus, once again we are dealing with conflicting motivations. This section is devoted to a discussion of the factors which motivate the choice of case marking to describe such situations.

In some cases, the semantic contrast between the accusative and the dative is clear and fully predictable from the meaning of the cases. The (a) sentences below indicate that the target's whole body was exposed to the action, whereas the (b) sentences describe situations which involve only a part of the body.

(307) a. *Umył dziecko.*
    'He washed the child (ACC).'

(307) b. *Umył dziecku rączki.*
'He washed the child's (DAT) hands (ACC).'

(308) a. *Przykryła go.*
'She covered him (ACC).'

(308) b. *Przykryła mu nogi.*
'She covered his (DAT) legs (ACC).'

(309) a. *Masował ją.*
'He massaged her (ACC).'

(309) b. *Masował jej plecy.*
'He massaged her (DAT) back (ACC).'

In other cases, however, the reasons for the choice of one case form over another are less obvious. For example, the accusative case is used in (310) and (311) in spite of the fact that only a part of the target's body (the beard or the hair) is directly involved in the action.

(310) *Ogolili go.*
'They shaved him (ACC).'

(311) *Uczesał ją.*
he combed her:ACC
'He combed her hair.'

In (312) and (313) the target of the action can be either dative or accusative. This does not result in any obvious differences in meaning in (312). The sentences in (313), on the other hand, do differ in meaning: (313a) implies that Piotr produced scratch marks on Robert's back, whereas (313b) means that he scratched Robert's back without causing any lasting effects, presumably to relieve itching.

(312) a. *Gorąca zupa parzyła Robertowi usta.*
hot   soup:NOM burned Robert:DAT mouth:ACC
'The hot soup burned Robert's mouth.'

(312) b. *Gorąca zupa parzyła Roberta w usta.*
hot   soup:NOM burned Robert:ACC in mouth:ACC
'The hot soup burned Robert's mouth.'

(313) a. *Piotr podrapał Robertowi plecy.*
Piotr:NOM scratched Robert:DAT back:ACC
'Piotr scratched Robert's back.'

(313) b. *Piotr   podrapał Roberta   w plecy.*
Piotr:NOM scratched Robert:ACC in back:ACC
'Piotr scratched Robert on the back.'

Finally, in some instances case selection seems entirely arbitrary. *Boleć* 'to hurt', *swędzieć* 'to itch', and *łamać w kościach* 'to have arthritis in one's bones' require accusative experiencers; *ścierpnąć* '[of limb:] to go to sleep' and *zdrętwieć* 'to go numb' govern the dative, and *strzykać w kościach* '[of bones:] to go crunch' can take either.

(314) a. *Boli mnie głowa.*
hurts me:ACC head:NOM
'I've got a headache.'

(314) b. **Boli mi głowa.*
hurts me:DAT head:NOM

(315) a. *Swędzi mnie ręka.*
itches me:ACC hand:NOM
'My hand itches.'

(315) b. **Swędzi mi ręka.*
itches me:DAT hand:NOM

(316) a. **Ścierpła/ Zdrętwiała mnie ręka.*
went to sleep/went numb me:ACC arm:NOM

(316) b. *Ścierpła/ Zdrętwiała mi ręka.*
went to sleep/went numb me:DAT arm:NOM
'I've got pins and needles in my arm./My arm is numb.'

(317) a. *W kościach mnie łamie.*
in bones:LOC me:ACC it breaks
'I've got a pain in my bones./My arthritis is playing up.'

(317) b. **W kościach mi łamie.*
in bones:LOC me:DAT it breaks

(318) a. *W kościach mnie strzyka.*
in bones:LOC me:ACC it crunches
'I can feel my bones going crunch.'

(318) b. *W kościach mi strzyka.*
in bones:LOC me:DAT it crunches
'I can feel my bones going crunch.'

114 *Dative and accusative targets*

All of the above sentences describe direct bodily experience. In some cases, the person having the experience must receive dative marking, and in others the corresponding NP must be accusative. How can the above data be reconciled with the claim that case selection is semantically motivated?

4.3.2. Affected body parts: Coding options

It will be useful to begin our discussion with some thoughts on the preliminary coding decisions that the speaker makes when describing actions which directly involve only a part of the passive participant's body.

One of the very first decisions that will have to be made is the designation of participants in the relationship to be described: in other words, the speaker has to decide whether she wants to describe a relationship between the agent and another person, or the relationship between an agent and an object (which, in the case we are considering, happens to be a part of another person's body). Once this choice has been made, the speaker must decide how to convey the relationship between the part of the body and the person to whom it belongs. The grammar of Polish offers three options:

1. The body part is given participant status, and its owner is specified by means of a possessive modifier (e.g. *Piotr podrapał plecy Roberta* 'Piotr scratched Robert's back').
2. The owner is given participant status and the part of the body is implicit in the meaning of the verb (*Ogolili go* 'They shaved him'), specified periphrastically (*Piotr podrapał Roberta po plecach* 'Piotr scratched Robert on the back'), or not specified at all (*Piotr podrapał Roberta* 'Piotr scratched Robert.').
3. Both the affected body part and the owner are given participant status, and the owner's involvement in the action is construed as a consequence of the affectedness of the body part (e.g. *Piotr podrapał Robertowi plecy* 'Piotr scratched Robert's (DAT) back').

In the subsequent discussion, I will refer to these as the *possessive, accusative*, and *dative construal*, respectively.

Each of these construals reflects some aspects of the situation quite faithfully and hides or even distorts others. The possessive construal explicitly specifies the relationship between the body part, which is coded as a patient, and the person to whom it belongs; however, it fails to code the experiencer's affectedness (thereby implicating that he was not affected).[53]

The accusative construal capitalizes on the fact that one is necessarily affected by any changes or processes within one's body. Moreover, wholes are cognitively more salient than parts, and human beings are more salient than inanimate objects, which further strengthens the affected person's claim to accusative marking. However, the decision to construe the "owner" of the body part, rather than the body part itself, as the tail of the action chain results in a somewhat unusual view of things because, although there is a totally affected entity, a less-than-wholly-affected participant is given patient marking, and the totally affected participant is sometimes not even named.

Finally, the dative construal allows explicit coding of both types of affectedness. However, it also offers a skewed picture of the event because it suggests that the human participant was affected indirectly (as a consequence of the agent's acting on an object belonging to his personal sphere) rather than directly.

The variability in the linguistic coding of processes affecting body parts stems from the unprototypicality of the event described – specifically, from the fact that the experiencer and the patient are not fully distinct. This kind of process can be construed in several different ways, and the different construals translate into different constructions at the linguistic level. Construal is partly a matter of linguistic convention and partly of the speaker's communicative objectives. Therefore, an adequate account of the choice of case-marking must explain why certain construals have a privileged status, and, when the language does allow coding options, explain the semantic consequences of a particular choice.

The possessive construal is rarely resorted to for several reasons. I have already indicated that it distorts reality in suggesting that the experiencer is not affected by the action. There is also a general preference for assigning participant status to humans rather than non-humans and to wholes rather than to parts. The experiencer is a more natural choice for participant status on both counts. Thus, although it is in principle possible to construe the body part as the patient and introduce the experiencer as a possessive modifier on the patient NP, such a choice – reflecting a purely objective, disembodied view of reality – is rather unusual in Polish.[54] In the following sections, therefore, I will only discuss the factors which determine the choice between the accusative and the dative construal.

4.3.3. *Focus on the affected body part vs. focus on the affected person*

I have indicated above that the accusative construal is more in line with general coding strategies in that it allows the speaker to focus on the affected person rather than an object and on the whole rather than a part. Such a coding decision results in a certain deviation from the prototypical value of the accusative, since the accusative-marked participant is only partially affected. Sentences such as (319), in which the partially affected person is coded by means of an accusative nominal, exhibit what Langacker (1984) calls *profile-active zone discrepancy*: although the entire passive participant is in profile, the active zone – i.e. the region directly involved in the process designated by the verb – comprises only a part of his body (in this case, the back). As Langacker shows, profile-active zone discrepancy is very common in language; it is also an extremely useful device precisely because it allows the conceptualizer to focus on the cognitively more salient entity. The down side of this is that (319) is less precise than its dative counterpart (320), since it doesn't explicitly code which part of Robert's body was affected, but this is easily remedied by adding a prepositional phrase which specifies which part of the body was involved in the action (321).

(319)   *Piotr drapał Roberta.*
'Piotr scratched Robert (ACC).'

(320)   *Piotr drapał Robertowi plecy.*
'Piotr scratched Robert's (DAT) back (ACC).'

(321)   *Piotr drapał Roberta po plecach.*
'Piotr scratched Robert (ACC) on the back.'

Thus the two construals differ in how much emphasis they accord to the two participants. The accusative highlights the affectedness of the non-active human participant while backgrounding the directly affected body part. The dative construal, on the other hand, places the body part in the center of the scene; the affectedness of the person to whom it belongs is portrayed as a consequence of the process affecting the body part. The choice of construal depends on the speaker's communicative objectives, but various other factors may limit the speaker's freedom of choice by making one of the options the preferred one or even the only possible one.

Somewhat trivially, if the verb designates an act of dismemberment, the dative construal is the only option, since it is the body part which is viewed as severed from the person and not the other way around – hence, the unacceptability of the (b) sentences below.

(322) a.   *Chirurg   amputował żołnierzowi   rękę.*
surgeon:NOM amputated soldier:DAT hand:ACC
'The surgeon amputated the soldier's hand.'

(322) b.   **Chirurg   amputował żołnierza   ręce /   od ręki.*
surgeon:NOM amputated soldier:ACC hand:DAT/from hand:GEN
'The surgeon amputated the soldier from the hand.'

(323) a.   *Mama obcięła Oli paznokcie.*
'Mother clipped Ola's (DAT) nails (ACC).'

(323) b.   **Mama   obcięła Olę   paznokciom/od paznokci.*
Mother:NOM clipped Ola:ACC nails:DAT/ from nails:GEN
'Mother clipped Ola from the nails.'

Another relevant factor is the *degree* of profile-active zone discrepancy. Actions involving vital organs, or parts of the body which are relatively large, are more likely to be given an accusative construal, since the whole person is obviously affected; the dative construal, however, remains an open possibility (see examples (324-325)). On the other hand, if the action involves a relatively small or unimportant part of the body – such as a tooth or the fingernails – the discrepancy between the active zone and the profile inherent in the accusative construal is too large, and dative coding on the passive human participant is the only option (326-328).

(324) a. *Chirurg   zoperował Ani   serce.*
surgeon:NOM operated   Ania:DAT heart:ACC
'The surgeon operated on Ania's heart.'

(324) b. *Chirurg   zoperował Anię.*
surgeon:NOM operated   Ania:ACC
'The surgeon operated on Ania.'

(325) a. *Lekarz   wyleczył Ani   nerki.*
doctor:NOM cured   Ania:DAT kidneys:ACC
'The doctor cured Ania's kidneys problem.'

(325) b. *Lekarz wyleczył Anię.*
'The doctor cured Ania (ACC).'

(326) a. *Fryzjerka ufarbowała Ani włosy.*
'The hairdresser dyed Ania's (DAT) hair (ACC).'

(326) b. ?? *Fryzjerka ufarbowała Anię.*
'The hairdresser dyed Ania (ACC).'

(327) a. *Dentysta zaplombował Ani ząb.*
'The dentist filled Ania's (DAT) tooth (ACC).'

(327) b. **Dentysta zaplombował Anię.*
'The dentist filled Ania (ACC).'

(328) a. *Kosmetyczka   polakierowała Ani   paznokcie.*
beautician:NOM put nail polish Ania:DAT nails:ACC
'The beautician put nail polish on Ania's nails.'

(328) b. **Kosmetyczka   polakierowała Anię*
beautician:NOM put nail polish   Ania:ACC.
'The beautician put nail polish on Ania.'

It should be noted, however, that larger profile-active zone discrepancies are tolerated in contexts in which it is quite clear which part of the affected person is directly involved in the action. Thus, it is fairly easy to imagine a woman saying to her hairdresser:

(329)   Czy   może mnie   pani   dzisiaj ufarbować?
        INTERROG can me:ACC madam:NOM today to dye
        'Can you dye my hair today?'

This is an unusual and slightly humorous usage, but it is a good illustration of the fact that linguistic rules can be bent (and broken) if the context provides appropriate motivation.

Finally, a speaker is more likely to choose the dative construal when the results of the action can be dissociated from the action itself – for example, if the action produces lasting changes in the affected body part. This can be illustrated with one of the recurring themes of this section, example (313), repeated here as (330). I observed in section 4.3.1 that the (a) sentence strongly implies that Piotr's action produced scratch marks on Robert's back, whereas (330b) does not have this implication. This, I suggest, is due to the fact that the accusative and the dative construals tend to combine with different senses of the perfectivizing prefix *po-*.

(330) a.   *Piotr   podrapał   Robertowi   plecy.*
           Piotr:NOM scratched:PF Robert:DAT back:ACC
           'Piotr scratched Robert's back.'

(330) b.   *Piotr   podrapał   Roberta   w plecy/   po plecach.*
           Piotr:NOM scratched:PF Robert:ACC in back:ACC/all over back:LOC
           'Piotr scratched Robert on the back.'

The perfective aspect is used with actions which, according to traditional grammar, are "delimited" in some way. I have argued elsewhere (Dąbrowska 1996) that an action be delimited in a variety of ways, e.g. spatially (i.e. by the spatial limits of the landmark, e.g. *przebiec ulicę* 'to run across a street/cross a street running', *dobiec do domu* 'run as far as the house'), temporally (by the temporal limits of the landmark, e.g. *przespać cały film* 'to sleep all through the film', *dospać do rana* 'to sleep until morning') or by the target state (e.g. *przebudować dom* 'to remodel the house', *dosolić zupę* 'to add salt to the soup to taste'). Most perfectivizing prefixes are polysemous (Rudzka-Ostyn 1985, Janda 1986, Pasich-Piasecka 1993), and the different senses reflect the different ways in which an action can be delimited. For the purposes of the following discussion, only two of the many senses of *po-* will be relevant: the "limited duration" sense ('to do X for a while', e.g. *pospać* 'to sleep for a while', *pobiegać* 'to run for a while') and the "change of state" sense (e.g. *poplątać* 'to tangle up', *pomalować* 'to paint [i.e. to cover the surface of the landmark with paint]').

The "change of state" sense tends to combine with the dative construal because it allows the results of the action (e.g. the scratch marks) to be conceptually separated from the action itself. This in turn makes it possible to distinguish between the different types of affectedness of the two participants: Robert's back was affected because its appearance changed as a result of the process designated by the verb, and Robert was affected because his back (a central part of his personal sphere) underwent a change of state. A "limited duration" interpretation of (330a) is also possible, but less likely.

The *po-* in (330b), on the other hand, tends to be given a "limited duration" interpretation because the prepositional phrase indicates that only a part of Robert's body was affected; therefore, the accusative case here signals not a participant that undergoes a change of state, but merely an entity that is acted on by the agent (cf. the discussion in section 4.1).[55]

I pointed out earlier in this chapter that the sentences in (312), repeated here as (331), do not exhibit a difference in meaning analogous to the contrast between (330a) and (330b). Since the special implications of (330a) arise from the interaction of the semantic structure associated with the dative and one of the senses of the perfectivizing prefix *po-*, this should no longer be a puzzle. As one might expect, the perfectivized counterparts of (331a) and (331b) contrast in exactly the same way as the sentences with *podrapać* 'to scratch' – see (332a) and (332b).

(331) a. *Gorąca zupa   parzyła   Robertowi   usta.*
         hot   soup:NOM burned:IMPF Robert:DAT mouth:ACC
         'The hot soup burned Robert's mouth.'

(331) b. *Gorąca zupa   parzyła   Roberta   w usta.*
         hot   soup:NOM burned:IMPF Robert:ACC in mouth:ACC
         'The hot soup burned Robert's mouth.'

(332) a. *Gorąca zupa   poparzyła Robertowi   usta.*
         hot   soup:NOM burned:PF Robert:DAT mouth:ACC
         'The hot soup burned Robert's mouth. (i.e., Robert's mouth is burned because of the hot soup.)'

(332) b. *Gorąca zupa   poparzyła Roberta   w usta.*
         hot   soup:NOM burned:PF Robert:ACC in mouth:ACC
         'The hot soup burned Robert's mouth. (i.e., the hot soup produced a burning sensation in Robert's mouth.)'

4.3.4. Dative vs. accusative construal: sublexical and explicit reference to affected body part

The verbs considered in the preceding section give the speaker the option of focusing either on the affected body part or on the whole experiencer. Some verbs, however, do not allow this choice, and the experiencer can only be coded by *one* of the two cases. I will presently show that this happens when the meaning of the verb is compatible with only one construal: either "holistic" (when the verb is "about" what happened to the whole person) or "local" (when the verb focuses on what happened to a body part).

(333) a. *Zdjął Kasi bluzkę.*
'He took off Kasia's (DAT) blouse (ACC).' [i.e. the blouse Kasia was wearing]

(333) b. *Rozebrał Kasię.*
'He undressed Kasia (ACC).'

(334) a. *Kat obciął głowę Marii Antoninie.*
'The executioner cut off Marie Antoinette's (DAT) head (ACC).'

(334) b. *Kat ściął Marię Antoninę.*
'The executioner beheaded Marie Antoinette (ACC).'

(335) a. *Bandyta   poderżnął   staruszce   gardło.*
bandit:NOM   cut open   old lady:DAT   throat:ACC
'The bandit slit the old lady's throat open.'

(335) b. *Bandyta   zarżnął   staruszkę.*
bandit:NOM   cut throat   old lady:ACC
'The bandit cut the old lady's throat [thus killing her]./The bandit killed the old lady by cutting her throat.'

The (b) sentences above describe situations in which the experiencer is totally affected: the final result is death or complete nakedness. This fits the patient prototype very closely, and the experiencer receives accusative case marking. In the (a) sentences, the action is aimed at only a part of the target's body. For example, in (333a) only a part of Kasia's body is uncovered. On the other hand, the blouse is affected as a whole (it changes location). Thus, the nominal *Kasia* receives dative marking and the blouse is coded by an accusative NP.[56] In (334a) the verb imposes a narrower perspective on the situation described in (334b): instead of describing an act of killing, (334a) describes an act of cutting off a part of the body (the head). Of course cutting off the head normally results in death, but this is an inference: the verb itself does not designate an act of killing. Similarly, in (335a) the action is directed at the victim's throat rather than the entire body; and though cutting the throat normally leads to death, the verb does not specifically state that the victim died. Thus, (336a), in contrast to (336b), is not contradictory:

(336) a. *Bandyta poderżnął staruszce gardło, ale udało się ją uratować.*
'The bandit cut open the old lady's (DAT) throat (ACC), but they succeeded in saving her life.'

(336) b. *Bandyta zarżnął staruszkę, ale udało się ją uratować.*
'The bandit cut the old lady's (ACC) throat, but they succeeded in saving her life.'

(333b-335b), like example (319), involve profile-active zone discrepancy. They differ from the sentences discussed in the preceding section in that the discrepancy is, as it were, written into the semantics of the verb. Consequently, the part of the body which is actually affected is implicit in the meaning of the verb itself.

Some verbs allow either explicit or sublexical reference to the affected body part:

(337)   *Ogolili Pawła.*
        'They shaved Paweł (ACC).'

(338)   *Ogolili Pawłowi brodę.*
        'They shaved Paweł's (DAT) beard (ACC).'

The verb *ogolić* 'to shave' does specify a default value of the affected body part: the beard.[57] However, it can also be used to describe an action of shaving any part of the body (cf. example (339)); when it is used in this extended sense, however, the affected body part must be explicitly mentioned.

(339)   *Ogolili Pawłowi głowę.*
        'They shaved Paweł's (DAT) head (ACC).'

4.3.5. Predicates of physical sensation

Throughout this section, I discussed the linguistic means available for describing situations in which an agent acts on a part of another participant's body. It should be pointed out that any action which involves a part of the body necessarily has a psychological dimension as well as a physical one. A person who is kicked or hit or licked experiences a sensation; and there is certainly more to kissing than just lip contact. In other words, the sphere of awareness is also relevant for physical actions involving body parts; the accusative construal, by focusing on the physical dimension, hides this aspect of the situation.

If, however, a predicate profiles not an action on another person's body which causes this person to experience certain sensations, but the sensations themselves, we would expect that the affected individual will be expressed by means of a dative nominal, since the sphere of awareness is undeniably a salient element of the semantic structure of such a predicate. This prediction is borne out in some cases (340-343), but not in others (344-346).

(340)   *Jest mi   gorąco/ciepło/zimno.*
        it is me:DAT   hotly/warmly/coldly
        'I'm hot/warm/cold.'

(341)   *Jest mi   słabo/niedobrze/mdło.*
        it is me:DAT   weakly/unwell/vapidly
        'I feel faint/sick/nauseaous.'

(342)　　Co　　　ci　　　dolega?
　　　　　what:NOM you:DAT cause discomfort
　　　　　'What's giving you trouble?'

(343)　　Dokucza mi　　　głowa/　　ból　　głowy.
　　　　　bothers　me:DAT head:NOM/ ache:NOM head:GEN
　　　　　'I'm suffering from a headache.'

(344)　　Boli　mnie　　głowa.
　　　　　aches me:ACC head:NOM
　　　　　'My head aches.'

(345)　　Swędzi mnie　　ręka.
　　　　　itches　me:ACC hand:NOM
　　　　　'My hand itches.'

(346)　　Uwiera mnie　　kołnierzyk.
　　　　　pinch　me:ACC collar:NOM
　　　　　'My collar is biting into my neck.'

The apparently arbitrary behavior of the verbs in examples (344-346) begins to make more sense when we look more closely at the linguistic properties of physical sensation predicates.

We should first note that there are very few "true" sensation predicates, i.e. predicates whose primary sense designates a physical sensation, such as *boleć* 'to hurt' or *swędzieć* 'to itch'. This is presumably due to the fact that bodily experience is entirely subjective: we have no way of knowing what another person's toothache feels like. It would thus be very difficult, if not impossible, for a community to fix constant meanings for a large set of physical sensation predicates. Consequently, most of the expressions used to talk about bodily experience are figurative extensions of physical action predicates. The sensation is described as similar to that experienced when the experiencer is the patient of the action designated by the basic sense of the predicate. For example, an individual suffering from stitch might describe his condition by using the word which normally designates the sensation experienced when a pointed object is pressed against the body (347); the sensation felt in the mouth or the throat after eating spicy food will be described as a "burning" sensation (348), and so on.

(347)　　Kłuje　mnie　　w boku.
　　　　　it pricks me:ACC in side:LOC
　　　　　'I've got a stitch.'

(348)　　Pali　mnie　　w gardle.
　　　　　it burns me:ACC in throat:LOC
　　　　　'I've got a burning sensation in my throat.'

(349) *W kościach   mnie   łamie. /Kości   mnie   łamią.*
       in bones:LOC me:ACC it breaks/bones:NOM me:ACC break
       'I've got arthritis in my bones.'

(350) *W gardle   mnie   drapie.*
       in throat:LOC me:ACC it scratches
       'My throat feels scratchy.'

(351) *W dołku   mnie   ściska.*
       in pit:LOC [of the stomach] me:ACC it compresses
       'My stomach is tight as a fist.'

(352) *Oczy   mnie   pieką.*
       eyes:NOM me:ACC burn
       'My eyes are smarting.'

(353) *Łupie mnie   w skroniach.*
       it chips me:ACC in temples:LOC
       'I've got a splitting headache.'

(354) *Mróz   szczypie mnie   w uszy.*
       frost:NOM   pinch   me:ACC in ears:ACC
       'The frost is biting my ears.'

(355) *But   mnie   gniecie.*
       shoe:NOM me:ACC presses
       'My shoe pinches.'

(356) *Noga   mnie   rwie.*
       leg:NOM me:ACC tears
       'I've got a twinge in my leg.'

Although the predicates in examples (347-356) designate bodily experience, in their primary senses they are used to describe physical actions. When they are used as experiential predicates, the verbs inherit the grammatical properties of the basic sense. Thus, the case marking on the experiencer is the same regardless of whether the sensation is due to the action of a human agent, as in (357), or an internal bodily process, as in (347).

(357) *Piotr   kłuł   mnie   w bok.*[58]
       Piotr:NOM pricked me:ACC in side:ACC
       'Piotr was pricking me on the side.'

This construal highlights the fact that, although the sensation may be localized in a particular part of the body, it is the person, not the body part, that has the sensation: it is impossible to separate the experience of pain from the bodily process itself. The part of the body where the sensation occurs is usually specified by means of a prepositional phrase, but sometimes it receives nominative coding. In the latter case, the body part is construed as the source – metaphorically, the cause – of the sensation.

Some physical process predicates which can be used metaphorically to designate bodily sensations take dative objects; these, however, are much less numerous.

(358) *W brzuchu   mi   burczy/bulgoce.*
       in belly:LOC me:DAT it rumbles/it bubbles
       'Me belly is rumbling/making bubbling sounds.'

(359) *W kościach   mi   strzyka.*
       in bones:LOC me:ACC it crunches
       'I can feel my bones going crunch.'

(360) *W uszach   mi   szumi/   dzwoni.*
       in ears:LOC   me:DAT   it buzzes/it rings
       'My ears are buzzing/ringing.'

In these examples, the experiencer is construed as a homunculus observing an autonomous process within his sphere of awareness. Among the bodily processes which best lend themselves to this kind of construal are those which have an externally perceptible aspect – for example, those which are accompanied by noises. The process described in (358) involves a sensation experienced in the stomach as well as an acoustic correlate which can be heard by other people. The twofold nature of the process makes it easier to construe the experiencer as dissociated from the process itself.

The dative form also occurs in a few idiomatic expressions in which the sensation is conventionally construed as a change of state or movement within the affected body part (examples (361) and (362)). Since the metaphor represents the sensation as an autonomous process, the only way to introduce the experiencer is through a dative nominal which invokes the concept of the sphere of awareness.[59]

(361) *Pęka mi   głowa.*
       cracks me:DAT head:NOM
       'I've got a splitting headache.'

(362) *W głowie   mi   się   kręci.*
       in head:LOC me:DAT INTR   it spins
       'I feel dizzy.'

However, predicates of physical sensation which govern the dative are rare in comparison to those which govern the accusative. In most cases, the sensation is likened to a physical action, and the person having the experience construed as patient-like and expressed by means of an accusative nominal. This puts strong analogical pressure on "true" sensation predicates, and partially motivates the use of the accusative case with *boleć* and *swędzieć* (examples (344-345)). The accusative construal capitalizes on the fact that physical sensations typically have physical causes, and highlights direct affectedness: it is impossible to dissociate the experience from the process.

Other "true" sensation predicates – *dolegać* 'to cause discomfort', *dokuczać* 'to bother' and *doskwierać* 'to afflict' – require dative experiencers. The high prominence of the sphere of awareness is, of course, one of the factors motivating the use of the dative case, but there are others. By themselves, these verbs do not designate any specific sensation, but a general discomfort; more specific information about the nature of the experience is usually provided by the subject nominal (363-364). The noun specifying the nature of the sensation is sometimes left out, as in (365), but the resulting sentence is understood to be elliptical.

(363) *Dolegał mu ból brzucha/ głód.*
caused discomfort him:DAT pain:NOM stomach:GEN/ hunger:NOM
'He was suffering from a pain in his stomach/from hunger.'

(364) *Dokucza mi ból głowy.*
bothers me:DAT ache:NOM head:GEN
'I'm suffering from a headache.'

(365) *Dokucza mi głowa.*
bothers me:DAT head:NOM
'I'm suffering from a headache.'

Thus, for symbolic purposes, the experience is broken up into two parts: an autonomous process (e.g. pain) occurring in a part of the experiencer's body, and the awareness of this process. This construal is highly compatible with the mental arena model, so the dative case is used to code the experiencer.

In addition to the three verbs discussed above, there is also another group of dative sensation predicates – complex expressions consisting of the verb *być* 'to be' and an adverb:

(366) *Jest mi mdło/ gorąco/ciepło/ chłodno/zimno/słabo.*
it is me:DAT insipidly/hotly/ warmly/coolly/ coldly/weakly.
'I feel sick/hot/warm/chilly/cold/faint.'

The experiencer in these constructions must be dative since the relationship designated by the adverb cannot be construed as an action. However, the accusative construal is required when a full-fledged verb is used to describe the very same sensation, as in (367).

(367) *Mdli mnie.*
it nauseates me:ACC
'I feel sick.'

4.3.6. Conclusion

This section was meant to illustrate the importance of construal in determining the choice of case marking. The choice of a particular case depends not only on the degree to which the properties of a participant in the event described match those of the prototype of one case category or another, but also on how the entire event is organized for expressive purposes – i.e. on whether it is construed as a single action in which the agent or agent-like participant causes another individual to experience something, or whether it is broken up into two parts: an autonomous process occurring in the experiencer's sphere of awareness and the experiencer's awareness of this process. Another construal decision has to do with the choice of participants: an event in which an agent acts on a part of the body of another participant can be conceptualized as involving the whole target person or just the directly affected part of the body. The speaker, as we have seen, has a certain degree of freedom in organizing the event for expressive purposes. However, the verb itself may impose a particular perspective. This does not mean that case selection is arbitrary: it is still motivated semantically, but it is the semantics of the verb rather than the semantics of the case itself that plays the decisive role.

Chapter 5: The dative and prepositional constructions

In the last two chapters I showed how the dative case contrasted with the nominative and the accusative, and argued that the occurrence of either one or the other with a specific verb can be explained in semantic terms. Polish also has prepositional constructions which express meanings similar to the dative: a participant cast in the beneficiary role can be introduced into the clause by means of the preposition *dla* 'for'; the recipient and the addressee can be signalled by the goal preposition *do* 'to'; and the person who "hosts" an event (i.e. on whose territory the event takes place) can be brought into the clause by means of the locative preposition *u* 'at'. It will come as no surprise to the reader that these prepositional constructions construe the situation described by the clause in rather different ways. It is to these contrasts that we now turn.

5.1. Expressing the beneficiary: the dative and prepositional phrases with *dla* 'for'

In section 2.2.4 we saw that the dative case is often used to designate a person who benefits from an action undertaken by the agent (368). The beneficiary relationship can also be signalled by the preposition *dla* 'for', as in (369) below. The most obvious difference between the prepositional construction and the dative is the fact that the former specifically designates the benefactive relationship, while the latter has a number of other uses as well. However, as we shall see, there are other, more subtle, differences as well.

(368)   *Piotr   wybudował   Ani   dom.*
         Piotr:NOM built   Ania:DAT   house:ACC
         'Piotr built a house for Ania [to live in].'

(369)   *Piotr   wybudował dla Ani   dom.*
         Piotr:NOM built   for Ania:GEN house:ACC
         'Piotr built a house for Ania./Piotr built a house for Ania's sake.'

Example (368) describes a situation in which the TP's personal sphere grows as a result of acquiring a new possession, from which one can plausibly deduce that the action was beneficial to the target person. The most obvious interpretation of (369) is also that Piotr built a house for Ania to live in – in other words, a house which is part of her personal sphere. Hence, the two sentences are perceived as very similar in meaning. Nevertheless, they are not fully synonymous. (369) states that Piotr's action was beneficial for Ania, from which we infer, by relying on our knowledge of the world, that it was beneficial because it made her personal sphere grow. In (368), on the other hand, the use of the dative indicates that Ania's personal sphere was affected. From the fact that the verb, *budować* 'to build', is a verb of creation, we infer that the personal sphere grew as a result of the action; and, since in our culture a swelling of the personal sphere is considered beneficial, we conclude that Ania benefited from Piotr's action. Thus, the perceived similarity in meaning is due largely to pragmatic implications, and we can expect the differences in meaning to show up more clearly when the verb designates an action that would normally be judged harmful. Compare:

(370)   *Piotr   spalił Ani   dom.*
        Piotr:NOM burned Ania:DAT house:ACC
        'Piotr burned Ania's house.'

(371)   *Piotr   spalił dla Ani   dom.*
        Piotr:NOM burned for Ania:GEN house:ACC
        'Piotr burned the house for Ania.'

In (370), the dative nominal introduces the concept of personal sphere, and the house is understood to be included in the dative participant's personal sphere (presumably, it belongs to Ania). On the other hand, because burning someone's house is generally harmful, without a special context (371) would be interpreted as meaning that he burned someone else's house – for example, the house belonging to Ania's worst enemy, and the two sentences would be perceived as very different in meaning. However, if, for example, Ania needed cash, couldn't sell her house, and was hoping to collect insurance money when it burned down, Piotr's action could be seen as benefiting Ania even if the house belonged to her; in this case, (370) and (371) conjure up very similar interpretations. (However, they still differ in terms of what is actually stated and what is merely implied; moreover, in (371), Piotr's action must have been volitional, whereas (370) could mean that he set fire to the house by accident.)

A similar semantic contrast arises in the following two examples:

(372)   *Piotr   obciął Dorocie   włosy.*
        Piotr:NOM cut   Dorota:DAT hair:ACC
        'Piotr cut Dorota's hair.'

(373)   *Piotr   obciął dla Doroty   włosy.*
        Piotr:NOM cut   for Dorota:GEN hair:ACC
        'Piotr cut his hair for Dorota./Piotr had his hair cut for Dorota.'

Neither sentence states explicitly whose hair was cut, but, barring certain unlikely contexts which might force a different reading,[60] (372) would be interpreted as stating that Piotr cut Dorota's hair and (373) that he cut his own. How does the listener arrive at this interpretation? The dative in (372) evokes the personal sphere and initiates a search for an entity by means of which Dorota was affected. Parts of the body are central elements of the personal sphere, so the reference to hair later on in the sentence is by far the most likely candidate for the trajector of the dative.

(373), on the other hand, states that Piotr performed the action of cutting an unspecified individual's hair for Dorota's sake. In choosing this form, and omitting any explicit mention of Dorota's affectedness, one conversationally implicates that she was not personally affected (otherwise (373) would be less than fully informative). The grammatical form of the sentence – the fact that the noun *Doroty* is separated from the main predicate by the preposition *dla* – iconically represents the same information. Therefore, the hair must belong to someone else – and since only one other participant is explicitly mentioned in the sentence, Piotr is the most likely candidate. However, in principle it is possible that Piotr cut a third party's hair for Dorota's sake, just like Delilah cut a third party's – that is, Samson's – hair for the benefit of the Philistines.[61]

Iconicity also partially motivates the contrast between (374) and (375).

(374)   *Magda   kupiła Wojtkowi   książkę.*
        Magda:NOM bought Wojtek:DAT book:ACC
        'Magda bought Wojtek a book.'

(375)   *Magda   kupiła książkę   dla Wojtka.*
        Magda:NOM bought book:ACC for Wojtek:GEN
        'Magda bought a book for Wojtek.'

Unlike (374), (375) does not necessarily imply that Wojtek got the book: the use of *dla* + nominal merely indicates that the action was undertaken for the beneficiary's sake without actually implying any affectedness on his part. Moreover, (375) strongly suggests that Wojtek was not present at the scene of the buying, and may not even know that it occurred. The presence of the dative in (374), on the other hand, indicates that Wojtek was or will be affected in some way, and although the sentence does not necessarily imply that Wojtek was present when Magda bought the book, it does not rule it out either. Thus, Wojtek's involvement in the action in (375) is more peripheral than in (374), and this is symbolized by the separation of the nominal *Wojtka* from the verb by the preposition. (In (375), the *dla* phrase also occupies the most peripheral position in the clause. Although other orderings of the constituents are possible, the one shown in (375) is the most neutral.)

5.2. Target person, source and goal: the dative and prepositional phrases with *do* 'to' and *od* 'from'

In several points earlier in this study I alluded to the fact that the dative was originally an allative case, and that many of its uses, even those that can be subsumed under the personal sphere schema, retain an allative flavor. This is natural enough, since transitive actions are construed as the transfer of energy from an agent to a patient, and so the action is seen as directed "towards" the dative participant's personal sphere in which the patient is located. Now Polish has a preposition, *do* 'to', which designates a very similar configuration: its landmark is the goal towards which the trajector is moving and near which it will eventually come to a rest. The main difference between *do* and the dative is that the former makes no reference to the concept of personal sphere (and consequently, unlike most uses of the dative, can take non-human landmarks). This leads to rather predictable semantic differences between pairs of sentences with verbs of transportation such as *zanieść* 'to take', *przynieść* 'to bring', *wysłać* 'to send', and others which express similar meanings.

(376) *Wysłał dokumenty   Robertowi.*
       he sent documents:ACC Robert:DAT
       'He sent Robert the documents.'

(377) *Wysłał dokumenty   do Roberta.*
       he sent documents:ACC to Robert:GEN
       'He sent the documents to Robert.'

The use of the dative, as in (376), indicates that Robert is a true recipient (he becomes the owner of the documents, or at the very least is entitled to use them). With *do* + the genitive, on the other hand, Robert is merely a spatial goal, no different from a location such as a city, and the documents are not intended for his use (they may have been sent to him for safekeeping, or perhaps someone else is going to collect them from him). Moreover, in (376) there is a stronger sense of the documents actually reaching Robert than there is in (377). This is presumably due to the fact that the overt mention of the personal sphere in the former focuses attention on the endpoint of the path traversed by the documents, while the preposition in the latter example profiles the entire path. The contrast between the two is thus similar to the semantic difference between English ditransitive sentences and their prepositional analogs (see Langacker 1991b and Goldberg 1992; for a brief summary of Langacker's argument, see section 1.2.2).

A similar distinction is found with verbs of transportation that denote movement away from a landmark: here the dative contrasts with the source preposition *od* 'from'.

(378) *Zabrał   dokumenty   Robertowi.*
       he took away documents:ACC Robert:DAT
       'He took the documents away from Robert.'

(379) *Zabrał   dokumenty   od Roberta.*
       he took away documents:ACC from Robert:GEN
       'He took the documents away from Robert's (place).'

Once again, the use of the dative indicates that Robert is to be construed as an individual endowed with a personal sphere. Hence, (378) would be appropriate if the documents belonged to Robert or were intended for his use. In contrast to this, in the prepositional construction (379), Robert is construed merely as a location: he is mentioned simply in order to help identify the place where the documents had been deposited, and there is no suggestion that he was affected in any way.

Do + the genitive can also occur with verbs of communication, and here the contrast with the dative is rather more subtle. As a general rule, only manner-of-speaking verbs can take *do* (380), while verbs of telling, which specify what message was communicated to the addressee, require the dative (381):

(380) a. *Coś   do mnie   krzyczał   /szeptał*
something:ACC to me:GEN he was shouting/he was whispering
ale nie mogłem   go   zrozumieć.
but not I couldn't him:ACC to understand
'He was shouting/whispering something to me, but I couldn't understand what he was saying.'

(380) b. **Coś mi krzyczał/szeptał...*
something me:DAT he was shouting/he was whispering...

(381) a. **Robert wspomniał do mnie   o   tym.*
Robert mentioned   to me:GEN about it

(381) b. *Robert wspomniał mi   o   tym.*
Robert mentioned me:DAT about it:LOC
'Robert has mentioned this to me.'

Mówić 'to speak', and *powiedzieć* 'to say, tell' can take both types of complement, but when they do, clear differences in meaning emerge. When *mówić* is used with the dative, the content of the message must be spelled out, as in (382); *mówić* + dative is thus a verb of telling. When used with a *do*-phrase, on the other hand, the verb is not used to specify what information was conveyed in the communicative act, but simply to identify its addressee (383).

(382) *Mówię   ci,   że nie masz   racji.*
I am speaking you:DAT that not you have right:GEN
'I tell you that you are wrong.'

(383) *Mówię   do ciebie!*
I am speaking to you:GEN
'I'm talking to you!'

With *powiedzieć* 'to say, tell', the content of the message can be specified in the prepositional construction, but only when the words are repeated verbatim (that is, when the words actually spoken appear to be more important than the message). If the speaker describes the content of the message in his own words – by using reported speech or simply by using an anaphoric pronoun in place of the reported utterance – only the dative can be used:

(384) a. *Powiedział mi:*   "*Przyjdę   jutro*".
         he told   me:DAT I will come tomorrow
         'He said to me: "I will come tomorrow".'

(384) b. *Powiedział do mnie:*   "*Przyjdę   jutro*".
         he told   to me:GEN I will come tomorrow
         'He said to me: "I will come tomorrow".'

(385) a. *Powiedział mi,   że   przyjdzie   jutro.*
         he told   me:DAT that he will come tomorrow
         'He told me he would come tomorrow.'

(385) b. **Powiedział do mnie, że przyjdzie jutro.*
         he told   to me:GEN that he will come tomorrow

(386) a. *Powiedział mi   o   tym.*
         he told   me:DAT about it:LOC
         'He told me about it.'

(386) b. **Powiedział do mnie   o   tym.*
         he told   to me:GEN about it:LOC

This is just what we would expect, given the semantics of the forms, as described above. The goal preposition *do* simply indicates that speech was directed towards the person specified in its landmark. The dative, on the other hand, places the words in the relevant part of the target person's personal sphere – the sphere of awareness, inevitably shifting the focus from the physical medium to the content of the message.

5.3. Personal sphere vs. location: the dative and prepositional phrases with *u* 'at'

Prepositional constructions with *u* are perhaps the most interesting for our purposes, as they reveal more clearly than the other three the role of construal in grammar. *U* was originally primarily a locative preposition meaning 'at' or 'near'; the original meaning still survives in expressions such as *u studni* 'at the well'. In contemporary Polish, it is used mainly with human landmarks to refer to spaces conventionally associated with people, as in (387) (cf. the French *chez Robert*). Since such spaces are part of the personal sphere, one might expect a fair amount of overlap between the two constructions.

(387)   *Jestem u Roberta.*
         I am   at Robert:GEN
         'I'm at Robert's.'

Actually they tend to occur in rather different contexts: *u* + GEN is typically used to specify where a person or thing is located, whereas the dative, as a rule, cannot be used with stative predicates. Furthermore, with verbs of transfer, *u* is replaced with the appropriate directional preposition (see the discussion of *do* and *od* above). However, they do contrast in some contexts, and the differences in meaning are rather revealing.

(388) a. *Piotr   stłukł Arturowi   okno.*
Piotr:NOM broke Artur:DAT window:ACC
'Piotr broke Artur's window [and Artur was affected].'

(388) b. *Piotr   stłukł u Artura   okno.*
Piotr:NOM broke at Artur:GEN window:ACC
'Piotr broke a window at Arthur's.'

(388a) and (388b) both state that a window-breaking event occurred which somehow involved an individual called Arthur. (388b) simply indicates that the action occurred in a place belonging to Arthur: presumably his home, but possibly another location which can be regarded as his territory, for instance his workshop or office. Arthur may have been affected by the event described in (388b), but the sentence does not explicitly specify this. In contrast, (388a) states that the action affected Arthur because it occurred in his personal sphere. We are not explicitly told the exact nature of the link between Arthur and the window-breaking event, but we can reasonably conclude that Arthur was affected because it was *his* window (recall that possessor-possessed is one of the most deeply entrenched of the linking strategies discussed in section 2.1), and hence presumably the event occurred in Arthur's house (or office etc.). Notice, however, that the concept of 'Arthur's place' is not directly evoked at all in (388a): we assume that the event occurred at Arthur's because it is part of our encyclopedic knowledge about windows that they usually come attached to buildings. (388a) could mean that, for example, Piotr broke a window that Arthur had bought and intended to take home with him. To summarize: both sentences could be used to describe the same event, but they construe it in different ways: (388b) is about what Piotr did in a particular place (at Arthur's); (388a) describes what Piotr did to Arthur (broke his window).

The contrast becomes even clearer when we consider a possession which is not attached to a particular location, as in (389) below.

(389) a. *Piotr   stłukł Wojtkowi   okulary.*
Piotr:NOM broke Wojtek:DAT glasses:ACC
'Piotr broke Wojtek's glasses [and Wojtek was affected].'

(389) b. *Piotr   stłukł u Wojtka   okulary.*
Piotr:NOM broke at Wojtek:GEN glasses:ACC
'Piotr broke his glasses at Wojtek's.'

Again, neither of these examples explicitly states *whose* glasses were broken: this must be inferred from the other elements present in the sentence – leading, in this case, to a very different interpretation.

In our final example, (390), the verb designates an activity which is often performed for an audience, and hence evokes the concept of a target person endowed with a sphere of awareness. Not surprisingly, therefore, the dative nominal in (390a) is interpreted as specifying the audience the singer performed for. Replacing the dative nominal *Adamowi* with a prepositional phrase, as in (390b), results in a very different meaning. The expression *u Adama* simply specifies where the performance took place: at Adam's house, or in a restaurant or a theater run by him. It could not refer to Adam's sphere of awareness, since any process that occurs in Adam's sphere of awareness would necessarily affect him, which is incompatible with being construed as an aspect of the setting rather than a participant.

(390) a. *Śpiewała Adamowi   francuskie piosenki.*
she sang Adam:DAT French   songs:ACC
'She sang Adam French songs.'

(390) b. *Śpiewała u Adama   francuskie piosenki.*
she sang at Adam:GEN French   songs:ACC
'She sang French songs at Adam's.'

5.4. Dative and prepositional constructions: A summary

We have seen that although sometimes it is possible to use either the dative or a prepositional construction to describe the same situation, the constructions differ in how the situation is construed, and hence they are not synonymous. The most obvious difference is that prepositional constructions express more specific meanings. This is hardly surprising, given the fact that there are only six cases in Polish (not counting the vocative) and several dozen prepositions.

Another more interesting difference stems from the fact that prepositional constructions do not assert, or even imply, the would-be target person's affectedness. In fact, because there is another construction available which specifically asserts affectedness, by choosing the prepositional construction rather than the dative the speaker conversationally implicates that the target was *not* affected. Not surprisingly, unlike the dative, the prepositions *do, od, u* and *dla* do not require the landmark to be human or even animate.

Prepositional phrases usually refer to aspects of the setting. The decision to bring a human participant into the sentence as an object of a preposition, therefore, reflects the speaker's decision to construe a potential actor as an aspect of the setting, no different from a reference point such as a crossroads. This is iconically reflected in the resulting construction by the fact that the would-be target person is physically separated form the verb by the preposition, which mediates its grammatical relationship with the rest of the sentence. Moreover, the prepositional phrase tends to occur in a peripheral position in the sentence, usually at the end, which further underscores the marginal role played by the person in the event.

A prepositional phrase such as *u Adama,* then, designates a location, while the dative nominal *Adamowi* designates a participant. This brings us to yet another difference between prepositions and case inflections. A preposition, unlike a case inflection, is a relational predicate: it designates a relationship between two entities. A case inflection, on the other hand, is a schematic nominal, though it contains a relation as part of its base. (A case-inflected noun is thus a kind of relational noun.) When the noun stem (which designates a kind of thing) combines with a case inflection (which designates a highly schematic thing which plays a particular role in the relationship designated by the verb or preposition), the result is, predictably, a kind of thing. However, the composite structure of the inflected nominal contains the relation present in the base of the case inflection, and hence it is no longer an autonomous predication. The trajector of the relation must be elaborated by another element – in the case of the dative, either an object belonging to the personal sphere or the process designated by the verb. The atemporal relation that is part of the inflected nominal's base has an important role to play in the process of assembling the clause, since it provides information about how the nominal should be integrated with the rest of the clause. The integration will involve establishing correspondences between the schematic trajector in the base of the inflected nominal and the entity which elaborates it. In the case of "governed" datives, the blueprint for the integration is available in the semantic representation of the verb; in other cases, correspondences will have to be established by following the linking strategies discussed in chapter 2.

5.5. Prepositional constructions with datives

We have seen in the preceding chapters that the presence of a dative nominal in a sentence can be sanctioned either directly by the verb (in which case it is said to be "governed" by the verb) or by the fact that the process designated by the verb is construed as impinging on some aspect of the dative participant's personal sphere. In either case, the dative nominal enters into a direct grammatical relationship with the verb, or, to use the established terminology, it is a sister of V and a daughter of VP. Dative forms also occur in prepositional constructions, and it is to these uses that we now turn.

In chapter 2, I reinterpreted the traditional notion of "government" in terms of semantic overlap: a verb governs a particular case when some substructure of its semantic representation corresponds to the meaning of the case.

With case forms occurring in prepositional constructions, the situation is slightly more complex, in that the choice of case marking may depend not only on the properties of what is traditionally regarded as the governing category, i.e. the preposition, but also on properties of the verb. This is seen most clearly with prepositions which can co-occur with more than one case form, as in the following example:

(391)   Piotr   siedział   na ławce.
        Piotr:NOM was sitting on bench:LOC
        'Piotr was sitting on the bench.'

(392)   Piotr   wskoczył na ławkę.
        Piotr:NOM jumped   on bench:ACC
        'Piotr jumped onto the bench.'

The preposition *na* 'on' takes the locative case in (391) and the accusative in (392). This well-known contrast is determined by the semantics of the verb: the locative occurs when the verb describes an action that is wholly contained within the region defined by the prepositional phrase, while dynamic verbs that describe a motion that originates outside this region and ends inside it require the accusative.[62] Thus the form of the object of the preposition is partly determined by the preposition itself and partly by the verb – a rather embarrassing situation for theories of grammar which require a single governor in a c-commanding position.[63]

Prepositional datives differ from datives occurring in verbal constructions in that they do not always designate a person, and hence do not necessarily evoke the personal sphere. Their status in the dative category is thus fairly peripheral: they are included in it because they bear family resemblance to somewhat more central uses, but they do not fit the category superschema proposed in chapter 2.

The four dative prepositions (*ku* 'to, towards', *dzięki* 'thanks to', *przeciw(ko)* 'against', and *wbrew* 'in defiance of, contrary to') are discussed in the following subsections.

5.5.1. Prepositional constructions with ku 'to, towards'

(393)   Podróżni   podążali ku   miastu.
        travelers:NOM hurried   towards town:DAT
        'The travelers hurried towards the town.'

The use of the dative with the preposition *ku* is a vestige of its earlier allative function (see section 2.2.11), now nearly obsolete[64] except in a few semi-idiomatic expressions such as *chylić się ku upadkowi* 'to be on the decline', *zbliżać się ku końcowi* 'to be drawing to an end', *ku mojemu zdziwieniu* 'to my surprise'. We have seen earlier (cf. section 2.2.11) that in the course of the development from Protoslavonic to what was to become Polish, the category center shifted to the 'target person' prototype, and therefore what we have today is a division of labor between the case marking and the preposition: the preposition specifies the direction of movement, and the dative nominal names the location with respect to which the direction is defined. This use of the dative is best regarded as an abstraction from the notion of personal sphere: the dative in the prepositional phrase designates a region defined with respect to any entity, whereas the personal sphere is defined with respect to a person.

5.5.2. *Prepositional constructions with* dzięki *'thanks to' and* przeciw(ko) *'against'*

(394) a. *Dzięki   Kasi...*
         thanks to Kasia:DAT
         'Thanks to Kasia...

(394) b. *Dzięki   pomocy   Kasi...*
         thanks to help:DAT Kasia:GEN
         'Thanks to Kasia's help...

(394) c. *Dzięki   dobrej pogodzie...*
         thanks to good   weather:DAT
         'Thanks to the good weather...

           ... udało   nam   się   skończyć   pracę   na czas.
           it succeeded us:DAT INTR   to finish   work:ACC   on time:ACC
           ... we succeeded in finishing the work on time.'

(395) a.. *Wystąpił   przeciw(ko) rządowi.*
          he came out against   government:DAT
          'He came out against the government.'

(395) b. *Wystąpił   przeciw(ko)   polityce   rządu*
         he came out against   policy:DAT   government:GEN
         'He came out against the goverment's policy.'

(395) c. *Wystąpił   przeciw(ko) nierówności   społecznej.*
         he came out against   inequality:DAT social
         'He came out against social inequality.'

The use of the dative in (394a) and (395a) can be easily subsumed under the umbrella of the personal sphere. In both of these examples, the object of the preposition refers to a participant endowed with a personal sphere – either an individual or a group of individuals – and the personal sphere (or, to be more precise, the sphere of potency) is highly relevant to the meaning of the proposition, which specifies, respectively, that the preposition's landmark makes it possible for the agent to accomplish the action, and that the agent's potency is pitted against that of the landmark. The occurrence of the dative with these prepositions, therefore, closely parallels its use with verbs of helping (cf. section 2.2.3) and verbs of resistance (section 2.2.7). It is also worth pointing out that both of these prepositions have verbal analogues which also require the dative case: *dzięki* is related to the verb *dziękować* 'to thank', and *przeciw(ko)* is related to *być przeciwnym* 'to be opposed to' and *przeciwstawiać się* 'to oppose'. (The link is particularly strong with *przeciw*: *być przeciwnym czemuś* 'to be opposed to something', is virtually synonymous with *być przeciwko czemuś* 'to be against something'.)

(394b-c) and (395b-c) are more problematic. In the (b)-sentences a human participant (Kasia or the government) occurs as a possessive modifier of the dative noun, and hence it could be argued that the personal sphere is evoked in this rather oblique way. However, this rather *ad hoc* solution will not work for (394c) and (395c), where the dative nominals designate abstract entities which clearly cannot experience the results of the action. On the other hand, the usages exemplified in the (b) and (c) sentences are clearly related to those illustrated in (394a) and (395a), and it seems that they are best viewed as extensions of, or abstractions from, these personal-sphere usages. The preposition *dzięki* specifies that the successful completion of the action described in the main clause was made possible by an ally, which can be either a person (as in (394a)) or an abstract entity (as in (394b) and (394c)). In the same vain, *przeciw(ko)* specifies that the action described in the clause was pitted against an enemy, and requires a landmark which is either a person or an abstract entity which can be construed as an enemy. Thus, in addition to the target person superschema and its instantiations (i.e. "enemy", "ally", etc.), the dative network also includes local schemas which allow the use of the dative to refer to any entity, concrete or abstract, which can be construed as an ally or an enemy. The "abstract ally" and "abstract enemy" senses do not fit the category schema of "target person". They are included in the category because they resemble other senses which do instantiate the superschema.

It should be observed that these two senses – "abstract enemy" and "abstract ally" – are extremely restricted: they only occur in construction with the prepositions *przeciw(ko)* and *dzięki,* respectively. One might object that the postulation of a distinct meaning for such restricted uses is highly wasteful – a flagrant violation of the principle of economy. This objection may be countered with two observations. First, as Langacker repeatedly points out (1987a, 1988, 1991b), economy is certainly desirable in linguistic description, but not at the expense of empirical adequacy or psychological reality. If an expression is polysemous/polyfunctional, then the description must capture all its meanings/functions: we still need to state that these two prepositions govern the dative. We could do this by means of diacritic features in the lexicon, but this is not only psychologically implausible, but would also fail to capture the semantic commonality between "ally" and "abstract ally" on the one hand and "enemy" and "abstract enemy" on the other – which of course is what motivated the extension in the first place. Secondly, it is quite typical of peripheral members of a category to occur in highly restricted contexts. We have already seen that this is the case with the allative senses (cf. section 2.2.11); Taylor 1990 provides further examples.

However, it is one thing to say that the occurrence of severe restrictions is rather unremarkable, given the peripheral status of these particular senses, and quite another to represent it explicitly in the grammar. How are we to capture the fact that the prepositions *przeciwko* and *dzięki* only occur with the dative case? This, I suggest, is best done by means of larger symbolic units consisting of the preposition and a schematic dative nominal. Thus, in addition to the symbolic unit DAT, which consists of the pairing of the target person network (which includes several "dangling" schemas that are not fully compatible with the superschema) and the various variants of the dative inflection, there are two larger units, [DZIĘKI + DAT] and [PRZECIWKO + DAT]. Both of these are composite relational predicates. [DZIĘKI + DAT] profiles a relationship between an event (elaborated by the main clause) and an abstract entity (elaborated by the dative nominal) and specifies that the abstract entitiy facilitated the occurrence of the event. [PRZECIWKO + DAT] profiles a relationship between an agent's action (elaborated by the main clause) and an abstract entity (elaborated by the dative) and specifies that the former was directed against the latter. The existence of these larger units, while not predictable from the general meaning of the dative, is motivated by the "resistance" and "assistance" uses.

5.5.3. Prepositional constructions with wbrew 'in defiance of, contrary to'

(396) a. *Ania   postąpiła wbrew   ojcu.*
Ania:NOM acted   in defiance of father:DAT
'Ania acted in defiance of (her) father.'

(396) b. *Ania   postąpiła wbrew   radom   ojca.*
Ania:NOM acted   in defiance of advice:DAT father:GEN
'Ania acted in defiance of (her) father's advice.'

(396) c. *Ania   postąpiła wbrew   temu,   co   radził*
Ania:NOM acted   in defiance of this:DAT that:ACC advised
ojciec.
father:NOM
'Ania acted in defiance of what (her) father advised.'

(397) a. *Wbrew   temu,   co   przewidywałeś,*
contrary to this:DAT what:ACC you predicted,
zabrakło nam   pieniedzy.
it lacked us:DAT money:GEN
'Contrary to what you predicted, we have run out of money.'

(397) b. *Wbrew   twoim przewidywaniom zabrakło nam   pieniędzy.*
contrary to your   predictions:DAT it lacked us:DAT money:GEN
'Contrary to your predictions, we have run out of money.'

The use of the dative with *wbrew* differs from the usages discussed in the previous subsection in several respects. Unlike *dzięki* and *przeciwko, wbrew* does not have a morphologically related verbal counterpart from which it could inherit a conventional image which determines case selection. Moreover, it tends to take abstract landmarks, although human landmarks are also possible, as in (396a). Finally, although it does resemble *przeciwko* in that it conveys a sense of confrontation, this sense is much more attenuated, particularly in examples such as (397). In spite of these differences, the use of the dative in the above sentences slots into the category network in exactly the same way as the dative governed by *przeciwko*. When used with a human landmark, as in (396a), the *wbrew*-governed dative is a special case of the "resistance" usages discussed in section 2.2.7. Example (398) below contains a verb-governed analogue of the use of the dative in (396a). In both cases, the target person's sphere of potency is affected because his wishes are opposed by another individual (the agent of the action).

(398)   *Ania   opierała się   ojcu/   woli   ojca.*
        Ania:NOM resisted INTR father:DAT/will:DAT father:GEN
        'Ania resisted her father/her father's will.'

The preposition *wbrew* in all three sentences in (396) indicates that the action described in the sentence took place in the presence of pressure to follow another course of action (in this case, whatever Ania's father wanted her to do). In (396a), the source of the pressure is a person (Ania's father); in (396b) and (396c), it is more abstract (his advice). Both uses can be subsumed under the same schema, which will merely specify that the landmark must be something that can be construed as a source of social pressure. Thus, (396b) and (396c) are related to (396a) in exactly the same way as (394b-c) and (395b-c) are related to (394a) and (394a) respectively.

In (397a) and (397b), *wbrew* is used is a slightly different sense: it no longer means 'in defiance of', but 'contrary to' – in other words, it no longer signals that the action designated by the clause occurs in opposition to social pressure, but merely that it is not what some person or persons specified in the dative nominal expected or believed would happen. Thus, *wbrew* in (397) designates an *epistemic* relationship between some aspect of reality and someone's beliefs about it. Apart from this domain difference, however, the two senses of *wbrew* are very similar, as illustrated in the schematic diagrams below.

In Figure 14(a), which corresponds to the "defiance" sense of *wbrew,* the trajector is a schematic event (and will be elaborated as a clause); the landmark is an abstract entity which is the source of social pressure (it will be elaborated as a nominal). The arrows are an *ad hoc* graphic device introduced to represent the "direction" of the pressure and the agent's actions; they point in opposite directions to represent the fact that the agent resists the pressure from the landmark entity. In Figure 14(b), which represents the "contrary belief" sense, the trajector is also a schematic actual event, and the landmark an abstract entity which represents a hypothetical course of events. The arrows point in opposite directions to indicate that what actually occurs is the opposite of what has been expected or believed.[65]

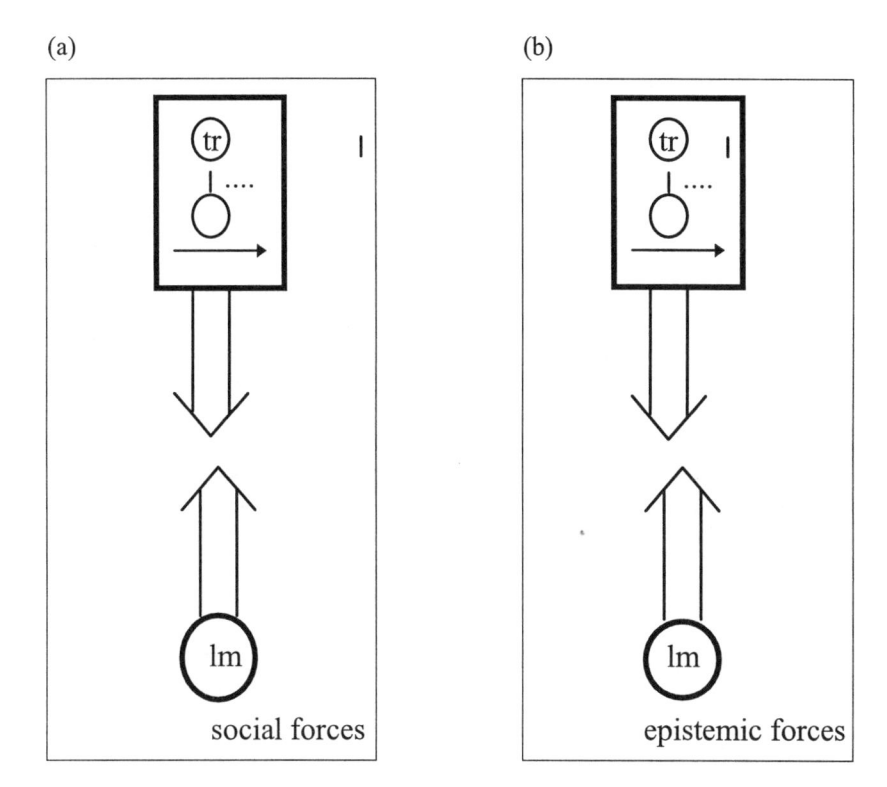

Figure 14. The 'defiance' (a) and 'contrary belief' (b) senses of *wbrew*

It should be noted that the extension of the use of [*wbrew* + DAT] found in (397) is anything but exceptional. It is quite common for linguistic expressions used to talk about pressures in the sociophysical world to acquire senses having to do with intellectual "forces". The expression *zgodnie z* 'in agreement/accordance with', provides another example of this pattern of polysemy:

(399) *Ania postąpiła zgodnie z wolą ojca.*
'Ania acted in accordance with her father's will.'

(400) *Ania postąpiła zgodnie z twoimi przewidywaniami.*
'Ania acted in accordance with your predictions.'

A more systematic example is provided by modal verbs, which frequently have epistemic as well as root (deontic) senses. For example, sentence (401) can mean either that Ania is under an obligation to come, or that she is likely to come.

(401) *Ania powinna przyjść.*
'Ania should come.'

Musieć 'must' and *móc* 'may' are ambiguous in exactly the same way (see Sweetser 1984, 1990 for a detailed discussion of this pattern of polysemy and the metaphor which motivates it).

To summarize: the use of the dative with *wbrew* in example (396a) is a special case of a fairly well-established use with predicates indicating resistance/opposition, also seen with verbs such as *opierać się* 'to resist', *oponować* 'to oppose' and the preposition *przeciw* 'against'. The prepositional constructions (396b-c) are sanctioned by a schema which is an abstraction of this usage: the target person is replaced by an abstract entity which is capable of playing the same role in the situation. This extension is paralleled by similar extensions of [*dzięki* + DAT] and [*przeciw* + DAT]. In all three cases, the abstract nominal "inherits" the case marking associated with the target person. Finally, the use of *wbrew* + DAT in (397) is an extension of the sense found in (396) motivated by the INTELLECTUAL FORCES ARE SOCIAL FORCES metaphor. Thus once again we have a chain of senses of which only the first (396a) is sanctioned by the superschema; the others are included in the category because they are extensions of an established sense.

Chapter 6: The personal sphere in other languages

The personal sphere, we saw in the preceding chapters, is a useful construct in that it allows a simple and intuitively appealing description of the semantics of the (Polish) dative. I have also suggested that is a rather natural conceptual category, a sensible concept for human beings to have, given that, as humans, we come with friends, families, beliefs, favorite possessions, etc. This raises the exciting possibility that the personal sphere may have linguistic repercussions in other languages as well. We will now explore this possibility.

In the following pages, I will examine two grammatical phenomena: constructions with the English verb *have* and 'external NP' constructions in Japanese. Both of these have been studied quite extensively in a variety of theoretical frameworks, including cognitive linguistics.[66] My purpose here is not to review the available literature or to provide a definitive analysis of either of these, but merely to demonstrate the relevance of the concept of personal sphere to the analysis of seemingly unrelated grammatical phenomena in other languages.

6.1. The English verb *have*

Many traditional grammarians have observed that the dative case often expresses the idea of possession. Although the dative cannot be used to assert possession in Polish (cf. the ungrammaticality in (402)), it is used when one wishes to state that something happened to an object belonging to the target person (403).

(402)   **Piotrowi jest samochód.*
        Piotr:DAT is   car:NOM
        'Piotr has got a car.'

(403)   *Robert   rozbił Piotrowi   samochód.*
        Robert:NOM   crashed Piotr:DAT car:ACC
        'Robert crashed Piotr's car [and Piotr was affected by this].'

We have seen in chapter 2 that, in addition to objects owned, the personal sphere includes parts of the body, objects held or used, one's friends and family, subordinates and subjects, "air bubble", territory, and so on. Now the English verb *have,* though prototypically used to indicate possession, can express many other relationships as well. Intriguingly, the range of its uses is remarkably similar to that of the Polish dative, as the following examples will illustrate.[67]

POSSESSION:
(404) a. *He has a very old car.*
(404) b. *He had his car stolen.*
(404) c. **He had his car crashed.*

PART OF THE BODY:
(405) a. *I have two hands.*
(405) b. *I have cold hands*
(405) c. *He had his head shaved.* ['They shaved his head and he was affected.']

OBJECT HELD/AVAILABLE FOR USE
(406)   *Have you got a pen?*

FRIENDS AND FAMILY:
(407)   *I have two children/many friends.*

SUBORDINATES, SUBJECTS, etc.:
(408) a. *We have two employees.*
(408) b. *We have two employees sick.* (Quirk *et al.* 1985: 1197)

AIR BUBBLE:
(409)   *Prof. Yamada has a lot of lice.*

TERRITORY:
(410)   *We had the bar to ourselves.*
(411)   *I have a doctor in my room.*
(412)   *We've had quite a lot of snow around here.*

SOCIAL SPACE
(413)   *I have a little boy here with me.*

MENTAL EXPERIENCE:
(414)   *Let's have a look.*
(415)   *She had an idea/doubts/a shock.*
(416)   *He has very vivid recollections of those events.*

ABILITY/CONTROL OVER OWN ACTIONS:
(417)   *It's worth having a try.*
(418)   *I had a little stroll round the garden this morning.*
(419)   *He has this amazing ability to make you laugh when a minute earlier you felt like crying.*
(420)   *I'll have it all done by Monday.*

CONTROL OVER EVENTS/ACTIONS OF OTHERS
(421)   *I had 3000 copies printed./I had John print 3000 copies.*
(422)   *I won't have it./I'm not having it.*

(423)   *We're having a party.*

PERSON AFFECTED BY SOMEONE ELSE'S ACTIONS
(424)   *I have a client coming at 4 o'clock.*
(425)   *Ken had his book stolen.* ['Someone stole Ken's book.']

BENEFICIARY
(426)   *Wherever she goes, she has fans opening doors for her, running to get her a coke, anticipating her every wish.*
(427)   *Pop stars always have thousands of fans write to them every day.*

This, I suggest, is due to the fact that the semantic structure of *have*, like that of the Polish dative, incorporates the notion of personal sphere: the semantic contribution of the verb *have* is to indicate that the landmark is located in the trajector's personal sphere.

Three of the constructions exemplified above are particularly interesting from our perspective and deserve special attention. First we have the "light verb" construction *have a N*, where N is a noun phonologically identical to the corresponding verb, and the subject names the agent of the action designated by the verb – cf. (414), (417) and (418). Expressions such as *He had a walk, I'll have a look* differ in meaning from the simpler *He walked, I'll look.* The most obvious difference is aspectual: the count noun in the light verb construction indicates that the action is bounded, and hence the sentence is understood to refer to a distinct episode rather than a type of activity. Other differences are more subtle. The light verb construction, Wierzbicka points out, "implies a subjective and experiential perspective" (1988: 297): in other words, it informs us not so much about what the subject participant *did*, but what he *experienced* and/or how he was *affected*. Consequently, the subject participant must be capable of subjective experience – that is to say, he must be human (or at least animate) and alive.[68] As Wierzbicka points out, Humpty Dumpty could have *had a fall*, but an apple could not;[69] similarly, Lazarus could *have a lie-down* after he was raised from the dead, but not in his grave. The experiential perspective evoked by *have* also determines which nouns can occur in the object position. Particularly suitable candidates are nouns derived from verbs of perception and cognition (*have a look, have a taste, have a think*) – with these, the notion of sphere of awareness is already present in the noun itself – and from verbs describing grooming actions *(have a wash, have a shave)*, since they necessarily imply that the agent was affected. On the other hand, nouns derived from verbs designating strongly agentive and inherently goal-oriented actions cannot be used in the construction: **have a find*, **have a work*, **have a speak*. Between the two extremes, we find a number of activity nouns which can occur in the construction: *have a walk, have a dance, have a cuddle.* The contrast in meaning between these and the corresponding lexical verbs is particularly instructive. The *have a N* construction implies that the agent finds the action enjoyable (or at least undertakes it because he believes it will be enjoyable). Thus, a soldier who walks ten miles with full gear to the next bivouac is not *having a* *walk;* and if during the march he has to lie down in a ditch to avoid being seen by the enemy, he is not *having a lie-down.*

Wierzbicka spells out these and other, more specific restrictions on the *have a N* construction in meticulous detail, and provides a very insightful description of its semantics. However, her analysis fails to explain *why* the construction should be subject to these restrictions or why it is associated with the "experiential" meanings discussed above.[70] On the other hand, the concept of personal sphere allows us to give a simple and intuitively plausible explanation of the special implications of this construction: they arise because the construction construes the subject's activity not as an action chain, but as a thing located in the subject participant's personal sphere. Consequently, the subject participant must be an entity endowed with a personal sphere and capable of experiencing the effects of the action, and the results of the action must not "spill" beyond the personal sphere.[71]

The second of the *have* constructions that I would like to discuss in more detail is the causative X *have* Y *do* Z, exemplified in (421). This construction has often been analyzed as simply stating that Y's actions were brought about by X. However, as we shall see shortly, this characterization is far from adequate. Let us once again take Wierzbicka's observations as our point of departure.

> In the *have* causative, the causer assumes the causee's 'readiness to serve'; the causee is treated here as a co-operative performer of the causer's will, as someone to whom the causer's will can be communicated (either directly or by an intermediary) and who will be neither unable to understand it nor unwilling to perform it. This explains why, as pointed out by Talmy (1976: 107), the causee of the *have* causative normally has to be human: **I had the squirrel leave its tree.* (Wierzbicka 1988: 241)

Implicit in Wierzbicka's statement, though never directly stated, is another semantic property of the construction: the *causer* is human as well (or resembles humans in some respects: animals and institutions also qualify).[72] Thus one cannot say

(428)   **Poverty had her work.*

though it is possible to say

(429)   *Poverty made her work.*

Moreover, the causer must intend the causee to carry out the action: incidental causation cannot be described with *have.* If John's neglect of Mary causes her to commit suicide, it is possible to say

(430)   *John made Mary jump off the bridge.*

(though it would be more accurate to say *John's indifference made Mary jump off the bridge*); however one cannot say

(431)   *John had Mary jump off the bridge.*

unless he specifically incited her to do it. Finally, the causal relationship itself must be fairly direct. Thus, it would be inappropriate to say

(432)   *John had Mary come to the party.*

if, for example, John had told Mary that Bill would be there and she came because she wanted to meet him – even if John knew that Bill's presence would be a strong incentive for Mary to come. On the other hand, the causer does not exercise direct coercion. In fact, the causer does not *need* to exercise coercion because he knows that the causee will comply with his wishes without being forced to. This is because *the causee is in the causer's sphere of influence.* One can have one's subordinates do things – but bosses can only be asked, persuaded, tricked, or blackmailed.

Thus, the English causative with *have* is used to describe a very special kind of causation: one in which a human participant *conceives* a certain (desirable) state of affairs and causes another human participant *within his sphere of influence* to bring it about. Again, these special properties derive from the meaning of the verb *have* and the notion of personal sphere that it evokes.

The sequence subject + *have* + agent + action can also receive a benefactive interpretation, as in (426-427). In fact, the benefactive sense can be regarded as the semantic invariant since this meaning is also implicit in the causative (one would not intentionally cause someone to do something one does not want done; therefore, the subject of the causative *have* benefits from the causee's actions in some way). However, the causative sense is more deeply entrenched and, unless specifically ruled out by the context, it usually pre-empts the benefactive. This ambiguity (vagueness?) is hardly surprising, given that the verb *have* simply evokes the personal sphere rather than a particular part of it (sphere of awareness, sphere of influence, private sphere). As we shall see later, it is characteristic not just of the English verb, but of personal sphere predicates in general.

Finally, the third special construction with *have* is the "affected subject" construction, exemplified in (404b), (405c) and (425). (The term comes from Palmer 1987.) In this construction, the subject of *have* represents a person indirectly affected by a process involving another participant included in his personal sphere. Once again the subject participant must be human and capable of experiencing something as a result of the action. The relationship between the target person and the patient is usually made explicit by means of a possessive pronoun modifying the patient noun and referring back to the subject of the sentence. This, however, is not necessary: (433), for example, does not directly specify the identity of the owner of the book, and the possessive relationship must be inferred by the addressee.

(433)   Ken had a book stolen.

It is worth noting that (433), as well as the other instances of the construction, is ambiguous: in addition to the "affected subject" reading ('Someone stole a book belonging to Ken and he was affected'), the sentence could also have a causative interpretation ('Ken had someone steal a book for him'). Much less likely, but still possible, is the agentive interpretation ('Ken managed to steal a book').[73] Finally, given the right context (for instance, if Ken is a librarian) it could also mean 'Someone stole a book entrusted to Ken [and he was affected]'. Again, the construction simply indicates that the process designated by the past participle occurred in the subject participant's personal sphere: the rest is inferred by the addressee.

The uses of the English verb *have*, then, closely parallel those of the Polish dative. These parallels in meaning and the restrictions on the various constructions with *have* are best explained by appealing to the concept of personal sphere. Before we proceed, a caveat is in order. I am *not* claiming that the Polish dative and the English *have* do not differ in meaning: they clearly do. What I am suggesting is that they share a common semantic substructure – the personal sphere – which accounts for the parallels in function. The most obvious *difference* between the dative case and *have* is the fact that the latter is a verb, and hence designates a *temporal relationship;* consequently, its semantic representation incorporates a substructure which represents a (highly schematic) *process* (see Langacker 1987a and 1991b for an detailed discussion of the semantic properties of verbs). Another difference – much more interesting from our point of view – is the way the personal sphere features in the semantic representations of these predicates.

I have argued in chapter 2 that the dative case presupposes the concept of personal sphere. However, the dative does not actually designate the personal sphere: the latter is merely a part of the knowledge structure, or base, with respect to which the dative is defined. What the dative profiles is the target person, i.e., the person affected by a process occurring in his or her personal sphere. This is why you cannot use the dative simply to state that someone possesses something – cf. the ungrammaticality of (402). A sentence with a dative nominal, then, states that something happened, and that the person designated by the dative was affected by this.

Sentences with *have*, on the other hand, assert that a person, an object, or a process is located in someone's personal sphere – in other words, *have* profiles the relationship between the personal sphere and an object or process occurring in it. Usages resembling Polish dative constructions, such as *He's had his car stolen* and *We have two employees sick* do sometimes occur, but they are rare and highly restricted, as evidenced by the ungrammaticality of (404c).

This brings us to another caveat. The fact that the dative case and the verb *have* share a semantic substructure results in certain parallels of function, since both of these items have uses motivated by various aspects of the personal sphere. It does not follow, however, that they both occur in exactly the same contexts – that is, that for every Polish sentence containing the dative there will be a corresponding

English structure with the verb *have,* or vice versa. This is clearly *not* the case. First, *have* has senses which cannot be subsumed under the umbrella of the personal sphere, such as those in (434)-(435) below.

(434)   *This room has five windows.*
(435)   *The house has a beautiful view.*

Secondly, the parallels in function between the dative case and *have* are not perfect: that is, certain usages that one might have been lead to expect do not occur or are fairly rare. (We have already seen one example of this: the comparative rarity in English of sentences such as (404b) and (408b).) I will show in section 6.3 that at least some of these differences in distribution follow from those aspects of their meanings that the two constructions do not share.

The concept of personal sphere, then, allows us to formulate a simple semantic description that will cover a wide range of seemingly disparate constructions with the verb *have*: it specifies that the landmark (which is prototypically a thing, but could also be a complex atemporal relation) is located within the trajector's personal sphere. However, we have just seen that this formulation is not general enough to accommodate all uses of *have.* Therefore, we now turn to another analysis of this verb in the cognitive framework, that in Langacker 1993 and 1995.

Langacker introduces the concept of *reference point*: an entity which allows the conceptualizer to establish mental contact with another entity (the target) – informally, the target's "mental address". For example, the expression *Sue's computer* allows the conceptualizer to establish mental contact (refer to, conceive of) a specific object in the universe – a particular member of the set of computers – by first accessing a cognitively more salient entity (*Sue*). The concept of reference point makes possible an insightful analysis of a variety of constructions, including possessive determiners, and provides a convincing explanation of why these should have so many different and seemingly disparate uses (possession, kinship, spatial proximity, part-whole relationships, subjective nominalization, objective nominalization, and many others). Langacker then proposes that *have* constructions are best seen as a type of reference-point construction. The difference between *Sue's computer* and *Sue has a computer,* he suggests, is due primarily to two factors: trajector/landmark alignment (with the Saxon genitive, the object possessed is the trajector and the possessor the landmark, while the verb assigns trajector status to the possessor) and to the fact that *have,* being a verb, has a positive temporal profile.

However, there are some difficulties with this analysis. First, not all Saxon genitives can be paraphrased with *have:* many subjective and objective nominalizations (*the boy's escape, the boy's release*), genitives of origin (*the boy's letter*), genitives of measure (*ten days' absence*), and many genitives with non-human reference points (*today's paper, next year's profits, duty's call, the poll's results*) do not have analogous usages with *have* (**The boy has an escape,* **The boy has a release...*). Conversely, some *have* constructions are not paraphrasable with genitives: *I have a little boy here with me; Let's have a look; I had John wash my car.* Most importantly, however, there are other semantic differences between the two constructions. *Have* doesn't merely signal the existence of a "possessed object": it also conveys the "dative" notions of control and affectedness. If you *have someone wash your car,* you don't merely have a clean car: you have also exercised your potency. If you are told that *Anne has a headache,* you are not simply informed of the existence of a headache which can be found wherever Anne is; you are also informed that she is suffering. If you tell someone that you *have a meeting at 10 o'clock,* you are not just informing them that a meeting has been planned which has something to do with you: you are telling them that your potency is somewhat diminished (you will not be free at ten o'clock). If you inform someone that *Peter first had a haircut and then a walk,* you are telling them that his body has been affected in a certain way (he looks different now) and that he has engaged in a pleasurable activity. *We have two employees sick* does not mean the same thing as *Two of our employees are sick:* the former, but not the latter, also indicates that we are affected by their illness.[74]

Thus, for the senses of *have* described above, a description in terms of personal sphere seems preferable. On the other hand, the personal sphere schema does not accommodate the various uses of *have* with non-human subjects, while Langacker's more general characterization does. However, the two descriptions are not really at odds, since it is possible to view the personal-sphere schema as a special case of the reference-point schema: after all, a person is a natural reference point for any object, person or event located in his personal sphere. Thus, a full description of the semantics of *have* must contain the over-all category schema as described by Langacker as well as the more specific personal-sphere schema. It appears that the latter is cognitively more basic: presumably it is acquired earlier and used more frequently. This, however, comes as no surprise: more specific local schemas tend to be more deeply entrenched than more abstract units.

So far, we have been concerned exclusively with the main verb *have.* Before we proceed, it will be worthwhile to consider briefly two grammatically very different uses of *have,* namely the semi-modal *have to* and the auxiliary verb *have.* These are generally assumed to be different lexemes which happen to be homophonous with the content verb. On the face of it, this appears to be the only reasonable solution, at least with regard to the main verb and the auxiliary: they express very different meanings and they have very different grammatical properties. Even phonetically, they tend to be realized differently: the auxiliary is usually contracted, while the main verb generally is not, and in many of its uses cannot be.[75]

While these differences must be noted and accounted for in the grammar, we should not allow them to prevent us from noticing similarities and links between the various uses of *have.* After all, the primary goal of linguistic analysis is not to provide a list of facts about language, but to explain these facts, to explore the relationships between different aspects of language and to show how grammatical morphemes come to have the functions that they do. In the remaining part of this section I will attempt to show that both the semi-modal and the auxiliary can, and should, be related to the personal sphere schema proposed above.

The semi-modal *have to* is the more straightforward of the two. Grammatically it patterns like a main verb, not like an auxiliary (in most dialects: *Do you have to* *go?* rather than **Have you to go?*). Semantically, it expresses obligation – that is, an infringement of the sphere of potency: if one is under an obligation to do something, one is not entirely one's own master (see the discussion of the use of the dative with verbs of ordering, obligation and allowing in Polish in section 2.2.5). The idea of obligation is expressed by indicating that a future action is "located" in the subject's personal sphere:

(436)   *Kate has to write a report.*

To appreciate the semantic affinity of the main verb *have* and the semi-modal, one has only to note that the former can also express a sense of commitment to a future action:

(437)   *Kate has a meeting this afternoon.*
(438)   *Kate has a report to write.*

(437) and (438) differ from the corresponding sentences with the semi-modal only in that the obligation is referred to by means of a noun rather than a verb.

Thus, the meaning of the semi-modal *have to* is fully compatible with the idea of personal sphere evoked by the content verb *have*. It should be stressed, however, that the relationship designated by *have to* is much more specific than that described by *have,* since it pertains to just one notion associated with the personal sphere – obligation – and is incompatible with others. For example, *have to V* cannot be used to talk about the subject participant's abilities, intentions, or knowledge. This means that the semi-modal must have a schema of its own, partially sanctioned by the personal sphere schema but distinct from it.[76]

The relationship between the content verb and the auxiliary is rather more complex. Langacker (1990, 1991a) argues that the auxiliary is most closely related to the sense of *have* exemplified in (439), which differs from other senses in that the notions of possession or control are almost completely bleached out, and the subject functions essentially as a "spatial reference point for establishing mental contact with the object" (1991a: 213-214). All that remains of the earlier, more concrete sense is a hint that the "occurrence of the object within the subject's dominion is potentially *relevant* to the subject in some fashion" (1991a: 214).

(439)   *We have a lot of skunks around here.*

The auxiliary differs from this use of *have* in three respects: (1) its landmark is an atemporal relation rather than a thing; (2) the relationship it profiles is temporal rather than spatial; and (3) the current relevance is no longer relevance to the subject of the predication, but to the conceptualizer – in other words, the auxiliary *have* has undergone subjectification.[77] The perfect construction, Langacker argues,

> .... describes a process as occurring prior to a temporal reference point, RP, at which time it nevertheless retains some current relevance. The process is construed atemporally and expressed by a perfect participle.... Through the

grounding of *have*, RP is situated with respect to the time of speaking (and so, indirectly, is the participialized process). *Have's* trajector is elaborated by the clausal subject and is further equated with the trajector of the participle – however, it is not identified as the individual(s) to whom the event is currently relevant at RP. Thus in (16)(a), *The water main has broken!,* the water main is understood as the trajector of *broken,* but the event is currently relevant to the speech-act participants (or some wider group of contemporaneous individuals). (Langacker 1991a: 220-222).

The description of the perfect that I am going to offer is inspired by Langacker's, but differs from his in two respects. First, I propose a different source of the perfect auxiliary – namely, the "affected subject" *have* discussed earlier. Secondly, I will argue that the perfect auxiliary does not have just one sense, but a whole family of related senses which can be arranged along a chain leading from uses which are only minimally different from the content verb *have* in the affected subject construction to the fully grammaticalized aspect marker. The proposed chain of senses is intended primarily as a synchronic description, but it could also be treated as an account of how the extension process might have proceeded diachronically.

At the beginning of the chain, then, we have the content verb *have* in the affected subject construction:

(440)   Herman had his nose broken.

This use of *have* resembles the auxiliary in that it has an atemporal relation rather than a thing as its landmark. The relationship between the trajector and the landmark is one of affectedness: the trajector (Herman) is affected by the landmark event (his nose being broken). The two events – the breaking of the nose and the affectedness – are not fully integrated, since the trajector of *have* is not the individual who is responsible for the nose-breaking; this is iconically reflected in the clause by the physical separation of the two verbs.[78]

In the corresponding construction with the perfect auxiliary (441), the nose-breaking and the affectedness *are* construed as one event, and the trajector of *have* is identical with the trajector of *broken;* the affected participant is also the person responsible for the nose-breaking. The complete integration of the two events is reflected by the contiguity of the verbs and the fact that *have* no longer needs to carry past tense marking to signal that the nose-breaking-cum-affectedness occurred prior to the speech event.

(441)   Herman has broken his nose.

The sense of affectedness is often quite attenuated, as in (442), where it is more appropriately glossed as "current relevance".

(442)   Nicola has lived in Brighton for 20 years now.

In these sentences, the affected persons are Herman and Nicola, not the speech act participants. Judging by the examples given in EFL textbooks, this, and not the subjectified version in (446), is the most prototypical use of the "current relevance" perfect. Of course both sentences could get a subjectified interpretation. In *Herman has broken his nose, so we can't come to your picnic,* what is at stake is the relevance to the speech act participants, not to Herman. However, it appears that when the subject of a perfect verb is a person, the default interpretation is that the event is relevant to this individual, not to the speech act participants. This would explain why it is odd to use the present perfect to talk about the actions of people who are no longer alive, as in the following examples taken from Palmer (1987:50).[79]

(443)   ? *Queen Victoria has visited Brighton.*
(444)   ? *Shakespeare has written a lot of plays.*[80]

The "experiential perfect" (445) provides another clear example.

(445)   *Tamara has visited New York.*

The implication of the use of the perfect is that Tamara's visit to New York has affected her in some way: now that she has seen the Statue of Liberty, she is not quite the person she used to be. Again, *have* seems to signal relevance to the subject, not to the speech act participants.[81]

When this attenuated version of the auxiliary becomes subjectified, we get the "true" perfect auxiliary. In (446), the notion of relevance is shifted to the subjective axis: the fact that the taxi has left is a matter of some relevance to the conceptualizer, not to the taxi.

(446)   *The taxi has (just) left.*

Finally, in some uses of the perfect, even the notion of "relevance" is largely bleached out. For example, (446) could mean that the taxi's departure is somehow relevant to the conceptualizer; but it could also mean simply that it occurred very recently. On this interpretation, *have* simply signals an indefinite recent past. All that remains of the notion of personal sphere is the idea of recency – the temporal analogue of spatial proximity.

The concept of personal sphere, then, has turned out to be extremely useful in describing the various senses of *have,* including the stative possessive sense, the causative, the "affected subject", the light verb *have,* the semi-modal and the various senses of the perfect auxiliary. It has also helped to explain how the various senses hang together to form a cohesive network. Although it is not abstract enough to cover all the uses of *have* (and thus the more inclusive reference-point schema is also necessary), it provides a structure which anchors the more peripheral members of the category.

6.2. External NP constructions in Japanese

6.2.1. The personal sphere in Japanese culture

Our second example of the linguistic repercussions of the personal sphere in other languages comes from Japanese and involves a pragmatic rather than a syntactic or lexical phenomenon. Japanese is a particularly interesting language for our purposes, because the personal sphere plays an extremely important role in Japanese culture. Like everyone else, the Japanese own objects, claim certain spaces for themselves and have mental experiences; but the distinction between the in-group (*uchi* lit. 'inside' or 'home') and the out-group (*soto* lit. 'outside') plays a much more important role in Japanese culture than it does in most other societies. These are two sharply delimited worlds, each associated with its own attitudes and norms of behavior: the Japanese will behave in a very different way within their in-group and in the company of strangers.[82]

The distinction has innumerable linguistic repercussions.[83] It partly determines the choice of speech-style (one normally uses the plain style only with members of one's own group) and the use of honorific forms. For example, one will use the word *uchi* 'house', to refer to one's own house, or to a house belonging to a member of one's own group, and *o-taku* 'house [honorific]', to refer politely to an outsider's house. There are also two sets of term for relatives, one used to talk about one's own family and the other reserved for other people's families.[84] (Interestingly, the choice of the humble or honorific form of a noun will often indicate possession, since the Japanese tend to avoid direct reference to themselves and their interlocutors.) There are also several different words for 'give', and the choice of the appropriate one depends on the group membership and relative status of the giver and the receiver as well as the speaker and the addressee. If the speaker or someone who belongs to the speaker's personal sphere is the giver, *ageru* is used (447) (or, if respect is to be shown to the receiver, its honorific equivalent *sashiageru*). If, on the other hand, the speaker or someone belonging to the speaker's social group is the receiver, the appropriate forms are *kureru* (when the giver has lower social status than the receiver) and *kudasaru* (when the giver has higher social status) (448).

(447) *Kanai-wa Yumiko-ni   hon-o   agemasu.*
 wife-TOP Yumiko-DAT book-ACC give:POLITE
 'My wife is giving Yumiko a book.'

(448) *Sensei-ga   musume-ni   kono hon-o   kudasaimashita.*
 professor-NOM daughter-DAT this book-ACC gave:POLITE
 'The Professor gave my daughter this book.'

The choice of the appropriate donatory verb involves careful social triangulation. The fact that the speaker uses *ageru* in (449a) indicates that she identifies more closely with Taro than with Yumiko; the opposite is the case in (449b). An even more interesting example is given by Loveday (1986a: 130). A woman who wishes to say that someone gave something to her father would normally use *kudasaru* or *kureru*; however, if she is talking to her husband, she will switch to *ageru* to indicate that she is no longer closely associated with her own family group. (However, it is all right for a man to show affiliation with his own family by using *kudasaru*.)

(449) a. *Taroo-wa Yumiko-ni kono hon-o agemashita.*
'Taro gave Yumiko this book.'

(449) b. *Taroo-wa Yumiko-ni kono hon-o kuremashita.*
'Taro gave Yumiko this book.'

Donatory verbs in Japanese are used not only to talk about giving things, but also when making requests, giving orders, or talking about actions performed for someone else's sake (i.e. in benefactive constructions). For example, *Please come quickly* is literally 'Give quick coming' (450); and 'John read the book for me' is 'John gave me the reading of the book' (451) or 'I received the reading of the book from John' (452).

(450)   *Hayaku kite   kudasai.*
        quickly coming give
        'Please come quickly.'

(451)   *John-ga   watashi-ni hon-o   yonde kureta.*
        John-NOM I-DAT   book-ACC reading gave
        'John read the book to/for me.'

(452)   *Watashi-wa John-ni   hon-o   yonde moratta.*
        I-TOP   John-DAT book-ACC reading received
        'I had the book read to me by John.'

It is no exaggeration, then, to say that "it is impossible to converse [in Japanese] without clearly indicating to which groups the interlocutors or the persons one is talking about belong" (Loveday 1986b: 304). Clearly, the concept of personal sphere (or, to be more exact, the sphere of empathy and the sphere of influence) plays a central role in Japanese culture.

6.2.2. Japanese particles

The relationships between the verb and its arguments are expressed in Japanese by means of particles which mark the basic syntactic relations of subject/nominative (*ga*), object/accusative (*o*), indirect object/dative (*ni*) and various adverbial functions (*ni* 'in, to', *kara* 'from', *de* 'in, by means of', and many others). Particles are also used to signal various discourse functions, including topic and focus. The topic particle *wa* replaces *ga* or *o* if the subject or direct object are topicalized, as in (453) but it is usually added to the adverbial particle if an aspect of the setting is topicalized, as in (454). (If the indirect object is the topic, the IO particle *ni* can be either retained or left out.)

(453) a. *Suzuki-san-ga   Asahi Shinbun-o   yomu.*
Suzuki-Mr-NOM Asahi Shinbun-ACC reads
'Mr Suzuki reads the Asahi Shinbun [a newspaper].'

(453) b. *Suzuki-san-wa   Asahi Shinbun-o   yomu.*
Suzuki-Mr-TOP Asahi Shinbun-ACC reads
'As for Mr Suzuki, he reads the Asahi Shinbun.'

(453) c. *Asahi Shinbun-wa   Suzuki-san-ga   yomu.*
Asahi Shinbun-TOP Suzuki-Mr-NOM reads
'Speaking of the Asahi Shinbun, Mr Suzuki reads it.'

(454) *Brighton-ni-wa   daigaku-ga   futatsu aru.*
Brighton-in-TOP university-NOM two   are
'In Brighton, there are two universities.'

An NP need not be a direct participant in the action or process designated by the verb to be a topic; all that is required is that an identifiable relationship of some kind hold between the topic and a direct participant (usually the subject of the sentence):

(455) *Zoo-wa   hana-ga   nagai.*
elephants-TOP nose-NOM is long
'Elephants have long trunks.'

(456) *Jishoo-wa   Webusutaa-ga ii.*
Dictionary-TOP Webster-NOM is good
'Talking about dictionaries, Webster's is good.'

(457) *John-wa   kodomo-ga byooki da.*
John-TOP child-NOM sick   is
'John's child is sick.'

The topic-marked constituents (455)-(457) are not directly evoked by the verb, and are external to the nuclear predication itself – that is to say, the two sentences have the structure NP + S. Some linguists (e.g. Kitagawa 1982) maintain that the same is true of (453b) and (453c), the only difference being that the latter two contain empty NPs coreferential with the preposed topic in the subject and direct object position, respectively. An analysis which postulates empty nodes for no other reason than the analyst's convenience is clearly not in the spirit of cognitive linguistics, but since topic constructions of this kind are of little interest to the following discussion, I will not pursue the matter here (though I will have more to say about Kitagawa's analysis further on).

The particle *ga*, in addition to signalling the subject, can also be used to mark the focus of the assertion.[85] Thus, example (453a), as well as having the more neutral reading of 'Mr Suzuki reads the Asahi Shinbun', could also mean 'It is Mr Suzuki who reads the Asahi Shinbun.' Like topical elements, nominals with the focus *ga* can occur outside the sentence (458).

(458) *Zoo-ga   hana-ga   nagai.*
       elephants-NOM nose-NOM is long
       'It is elephants that have long trunks.'

In the following discussion, I will be primarily concerned with clause-external *wa-* and *ga-*marked nominals of the type found in (455-457). For the sake of simplicity, I will concentrate on topic constructions, but what I will have to say applies equally well to sentences with focus-marked NPs such as (458).

Any adequate description of external-NP constructions in Japanese must answer two questions. First, it has to explain how the addressee works out the relationship between the *wa-* or *ga-*marked nominal and the rest of the sentence. The topic or focus of an assertion is by definition central to the conceptualization, but the external participant is not directly involved in the process designated by the verb, and the verb does not require it. Secondly, the description must specify which NP + S combinations are possible and which are not. Clearly, one cannot add any *wa-* or *ga-*marked NP in front of a sentence and hope that the result will be grammatical, because in most cases it will not be. The problem is compounded by the fact is some cases it is possible to have more than one external NP, as in (459).

(459) *Mary-ga   me-ga   hitomi-ga iro-ga   kirei   da.*
       Mary-NOM eye-NOM pupil-NOM color-NOM beautiful is
       'Mary – her eyes – their pupils – their color is beautiful.'
       (Song 1993: 67)

Works on Japanese syntax are singularly vague in their treatment of these questions. All that Kuno has to say on the subject is that "at present it is not clear what kind or relationship the [topic] and the comment must hold for the sentence to be grammatical" (73:254). Kitagawa is only slightly more explicit. He proposes a rule of "topic binding", a well-formedness condition on sentences with NP-*wa*: "The topic X-bar must be pragmatically bound to an X-bar which is in the domain of Predication (Pred)" (1982: 184). Thus in (453c) the topic would be bound with an empty NP in the Pred which corresponded to the patient, and in (457) it would be bound with the NP *kodomo ga*. However, he has very little to say about the way topic binding is actually accomplished: "A question may be raised as to how exactly we can characterize the sense of pragmatic connection that is assumed in Topic Binding. The precise answer to this is yet to be formulated," but it involves "a strong sense of identification in terms of real-world knowledge" (186). "The referent of the target NP is understood, in some relevant sense, to belong to the topic NP referent" (187; the target NP is the pragmatically bound X-bar in the predication).

There are two problems with Kitagawa's formulation. The obvious one is its vagueness: what exactly does "in some relevant sense" mean? Like Kuno, Kitagawa hints that a pragmatic phenomenon of some kind is involved, and then leaves it to someone else to work out the exact nature of the relationship between the topic and the rest of the sentence.[86] Another difficulty, pointed out by Oehrle and Nishio (1981:175), is that not all topics stand in an anaphoric relationship to one of the nuclear participants. In indirect passives such as (460) and (461) below, it appears that the entire predication, rather than any one NP, is "within the scope," as it were, of the topic NP. (A similar point is made in Farmer 1984.)

(460)   *Taroo-wa ame-ni   furareta.*
         Taro-TOP rain-DAT fell:PASS
         'Taro had it rain on him./Taro got rained on.'

(461)   *Taroo-wa Hanako-ni   piano-o   hikareta.*
         Taro-TOP Hanako-DAT piano-ACC played:PASS
         'Hanako played the piano and Taro suffered.'

What, then, is the relationship between the topic and the rest of the sentence when the topic is not a direct participant or an element of the setting? Writers of reference grammars intended for foreign learners of Japanese are much more explicit than theoretical linguists in this regard. Makino and Tsutsui (1986: 526) offer the following rough guide:

When the referent of topic NP is neither a direct participant nor an element of the setting, it bears one of the following relationships to the rest of the sentence:
1. It is the whole of which the subject NP is a part.

2. It is the set of which the subject NP is a member.

3. It is the person who has the mental experience described in the sentence.

As we shall shortly see, this characterization does not cover all topics, and therefore I would like to propose the following refinement:[87]

When the referent of topic NP is neither a direct participant nor an element of the setting, it bears one of the following relationships to the rest of the sentence:
1. It is the whole of which the subject NP is a part.
2. It is the set of which the subject NP is a member.
3. It is the person in whose personal sphere the process designated by the verb occurs.

Needless to say, it is the third case which will be the focus of our interest in the remaining parts of this chapter.

6.2.3. External NP constructions and the personal sphere

Perhaps the most startling fact about "external" topic constructions (i.e. sentences with topics which cannot be regarded as arguments of the verb or elements of the setting) is the close parallels which they exhibit with dative constructions and generalized verbs of possession. Like the Polish dative and the English *have*, they can be used to symbolize the relationship between a person and part of the body (examples (462-463)), the possessor and the object possessed (464) and a person and an object held or available for use (465).

(462)   *Watashi-wa te-ga   tsumetai.*
        I-TOP   hands-NOM are cold
        'My hands are cold.'

(463)   *Watashi-wa ke-ga   usuku-naru.*
        I-TOP   hair-NOM thinly-becomes
        'I'm losing my hair.'

(464)   *John-wa   kuruma-ga aru.*
        John-TOP car-NOM   is
        'John has a car.'

(465)   *Tanaka-san-wa empitsu-ga arimasu   ka.*
        Tanaka-Mr-TOP pencil-NOM is:POLITE INTERROG
        'Have you got a pencil, Mr Tanaka?'

Like the other two personal-sphere constructions, sentences with external topics are used to signal inclusion in the sphere of empathy and/or the sphere of influence – that is to say, they indicate that the subject NP belongs to the topic NP's family or social group (466-467) or some group that the topic-marked NP has control over, such as his employees, subordinates, subjects, etc. (468)

(466)   *John-wa kodomo-ga aru.*
        John-TOP child-NOM be
        'John has a child.'

(467)   *John-wa kodomo-ga byooki da.*
        John-TOP child-NOM sick   is
        'John's child is sick.'

(468)   Watashi-wa hisho-ni   byooki-ni narareta.
        I-TOP   secretary-DAT ill-in   became:PASS
        'My secretary has fallen ill on me.'

Like the dative and *have* constructions, external topics are used when the process designated by the verb occurs in a space closely associated with an individual – his "air bubble" (469-470) or territory (471).

(469)   Yamada-sensei-wa shirami-ga takusan iru.
        Yamada-Prof.-TOP lice-NOM lots   are
        'Prof. Yamada has a lot of lice.'

(470)   Kare-wa dangan-ga mimi-no soba-o   tsuukashita-no-de
        he-TOP bullet-NOM ear-GEN side-ACC passed-NOMIN-because
        kowakunatta
        got scared
        'A bullet flew right by his ear and he got scared.'

(471) a. Watashitachi-wa gakusei-ga   imasu   kara,
         we-TOP   student-NOM is:POLITE since
         taihen urusai desu.
         very noisy is:POLITE
         'We have students [living] with us, so it's very loud.'
         [lit., 'As for us, because there are students, it is noisy.']

(471) b. Watashitachi-wa gakusei-ga   kite   kara
         We-TOP   student-NOM coming since
         taihen urusaku narimashita.
         very noisily became:POLITE
         '[We were affected because] Students came and it got very loud.'
         [lit., 'As for us, because some students came it got very noisy.']

We have already seen (cf. example (452)) that topic constructions can be used to describe actions undertaken for the benefit of another person. In the following subsections, I will discuss external NP constructions used to talk about mental experience (i.e. events which occur in the sphere of awareness) and control (or lack of control) over one's own actions and those of others.

6.2.4. Linguistic construal of mental experience in Japanese

With most Japanese mental experience verbs, the nominative particle *ga* marks the *object* rather than the subject of the experience; the experiencer himself, if mentioned at all, occurs as a topic (or focus) outside the nuclear predication.

(472) *Taroo-wa kokuban-no zi-ga miemasu.*
Taro-TOP blackboard-GEN letters-NOM be visible:POLITE
'Taro can see the letters on the board.'

(473) *Boku-wa sono inu-ga kowai*
I-TOP this dog-NOM is scary
'I am afraid of that dog.'

(474) *Boku-wa futtobooru-ga suki-da.*
I-TOP football-NOM liking-is.
'I like football.'

(475) *Tanaka-san-wa eigo-ga wakaru.*[88]
Tanaka-Mr-TOP English-NOM is understandable
'Mr Tanaka understands English.'

The same pattern (object of mental experience as grammatical subject, experiencer in topic or focus position outside the nuclear predication) can also be used when the nature of the experience is specified by means of a nominal (476-477). The resulting structure parallels the normal possessive construction (cf. (464)), and can also be extended to experiential sentences such as (478-479), where the entire clause describing the experience is nominalized and made the subject of *aru* 'to be'.

(476) *Watashi-wa ii kangae-ga aru.*
I-TOP good thought-NOM is
'I have a good idea.' [lit., 'As for me, there is a good idea.']

(477) *Watashi-wa ichido ano hito-ni atta kioku-ga aru*
I-TOP once that person-DAT met memory-NOM is
'I have a memory of once meeting him.' [lit., 'As for me, there is a memory of meeting that person once.']

(478) *Watashi-wa Nippon-e itta-koto-ga aru.*
I-TOP Japan-to went-NOMIN-NOM is
'I have been to Japan.' [lit., 'As for me, there is the having-gone-to-Japan thing.']

(479) *Kare-ga gakkoo-de furansu-go-o oshieta-koto-ga aru.*
He-NOM school-in France-language-ACC taught-NOMIN-NOM is
'He has taught French in a school.' [lit., 'As for him, there is the having-taught-French-in-a-school thing.']

It is also used with "secondary" mental experience predicates derived from ordinary verbs by adding the desiderative suffix *-ta(i)*. Corresponding to the ordinary transitive sentence (480)

(480)   Watashi-wa kimono-o   kau.
        I-TOP   kimono-ACC buy
        'I'm buying a kimono.'

is the desiderative (481), in which the desired object is given the nominative marker *ga:*

(481)   Watashi-wa kimono-ga   kaitai.[89]
        I-TOP   kimono-NOM want to buy
        'I want to buy a kimono.'

The *NP-ga V-tai* construction is used in affirmative sentences when the experiencer is the speaker and in interrogative sentences when the experiencer is the addressee. In other cases, the verb, in addition to the desiderative suffix, normally carries the auxiliary verb *garu*. *Garu* means something like 'to show signs of, behave like *-ing*', and it "changes verbals of internal feeling into those of outward manifestation of internal feeling" (Kuno 1973: 84). Interestingly, verbs with *garu* are transitive:

(482)   Mary-wa kimono-o   kaitagatta.
        Mary-TOP kimono-ACC showed signs of wanting to buy
        'Mary wanted to buy a kimono.'

Japanese linguists disagree about the grammatical status of the *ga*-marked participant in the NP-*wa* NP-*ga* construction. Many traditional grammars, including Martin 1962, maintain that it is the subject of the sentence; others, for example Kuno 1973 and Farmer 1984, consider it the object. Both analyses have their problems. Martin's approach has the obvious advantage of being faithful to the surface syntax (*ga* consistently marks subjects and *o* objects) but founders on the status of the sentence-initial NP-*wa*, which, unlike the topic NPs discussed in the previous section, is arguably an argument of the verb. Since the delinquent nominal also has many subject properties, Martin concludes that sentences such as (472-475) have *two* subjects – a claim which is rather difficult to defend on theoretical grounds. Kuno gets around the difficulty by claiming that the problematic sentences are structurally similar to their English equivalents – i.e. that the sentence-initial NP-*wa* is the subject and the following NP-*ga* the object. Since objects normally take the particle *o*, he needs a rule which changes the underlying *o* to *ga* when the verb is marked [+stative]. This is not a very satisfactory solution either. First, it does not explain *why* stative verbs should behave like this. Secondly, since not all stative verbs have this curious property, the description will have to distinguish between syntactically stative and semantically stative verbs. Thirdly, it commits him to some rather peculiar analyses. For example, he claims (1973: 92) that *watakushi* 'I' is the subject in (483): this makes *kono hon-no suzi-ga* 'the plot of this book' the object of the adjective *omoshiroi* 'interesting' (!). However, if the sentence-initial NP-*wa* is absent, as in (484), *omoshiroi* behaves like an ordinary adjective and *kono hon no suzi ga* is its subject. In other words, according to Kuno, there are two adjectives *omoshiroi*, which presumably just happen to be homophonous: *omoshiroi$_1$*, which designates the objective property of being interesting and which takes *ga*-marked subjects, and *omoshiroi$_2$*, which designates the subjective feeling of the experiencer towards the object of experience and which requires *ga*-marked objects.

(483)   *Watakushi-wa kono hon-no   suzi-ga   omoshiroi.*
        I-TOP   this book-GEN plot-NOM is interesting
        'I find the plot of this book interesting.'

(484)   *Kono hon-no   suzi-ga   omoshiroi.*
        this book-GEN plot-NOM is interesting
        'The plot of this book is interesting.'

To make things worse, Kuno still needs the NP+S rule to handle other topic constructions, such as (455-457). In fact, Kuno acknowledges that *some* sentences describing mental experience, e.g. those with the verb *mieru* 'to be visible', have this structure. Thus, in spite of the fact that (472-475) appear to have the same structure (NP-*wa* + NP-*ga* + verb), he claims that (472) is entirely different from (473-475) : while the former consists of a sentence external topic NP and an intransitive verb with the object of experience as subject, the latter are transitive constructions with the experiencer in the subject position and the object of experience as the grammatical object. He argues for the distinction on the basis of the intuition that if the topic NP in (473-475) is left out, the resulting sentences feel elliptical, whereas (472) appears to be complete even without the *wa*-phrase, which suggests that the topic is an optional adjunct. In other words, Kuno claims that a string such as

(485)   *Sono inu-ga   kowai.*
        that   dog-NOM is scary

could be either a truncated version of (473) meaning '(I) am afraid of that dog', in which the noun *inu* is the object, or a non-elliptical intransitive sentence meaning 'That dog is scary', in which the *inu* is the subject. However, he is treading on shaky ground here. All of the sentences are perfectly acceptable in their truncated versions – in fact, the truncated versions are preferred when the topic is a personal pronoun – but native speaker intuitions about the status of the truncated versions of these sentences differ. In particular, few people appear to share Kuno's view that (483) feels incomplete without the topic phrase. The truncated versions of the above sentences do not fall into two distinct classes ("elliptical" and "non-elliptical"), but rather seem to vary along a continuum: the truncated counterpart of (475) is clearly elliptical, that of (472) appears to be complete, while the other examples occupy various intermediate points.

In more recent analyses (e.g. Gunji 1987, Kitagawa 1982), the *ga*-marked participant is assumed to be the subject, and the topic NP is considered to be sentence-external. This avoids some of the pitfalls outlined above, but still leaves unanswered the fundamental question of *why* mental experience verbs should have the peculiar property of requiring that the stimulus be the subject of the verb and the experiencer appear as a topic outside the nuclear predication. In fact, this property of mental experience predicates will appear to be entirely arbitrary in any purely syntactic account. However, given what has already been said about the role of the personal sphere in motivating external-NP constructions, the special grammatical properties of these predicates emerge naturally from their semantics.

Mental experience, I argued in chapter 3, is often construed as an independent process occurring in the sphere of awareness. Thus, the obvious way to organize a mental-experience event linguistically is to specify the nature of the experience by means of an independent predication and bring the experiencer into the picture by whatever means is available in the language for expressing the relationship between an individual and aspects of the personal sphere – in Japanese, the external NP construction.[90] In other words, it is only natural that mental experience predicates should favor the external NP construction, since they evoke the sphere of awareness, and the sphere of awareness is a central element of the personal sphere. This account captures the fact that the "external" participant is argument-like in that it is strongly evoked by the verb without doing violence to the observable grammatical facts – i.e., that the object of the experience is the grammatical subject, as evidenced by the presence of the nominative particle *ga*. Moreover, since a predicate can evoke the experiencer more or less strongly, depending on the prominence of the sphere of awareness in its semantic structure (it is absolutely central for *wakaru* 'to understand', and fairly marginal for *omoshiroi* 'interesting'), the analysis predicts that some predicates will occur with the experiencer nominal quite frequently (and feel elliptical without it), while others will tend to occur in simple intransitive constructions without an external nominal.

6.2.5. The sphere of potency

In the construction discussed in the previous section, the mental experience predicate makes schematic reference to the sphere of awareness and the sentence initial NP-*wa* or NP-*ga* specifies the individual in whose sphere of awareness the process occurs. Not surprisingly, verbs which evoke the sphere of potency require the same construction:

(486) a. *Taguchi-san-wa chuugoku-go-o hanasu koto-ga dekiru.*
Taguchi-Mr-TOP China-language-ACC speak thing-NOM is possible
'Mr Taguchi can speak Chinese.'

(486) b. *Taguchi-san-wa chuugoku-go-ga dekiru.*
Taguchi-Mr-TOP China-language-NOM is possible
'Mr Taguchi can speak Chinese.'

Here the sphere of potency is evoked by the verb *dekiru* 'to be able to, to be possible'. Located within this sphere is either a hypothetical action (speaking Chinese) construed as an object (note the nominalizing morpheme *koto*) or the language itself.[91] One can also express ability by using the potential form of the verb (487b); the latter, like *dekiru,* requires that the object of experience be expressed by means of a nominative nominal.

(487) a. *Taguchi-san-wa chuugoku-go-o   hanasu.*
          Taguchi-Mr-TOP China-language-ACC speaks
          'Mr Taguchi speaks Chinese/is speaking Chinese.'

(487) b. *Taguchi-san-wa chuugoku-go-ga   hanaseru.*
          Taguchi-Mr-TOP China-language-NOM speak:POTENTIAL
          'Mr Taguchi can speak Chinese.'

6.2.6. Causatives

In addition to the external topic and focus constructions discussed above, Japanese has two other sentence types in which an extra NP, marked with either *wa* or *ga*, appears at the beginning of the sentence: the so-called indirect (or adversative) passive, discussed in the next section, and the causative (488).

(488) *Taroo-ga   Hanako-o/ni   hatarakaseta.*
       Taro-NOM Hanako-ACC/DAT caused to work
       'Taro made/let Hanako work.'

In addition to the extra sentence-initial NP, the causative construction contains the auxiliary verb *saseru;* and the agent of the action, which would have been nominative in a simple active sentence, is marked either by the dative particle *ni* or the accusative *o.*

In most standard descriptions (e.g. Comrie 1976, 1985, Inoue 1969) causitivization is treated as a process which increases the verb's valence by one: the new argument becomes the subject, while the "original" subject is "demoted" to direct object or indirect object. This account is correct only at a very superficial level. As we shall see shortly, there is more to causatives than meets the formal linguist's eye.

First of all, the formal approach to causativization cannot explain certain curious restrictions on the construction. There is nothing semantically incoherent about an inanimate cause (for example, poverty) causing a person to undertake an action (for example, to take up a job); however, a situation of this kind cannot be described using the causative construction. The causer in the causative construction must be human – cf. the ungrammaticality of (489). Even more curiously, the causative construction cannot be used when the causer is lower in status than the causee. If the teacher referred to in (490) is the speaker's teacher,

166 *The personal sphere in other languages*

the sentence is unacceptable. Thus, Japanese causatives are subject to the same restrictions as English personal sphere causatives (see the discussion in 6.1 above).

(489)   **Bimbo-ga   Hanako-o/ni   hatarakaseta.*
        poverty-NOM Hanako-ACC/DAT caused to work
        'Poverty made Hanako work.'

(490)   **Watashi-wa sensei-o/ni   paatii-ni kosaseru   tsumori da.*
        I-TOP   teacher-ACC/DAT party-to cause to come intention is
        'I am going to make/let (my) teacher come to the party.'

Moreover, like the constructions with *have* discussed in the previous section, the "causative" construction also has other, non-causative interpretations. Oehrle and Nishio (1981) observe that (491) has no fewer than four readings, viz. (1) the father intentionally brought about the child's death; (2) the father let the child die; (3) the father accidentally caused the child's death; and (4) the father was affected by the child's death (but he didn't cause it).

(491)   *Chichioya-wa kodomo-o   shinaseta.*
        father-TOP   child-ACC   caused to die

Most curiously of all, the adversative interpretation is not possible when the roles are reversed, i.e. when the child is the subject and the father the object. (492) can only mean 'The child caused his father's death', not 'The child suffered the loss of his father.' Or to take another example, in (493) the adversative interpretation is possible only if Taro owns the company; if he is merely an employee, the sentence can only mean that he was responsible for the bankruptcy.

(492)   *Kodomo-wa chichioya-o shinaseta*   (Oehrle & Nishio 1981: 168)
        child-TOP   father-ACC caused to die
        'The child caused the father to die.'

(493)   *Taroo-wa (fukeiki-de)   kaisha-o   toosansaseta.* (*ibid* p. 167)
        Taro-TOP (depression-with) company-ACC caused to go broke
        'Taro had his company go broke on him (because of the depression).'

How are we to account for this curious set of restrictions? I suggest that *saseru* indicates that either the whole process designated by the main verb or some part of it is located in the external participant's sphere of potency. If the entire action is included in the sphere of potency, we get the intentional-causative interpretation: the external participant indirectly controls the action. If only some stages of the process occur in the external participant's sphere of potency, we get the accidental-causative interpretation: the external participant is construed as affected because his potency diminishes when the process gets out of hand. Finally, if the sphere of potency contains only the direct participant, but not the process itself, we get the adversative interpretation.

The above analysis neatly accounts for both the semantic restrictions on the "causative" constructions and the seemingly contradictory range of meanings associated with it. Both are fully compatible with the semantic contributions of the linguistic forms that make them up; and – what is perhaps even more interesting – both have analogues in various uses of the dative in Polish and in constructions with *have* in English.

6.2.7. Indirect passives

The passive construction is one of the most widely studied, as well as the most problematic, aspects of Japanese grammar. It comes in two variants, the so-called direct (494) and the indirect, or "adversity" passive (495-496).

(494)   *Kodomo-ga   sensei-ni   shikarareta.*
        child-NOM   teacher-DAT scolded:PASS
        'The child was scolded by the teacher.'

(495)   *Taroo-ga   sensei-ni   kodomo-o   shikarareta.*
        Taro-NOM teacher-DAT child-ACC scolded:PASS
        'Taro was (adversely) affected by the teacher's having scolded his child.'

(496)   *Taroo-ga   ame-ni   furareta.*
        Taro-NOM rain-DAT fell:PASS
        'Taro got rained on.'

Both variants require the presence of the bound auxiliary verb *rareru;* the agent is case-marked with the dative particle *ni* rather than the nominative *ga.* In the direct variant, the verb must be transitive and the subject is the patient of the action. In the indirect variant, the verb can be either transitive (495) or intransitive (496); if it is transitive, the patient retains its direct object status (note the accusative particle *o* in (495)). The most peculiar feature of the indirect passive is the presence of an extra NP at the beginning of the sentence ("extra" in the sense of not being required by the verb). The construction is used to indicate that this external participant was affected by the action, usually adversely (hence the term "adversity passive").

There is a great deal of disagreement in the literature – most of it in the generative tradition – about whether or not the two passives are variants of the same construction (and hence should be derived from the same source) and about the status of the "extra" NP in the indirect passive and its relationship with the rest of the clause.[92] In what follows, I will attempt to show that by appealing to the concept of personal sphere, we can offer a revealing account of both the syntactic and the semantic properties of the construction.

The passive auxiliary *rareru* restricts the temporal profile of the verb to the final state and designates the relationship between the affected participant (its trajector) and the resulting atemporal relation (its landmark). In other words, the effect of adding *rareru* to the verb is to separate the agent's action from its results and to focus on the results, thus backgrounding the agent and foregrounding the affected participant. The structure of the passive construction could be informally summarized by the formula AFFECTED PARTICIPANT + SITUATION, where "Situation" refers to the state resulting from the agent's action. In the direct passive, the affected participant is the patient: the construction differs from the corresponding active in that it describes not what the agent did to the patient, but how the patient was affected by the agent's action. The indirect passive describes a relationship between an external participant and either the results of a process directly involving an entity belonging to his personal sphere (as in (495), where *kodomo* 'child' is understood to refer to Taro's child) or a process occurring in his personal sphere (as in (496), where the entire event, i.e. rain falling, not just the rain drops, is located in Taro's air bubble).

This analysis provides a natural account for the various semantic properties of the passive construction which have been commented on in the literature. First of all, since the indirect passive crucially depends on the concept of personal sphere for its interpretation (the personal sphere is, as it were, the glue that connects the external participant with the rest of the clause), the sentence-initial nominal must be an entity that is endowed with one – i.e. it must be human, or at least animate.[93] In contrast, in the direct passive, the verb itself provides information about how the sentence-initial nominal is to be integrated with the rest of the sentence, and the concept of personal sphere need not be invoked; consequently, the subject of the direct passive can be inanimate. Secondly, the personal-sphere analysis of indirect passives predicts the kinds of relationships that can hold between the external and the direct participant: the latter can be a part of the former's body, a member of his family, his subordinate, a possession, and so on. Without the concept of personal sphere, we would have no way of establishing the possible relationships other than simply listing them – and even this would be inadequate since, as we have seen in chapter 2, the personal sphere is an open-ended concept.

The indirect passive, then, portrays the event designated by the clause as occurring in the external participant's personal sphere. This explains why the external participant is understood to be (indirectly) affected by the event; however, it does not account for another interesting property of the construction: the fact that it generally implies that the effect on the external participant was adverse. Indirect passives are not *always* adversative: in (497) and (498) below, the positive connotations of the lexical items *homaru* 'to praise' and *kawai* 'pretty', coupled with pragmatic knowledge about how a man is likely to be affected when his child is praised or when an attractive girl sits next to him, force a propitious interpretation. However, the default interpretation is adversative: when there is nothing in the sentence to suggest that the external participant benefited from the action, as in (499), the effect is understood to be negative. How, then, does the indirect passive acquire such negative connotations?

(497)   *Taroo-ga sensei-ni kodomo-o homarareta.*   (cf. (495))
           'Taro's child was praised by the teacher [and Taro was affected by it].'

(498)   *[Boku-wa] Eigakan-de kawai ko-no   tonari-ni suwarareta.*
        [I-TOP]   cinema-in pretty girl-GEN beside   sat:PASS
        'A pretty girl sat next to me at the cinema [and I was affected].'
        (Alfonso 1971)

(499)   *John-wa   kodomo-ni nerareta.*
        John-TOP child-DAT slept:PASS
        'John was inconvenienced by the child's falling asleep.'

One possibility is that they arise through conversational implicature. If an action affecting another person has favorable consequences for the latter, the rules of politeness require that one acknowledge the favor. By failing to acknowledge it explicitly, one conversationally implicates that the action was not favorable. Something along these lines was proposed by Alfonso (1971), who points out that a situation in which a third party benefits from the agent's action calls for the use of the benefactive *-te morau* construction (see example (452)). It is worth noting in this connection that when the verb or some other element in the sentence forces a benefactive interpretation, it is understood that the positive effect on the external participant was not intended. For example, the teacher in (497) did not intend to please Taro by praising his child: he was merely expressing his approval of the child's behavior, and Taro's affectedness was entirely accidental.

However, as Wierzbicka notes, adversative connotations also arise in indirect passives with non-agentive verbs, such as (500) below, where there is no question of acknowledging a favor. (500) by itself is not a problem, since its adversative connotations could plausibly be attributed to the fact that the verb *shinu* 'to die', designates an event which is intrinsically inauspicious. However, if it were *shinu* that triggered the adversative interpretation, substituting a positively-charged verb such as *naoru* 'to recover', should result in a sentence which suggests that the effect on John was propitious. This, however, is not the case: speakers find (501) decidedly odd, precisely because it suggests that John was adversely affected by his wife's recovery.

(500)   *John-wa   tsuma-ni   shinareta.*
        John-TOP wife-DAT died:PASS
        'John was [adversely] affected by his wife's death.'

(501)   ? *John-wa tsuma-ni   naorareta.*
        John-TOP wife-DAT recovered:PASS
        'John was [adversely] affected by his wife's recovery.'

In at least some uses, therefore, the adversative connotations arise from the meaning of the indirect passive construction itself, not through a combination of lexical and pragmatic factors. On the other hand, as Alfonso (1971) painstakingly documents, there are also many contexts in which the indirect passive does not carry adversative overtones. This suggests that the construction's semantic properties cannot be captured by means of a single schema. In fact, I suggest that what is required is a network of at least six interrelated schemas of varying degrees of generality (see figure 15). The most deeply entrenched schema (the category prototype) is the agentive-adversative variant, exemplified in (495). The adversative connotations presumably originally arose through conventionalization of implicature; once they became conventionally associated with the construction, they spread to the non-agentive variant illustrated in (496) and (500). The adversative schema captures the properties shared by the two variants: namely, the fact that the process designated by the verb had an adverse effect on the participant in whose personal sphere it occurred. The third local schema, which corresponds to the agentive-auspicious variant of the construction, resembles the category prototype in a different way: like the agentive-adversative variant it specifies that the indirect participant was affected by someone undertaking an action which impinged on the latter's personal sphere. The common properties of these two schemas are captured by the intermediate-level agentive schema. Finally, the 'neutral' schema – the most general description of the indirect passive – merely specifies that the external participant is affected in some way by a process which takes place in his personal sphere, thus neutralizing the distinction between agentive and non-agentive on the one hand and adversative and non-adversative on the other.

It must be stressed that although the 'neutral' superschema captures what all the variants of the indirect passive have in common, it cannot be taken as the one and only characterization of the category: a full description must include local and intermediate-level schemas as well as the superschema. This is because the most general description of the category is fully compatible with usages that most speakers find unacceptable, such as (501). As explained in section 1.2.1, the main function of superschemas is to hold categories together; to assemble novel expressions, speakers generally rely on the more deeply entrenched local schemas. Because there is no local schema to sanction (501), it is extremely unlikely (though not altogether impossible) that such a sentence should occur. Finally, the fact that the agentive-adversative schema is more deeply entrenched (that is, more accessible as a cognitive routine) than the more abstract neutral superschema also explains why the adversative interpretation pre-empts a propitious one unless it is specifically ruled out by the context.

6.2.8. *The honorific use of* rareru

Before we conclude the discussion of the Japanese data, it is worth noting that the auxiliary verb *rareru* also has another function: that of elevating the subject of the sentence. Thus, (502) can have an adversative interpretation, in which the teacher is an external participant indirectly affected by the action, or a honorific interpretation, in which the teacher is the agent of the action.

External NP constructions in Japanese 171

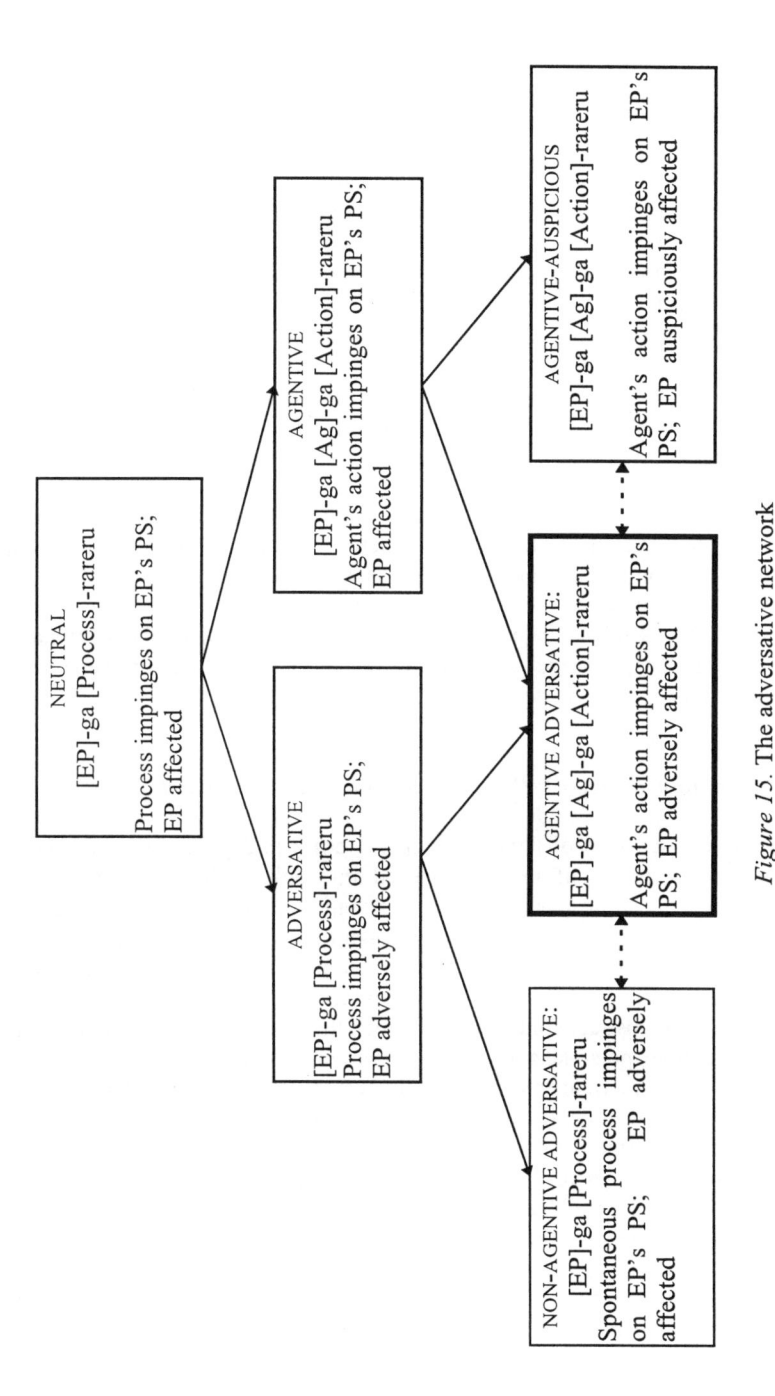

```
                    ┌─────────────────────┐
                    │      NEUTRAL        │
                    │ [EP]-ga [Process]-  │
                    │      rareru         │
                    │ Process impinges on │
                    │ EP's PS; EP affected│
                    └──────────┬──────────┘
                       ┌───────┴───────┐
                       ▼               ▼
        ┌─────────────────────┐   ┌─────────────────────┐
        │      AGENTIVE       │   │     ADVERSATIVE     │
        │ [EP]-ga [Ag]-ga     │   │ [EP]-ga [Process]-  │
        │  [Action]-rareru    │   │      rareru         │
        │ Agent's action      │   │ Process impinges on │
        │ impinges on EP's PS;│   │ EP's PS; EP         │
        │ EP affected         │   │ adversely affected  │
        └──────────┬──────────┘   └──────────┬──────────┘
                   └──────────┬──────────────┘
                              ▼
                    ┌─────────────────────┐
                    │ AGENTIVE ADVERSATIVE│
                    │ [EP]-ga [Ag]-ga     │
                    │  [Action]-rareru    │
                    │ Agent's action      │
                    │ impinges on EP's    │
                    │ PS; EP adversely    │
                    │ affected            │
                    └─────────────────────┘
                     ▲                   ▲
                     ┆                   ┆
                     ▼                   ▼
    ┌─────────────────────┐   ┌─────────────────────┐
    │ AGENTIVE-AUSPICIOUS │   │ NON-AGENTIVE        │
    │ [EP]-ga [Ag]-ga     │   │   ADVERSATIVE:      │
    │  [Action]-rareru    │   │ [EP]-ga [Process]-  │
    │ Agent's action      │   │      rareru         │
    │ impinges on EP's    │   │ Spontaneous process │
    │ PS; EP auspiciously │   │ impinges on EP's PS;│
    │ affected            │   │ EP adversely affected│
    └─────────────────────┘   └─────────────────────┘
```

Figure 15. The adversative network
(Solid lines indicate schematicity; double headed dotted lines indicate mutual similarity; EP = external participant; Ag = agent)

(502)   *Sensei-wa   sashimi-o   taberareta.*
teacher-TOP sashimi-ACC ate:PASS
'The teacher was [adversely] affected by the sashimi having been eaten.'
'The teacher ate the sashimi.'

The honorific function of *rareru* is traditionally explained by appealing to the idea of *indirectness:* (502) is felt to be more polite than the corresponding sentence without *rareru* because it is indirect, and indirect expressions are considered more polite by the Japanese. This, however, begs the question of what exactly makes this usage "indirect": it is without doubt *marked,* but why indirect?

I have claimed earlier that the semantic contribution of *rareru* in passive constructions is to focus on the results of the action rather than the action itself, thus backgrounding the agent. It seems that the honorific effect is achieved in exactly the same way: by backgrounding the subject participant's agentive involvement in the action. The action in (502) is construed not as a transfer of energy from the agent to the patient, but as a process occurring in the agent's personal sphere. The usage is "indirect" in that it is vague, since *rareru* doesn't specify which region of the personal sphere is involved. The subject participant's role in the action is only hinted at, and it is up to the addressee to work out that the process designated by the verb occurs in the external participant's sphere of potency. This kind of vagueness is fully compatible with the personal-sphere analysis; indeed, as we have seen, it is characteristic of personal-sphere constructions.

6.2.9. Additional support: Parallels with locative constructions

The above discussion of "non-participant" topics in Japanese fits in rather nicely with the description of topics proposed in Cook 1989. Cook argues that the meaning of the topic particle *wa* is best captured by means of a Langackerian network which comprises four schemas: that of a whole (which contains a part), a set (which contains a singled out member), a physical setting (which "contains" a participant), and an experiencer-setting (which "contains" the experience), plus a superschema ("abstract container") of which these are more concrete instantiations. If we substitute "personal sphere" for "experiencer setting" (a much more inclusive concept than "experiencer setting", which corresponds to what I have been calling the sphere of awareness), this characterization covers the data remarkably well, though further refinements will almost certainly prove to be necessary.

It is worth noting in this connection that Japanese topic constructions exhibit certain structural parallels to locative constructions, as the following schematic formulas make clear (cf. Ikegami 1984: 59-60):[94]

Location in space: [Location] *ni* [Person/thing] *ga aru/iru.*
Location in personal sphere: [Person] *ga/wa* [Person/thing] *ga aru/iru.*

Both of these are elaborations of the existential sentence pattern, which can be represented as

    Existence: [Person/thing] *ga aru/iru*.

It is also worth noting that in some of the sentences discussed above the experiencer can be marked with the dative/locative particle *ni*. For example, instead of uttering (475), repeated here as (503), one could also say (504), which literally means 'In Mr Tanaka, English is understandable'.

(503)   *Tanaka-san-wa   eigo-ga   wakaru.*
         Tanaka-Mr-TOP English-NOM is understandable
         'Mr Tanaka understands English.'

(504)   *Tanaka-san-ni   eigo-ga   wakaru.*
         Tanaka-Mr-in   English-NOM is understandable
         'Mr Tanaka understands English.'

6.3. The personal sphere in Polish, English and Japanese

The Polish dative and the English verb *have* express a variety of meanings which seems to defy the linguist's efforts to systematize and to capture significant generalizations. Similarly, sentence-external NPs in Japanese can be related to the rest of the clause in many different ways, and whatever principles determine the possible links have long remained elusive. The fact that any one of these three forms should have so many different functions is intriguing; the fact that the same constellation of functions occurs in very different areas of linguistic organization in three different languages is positively astounding. We have seen that the concept of personal sphere makes it possible to provide a unified description of the semantics of the dative, the verb *have,* and external-NP constructions, which of course is highly desirable. What is more, it provides an explanation for why the same pattern of polysemy should recur in different languages, which is a further argument for its utility in linguistic description.

It should be noted that some of the cross-linguistic parallels discussed here have been commented on by other linguists. For example, Palmer (1994: 235) notes a vague similarity between the Japanese causative and passive on the one hand, and English constructions of the form *have a book stolen* on the other. However, he seems to be unaware that Japanese causatives can also have an adversative interpretation, so he does not take the analogy as far as he might have done. Wierzbicka (1988: 278) observes that the Japanese adversity passive resembles dative constructions in various languages, including Polish: "other languages, unrelated to Japanese, tend to use one morphological exponent to codify a set of meanings similar to that served by the Japanese passive." She also points out that the English "light verb" construction with *have* and the Polish ethic *sobie* express very similar meanings. However, without the concept of personal sphere proposed here these two linguists could only see certain similarities but were unable to explain them.

The concept of personal sphere also helps to explain certain characteristic ambiguities exhibited by constructions which depend on it for their interpretation, specifically their tendency to be ambiguous between an "active" (i.e. agentive or causative) reading and a "passive" ("affected person") reading. *Kate had a book stolen* can mean either that she had caused someone to steal a book or that one of her own books was stolen; *Kate had a wash* can mean that she washed herself or that someone washed her (if, for example she is a baby or a patient in a hospital). Examples from Japanese include the causative, which, as we have seen sometimes expresses adversative meanings, and the indirect passive, in which the sentence-initial nominal can specify either the indirectly affected participant or, in honorific usage, the agent. Finally, in Polish, the dative-patient subject construction is ambiguous between an "unlucky agent" and an "unlucky recipient" interpretation.

At this point I should perhaps repeat a caveat made earlier in this chapter: I am not claiming that the dative, the verb *have* and external topic constructions do not differ in meaning (they clearly do); nor am I claiming that their uses are fully parallel, i.e. that for every use of the Polish dative there will be a corresponding sense of *have* and a corresponding variant of the external NP construction in Japanese. What I am saying is that there are certain broad parallels of function between the three, and that many of the differences in distribution are attributable to the differences in the meanings of the expressions themselves and of the other linguistic units with which they combine in constructions. This does not rule out language-specific idiosyncrasies – for example the fact that one cannot use an external NP construction in Japanese to describe a situation in which, say, a man is positively affected by his wife's recovery from an illness (cf. the unacceptability of (501) above), while the corresponding dative construction in Polish is perfectly grammatical (cf. example (519) in section 7.1). These will be captured in the grammar by lower-level schemas which co-exist with the more abstract personal-sphere schema.

It seems only appropriate to conclude this chapter with a brief discussion of the differences between the three units we have been studying. Let us begin with the semantic differences. The dative, I proposed in chapter 2, is defined relative to a knowledge structure which includes a person, his or her personal sphere, and a process impinging on this sphere. The person is construed as affected by the process impinging on the personal sphere, and the dative ending profiles this person. *Have*, on the other hand, designates the inclusion relationship between an individual and an entity located in his personal sphere. Since *have* is a verb, it has a positive temporal profile and its trajector (the "owner" of the personal sphere) is also the clausal trajector, i.e. the subject. Its landmark is typically a thing or (in certain constructions such as the causative) an event construed atemporally. Loosely speaking, a sentence with a dative presupposes that an entity (i.e. a process or a thing) is located the TP's personal sphere and asserts the TP's affectedness, whereas *have* asserts that that entity is in an individual's personal sphere (from which, if the entity in question is a process, one may reasonably infer that the individual was affected). In contrast to this, the topic and focus particles in Japanese do not specifically designate any aspect of the relationship between an individual and his personal sphere: they merely exploit a salient conceptual relationship not directly evoked by any of the lexical items in the construction. (However, it is perfectly possible – indeed probable – that the construction itself evokes the personal sphere.)

Grammatically, perhaps the most obvious difference between the English content verb *have* on the one hand and the Polish dative and the Japanese external NP construction on the other is the fact that *have*, being a transitive verb, requires an object. Hence, although *have* can be used to locate a mental experience in the personal sphere, this is only possible when there exists a noun to designate the experience. One can *have a look* at something, but not **an admire* or **a double-see*, although one can *admire a building* and *see double*. In Polish and Japanese, the nature of the mental experience is specified by the verb, so the personal-sphere conceptualization will be possible if the language has an appropriate verb (i.e. a verb which construes mental experience as an autonomous process rather than an action).

The fact that the dative nominal cannot, while the trajector of *have* must be the subject leads to some interesting differences between Polish and English with regard to the options available to indicate that an individual is in control of an action or event. There are two basic ways to conceptualize the relationship between an individual and an action that he is in control of. One is to construe the event as located in the individual's personal sphere, or, to be more exact, his sphere of potency. The other is to construe the participant as an abstract source of the action, i.e. the head of an action chain. Now in an active sentence, the head of the action chain will always be the subject, while the centre of the personal sphere will be the subject in English but a dative nominal in Polish. This means that in English it is possible to represent a participant as simultaneously the head of an action chain and the centre of the personal sphere. The two images are compatible and are be superimposed over each other in expressions such as *I had a walk* or *I had him wash my car*. In Polish, on the other hand, since a nominal cannot be both nominative and dative at the same time, construing an event as an action chain normally pre-empts explicit mention of the personal sphere. When the action in question is the target person's own action, it is possible to bring the personal sphere in through the back door, as it were, by introducing a dative nominal coreferential with the subject, i.e. the reflexive pronoun *sobie*; however, the semantic contribution of the dative pronoun here is to add a nuance of self-indulgence rather than potency – presumably because the effects of the action are confined to the personal sphere (see section 2.3.4). One cannot use the dative in Polish to refer to an individual who controls someone else's actions – that is to say, there is no dative analogue of *I had him wash my car*.

In contrast, the dative is often used to refer to agents of involuntary actions, as in *Adamowi trzęsły się ręce* 'Adam's hands were shaking' (lit., 'Hands were shaking to Adam') or *Adamowi wylała się herbata* 'Adam (accidentally) spilled his tea' (lit. 'The tea spilled itself on Adam'), where the nominal *Adamowi* is in the dative case. (See section 3.1.1 for a discussion of this construction.) Predictably, because the subject position in English is associated with high potency, the *have a N* construction in English cannot be used to describe involuntary actions. Thus, one cannot say **He had a spill of the tea* to mean that he accidentally spilled the tea.

In Japanese, *wa-* and *ga-*marked nominals can be action-chain heads (in standard transitive clauses such as (453a) and (453b) and in causative constructions such as (488)), but they need not be (when they mark the external participant in most of the examples discussed in the previous section). Predictably, *wa-* and *ga-*marked nominals are compatible with both high-potency and low-potency situations.

These brief comments should make it clear that, although there are clear parallels between the uses of the dative, the verb *have*, and clause-external NPs, there are also significant differences. These are largely attributable to the semantic properties of the linguistic units themselves and other units with which they combine in constructions, though some differences are due to the presence or absence of more specific local schemas in a particular language.

6.4. A word on English ditransitives and the "dative" *ni* in Japanese

We have seen in the preceding chapters that the special properties of the Polish dative are best explained by appealing to the concept of personal sphere. The purpose of this chapter was to provide further evidence for the validity of this concept by showing that it can be invoked to help explain other linguistic phenomena as well. To do this convincingly, it was necessary to choose linguistic items as different as possible from the Polish dative. This may have left the reader wondering about the status of the personal sphere in some more obvious equivalents of the dative, such as the English ditransitive construction and the Japanese particle *ni*, which I have glossed as "dative" throughout this chapter.

The "first object" in the English ditransitive construction indeed expresses ideas very similar to the Polish dative: recipient in an act of giving, addressee in a communicative event, and beneficiary. Perhaps the most obvious difference between the two languages is that in English, there is no one phonological element corresponding to the dative – the meaning of "personal sphere" is associated with the whole construction (cf. Goldberg 1992). Furthermore, the English construction is much more restricted than the Polish dative: it generally cannot be used with verbs of loss (cf. (505)); and even within the broad category of verbs of coming into possession or prospective possession there are many verbs which do not allow the would-be possessor in the direct-object position (examples (506) and (507)).

(505) a. *Podwędził mi okulary.*
  'He pinched my (DAT) glasses.'
(505) b. **He pinched me the/my glasses.* ['He stole my glasses.']

(506) a. *Powierzyłem mu rękopis.*
'I entrusted him (DAT) with the manuscript.'
(506) b. **I entrusted him the manuscript.*

(507) a. *Wybrałam jej sukienkę.*
'I chose a dress for her (DAT).'
(507) b. ? *I chose her a dress.*

On the other hand, membership in the class of verbs that allow two objects is not entirely a lexical matter, since, as pointed out in Gropen et al. 1989 and Goldberg 1992, the pattern is partially productive: for example, it is readily extended to new verbs such as *fax* and to nonsense verbs in experimental conditions. Gropen et al. and Goldberg both argue, therefore, that an adequate description of the English construction requires both a broad characterizaton which captures its general properties and a set of fairly narrow rules – that is to say, local schemas – which spell out in fine detail the semantic properties of the verbs which can occur in the construction. The differences between Polish and English, therefore, would follow from the fact that English lacks many of the local schemas that exist in Polish.

I believe that this account is basically correct, though the following refinement will help to explain some more general differences between the two languages, especially the English tendency to avoid the ditransitive construction with verbs of loss and damage. Goldberg points out that *give* is by far the most prototypical ditransitive verb, and argues that this is because "its lexical semantics is identical with the construction's semantics" (1992: 54), by which she appears to mean that the prototypical sense of *give,* like the prototypical variant of the ditransitive construction, designates a situation in which an agent causes a patient to enter the recipient's sphere of influence. She then argues that the ditransitive construction is polysemous – that is to say, that the variants or local schemas referred to above form a network of distinct, though related senses, and shows that the links between the nodes in the network are independently motivated, since the same patterns of polysemy are found elsewhere in the language.

Goldberg's account thus explains why the ditransitive construction has overtones of benefit and control: they are inherited them from the lexical meaning of the verb *give*.[95] On the other hand, connotations of loss, reduced potency, and adverse affectedness, so characteristic of the Polish dative, are incompatible with *give*. This is not to say that variants with just these connotations are impossible: extended senses are by definition not fully compatible with the basic sense. In fact, there is an established variant of the ditransitive construction that specifies that the agent causes the potential recipient *not* to receive the patient (e.g. *They refused/denied her a permit*). Such uses, however, are restricted to only a few verbs.

In contrast to the English ditransitive construction, the Japanese particle *ni* covers a much wider semantic space than the Polish dative case, and its uses are even more heterogeneous than those of the dative. We have already seen that it is associated with the typically "dative" roles of recipient and addressee as well as what is traditionally referred to as the source, i.e. the agent in causative, passive, and benefactive constructions (cf. sections 6.2.5, 6.2.6 and 6.2.1, respectively). Apart from these, the particle *ni* also signals location in space and time (*Kobe-ni* 'in Kobe', *goji-ni* 'at five o'clock'), goal (*Kobe-ni* 'to Kobe') and purpose (*okurimono-o kai-ni* 'in order to buy a present'). Most traditional grammars treat these various senses as homonyms, thus tacitly assuming that it is purely accidental that they should have the same phonological exponent. However, even a cursory glance at the semantics of the various senses reveals numerous links: location in space and location in time are related through the TIME IS SPACE metaphor; a purpose is a metaphorical goal (note the ambiguity of the word *goal* itself); the goal of movement is a type of location (the final location of the moving object). All of these are well-attested patterns of semantic extension, in that many linguistic items in a number of languages have been found to exhibit similar patterns of polysemy.[96] The relationships between the locative and directional senses of *ni* and its use to mark the recipient, addressee and other "dative" roles may appear puzzling at first, but becomes understandable once it is acknowledged the personal sphere is an abstract *region*;[97] hence, what is traditionally known as the "indirect object" *ni* simply marks the abstract goal towards which the patient moves.

This leaves us with the *ni* in indirect passives, causatives, benefactives, and "receiving" constructions such as (508), often called the "source" *ni* because it marks a participant who can be thought of as an abstract source – the agent, the causer, or the original owner. Furthermore, this sense of *ni* can sometimes be replaced with the source particle *kara* without any obvious change of meaning.

(508)   John-wa   Mary-kara/ni   nekutai-o   moratta.
        John-TOP Mary-from/DAT necktie-ACC received
        'John received a necktie from Mary.'

For some linguists, the existence of this sense is the clinching argument for homonymy: since *ni* also marks the goal, the two senses cannot possibly belong to the same lexical item. We might observe in passing that saying that the source *ni* and the goal *ni* are homonyms hardly explains anything, and still leaves us with a homonymic clash. But how could this apparent incongruity be accounted for? I suggest that in fact there is no incongruity: the offending sense, as we will see shortly, fits quite comfortably into the *ni* network. The real culprit is the label "source", which is highly misleading. We have seen earlier that the agent *can* be conceptualized as the source of the action (cf. the discussion of action chains in section 1.2.3). However, it can also be given another construal: it can be thought of as the individual in whose sphere of potency the action takes place. The Polish dative patient-subject construction and English expressions such as *have a walk*, *have a drink* embody precisely this construal (see sections 3.1.1 and 6.1, respectively). I suggest, then, that this particular sense of *ni* marks not the source, but an agent construed as the owner of a sphere of potency.[98],[99]

This contention is supported by two independent lines of evidence. First, although the relevant sense of *ni* can sometimes be replaced with *kara* 'from', in most cases such a substitution is not possible. *Kara* works best in situations involving fairly concrete movement (such as that described in (508)); it is rare in passives and cannot mark the agent in causative sentences. When the substitution is possible, the resulting sentences are not fully synonymous: the sentence with *kara* gives greater prominence to the actual transfer from the giver to the receiver, while the *ni* variant primarily highlights the receiver's affectedness. Needless to say, this subtle difference in emphasis results from different construals of the same content. Secondly, *ni* can only be used when the "source" is an entity endowed with a personal sphere; when the giver is an abstract entity (for example an institution), only *kara* can be used:[100]

(509)   *John-wa   monbushoo kara/*ni   shoogakukin-o   moratta.*
John-TOP Ministry of Education-from scholarship-ACC received
'John received a scholarship from the Ministry of Education.'

The various uses of *ni*, then, form a network of interrelated senses of which the personal-sphere uses form an integral part. A discussion of the various senses and the relationships between them in the detail they deserve would take us too far beyond the subject of our enquiry; the interested reader is referred to Kumashiro 1993. We might note in passing, however, that the "dative" part of the network does not exhibit the whole constellation of personal sphere uses that we might expect. For example, *ni* does not occur in constructions analogous to the Polish dative patient-subject construction:

(510)   *Johnowi   umarła żona.*
John:DAT died   wife:NOM
'John was [adversely] affected by his wife's death.'

(511)   **John-ni tsuma-ga shinda.*
John:DAT wife:NOM died

To express a meaning like that in (510) in Japanese, one would have to use the indirect passive (cf. (500)): the *ni* network lacks this particular local schema. This once again demonstrates that an adequate description requires local as well as more general schemas which capture higher-level generalizations.

Chapter 7: Conclusion

The purpose of this concluding chapter is twofold. First, by showing how the analysis proposed here compares with descriptions of the dative conducted in several cognate frameworks, I highlight the contributions of this monograph to the study of the semantics of case. Secondly, I discuss in greater detail several general issues that have been touched upon in the preceding chapters: the sources of prototype effects, the need for schemas of various levels of generality, and the role of imagery in grammar. To a linguistic theory that strives to elucidate the relationship between grammar and conceptualization, these questions are of fundamental importance. Hopefully the comments that follow will help further the cognitive enterprise.

7.1. Comparison with other analyses

7.1.1. Wierzbicka

Wierzbicka 1988 is a very subtle and insightful description of the semantics of the Polish dative, and therefore it will be an excellent point of departure for our discussion.

Wierzbicka begins by pointing out that although the *core* meaning of the dative ("recipient in sentences of GIVING") is the same in many European languages, the *extensions* from the core are language-specific, since each language has a unique array of uses. Therefore, she argues, "if we want to predict the entire range of uses that the dative has in a particular language, we have to establish a full list of semantic constructions permitting the use of the dative in this language" (393). She then proceeds to enumerate the "semantic constructions" with the dative in Polish, and comes up with a list of no less then thirty-one.

It is impossible to do justice to Wierzbicka's analysis in a short critique such as this one; the following comments will concentrate, somewhat unfairly, on what I regard as its weaknesses. What I hope to demonstrate is that her analysis fails in some points because the view of meaning that it embodies is too narrow.

First, many of the distinctions that she proposes are unnecessary and actually obscure the picture. For example, the semantic difference between 'causing a change in someone's possessions' (512) and 'accidental change in someone's possessions' (513) is due to the presence or absence of an agent, and has nothing to do with the semantics of the dative. What led Wierzbicka to treat the latter as a different function of the dative is the observation that the change in sentences such as (513) is for the worse. While this is usually true, it is not invariably the case (cf. (514)), and it seems to be a consequence of the fact that things do not normally change for the better of their own accord.

(512)   *Zepsuła/   Zreperowała mu   zegarek.*   (Wierzbicka 1988: 429)
        she wrecked/she repaired   him:DAT watch:ACC
        'She wrecked/repaired his watch.'

(513)   *Zepsuł mi   się   zegarek.*   (Wierzbicka 1988: 429)
        wrecked me:DAT INTR watch:ACC
        'My watch broke down.'

(514)   *Za dwa-trzy   dni   dojrzeją nam   pomidory.*
        in two three days ripen   us:DAT tomatoes:NOM
        'Our tomatoes are going to get ripe in two or three days.'

The same point can be made with regard to the distinction between 'causing a change in a related person' (515), 'something bad happening to a related person' (516), and 'bad actions of a related person' (517). All that is needed to motivate the use of the dative is for the target person to be affected by an action or process occurring in his or her personal sphere; whether the action involves a third party or not and whether the consequences are beneficial or adverse is irrelevant from the point of view of the semantics of the dative.

(515)   *Zabili/Uratowali mu syna.*   (Wierzbicka 1988: 430)
        'They killed/saved his (DAT) son.'

(516)   *Żona mu umarła.*   (Wierzbicka 1988: 430)
        'His (DAT) wife died.'

(517)   *Syn mu się rozpił.*   (Wierzbicka 1988: 430)
        'His (DAT) son turned into a drunk.'

Wierzbicka claims that the dative can be used to refer to a person affected by an agentless event involving a related person only if "the effect is bad, both for the person directly involved and for the indirectly affected" (405). Thus, she maintains, although (516) is perfectly normal, one cannot say (518) "unless in jest". She seems to have got the facts wrong here: (518) is slightly odd as it stands, but it becomes perfectly acceptable given the right context (cf. (519)). (520) provides another example of the dative being used to designate a person indirectly affected by a spontaneous process whose effects are not necessarily bad for the individual in question.

(518)   (?) *Żona mu wyzdrowiała.*
        'His (DAT) wife has recovered.'

(519)   *Kowalski powiedział, że jeżeli żona mu wyzdrowieje, to da 50 milionów na budowę kościoła!*
        'Kowalski said that if his (DAT) wife recovers [from her illness], he will donate 50 million for the construction of a [new] church.'

(520)   *Dzieci nam rosną/dojrzewają.*
'Our (DAT) children are growing/growing up.'

A positive counterpart of (517) ("a good action of a related person") is also possible, given the right context:

(521)   A: *Dlaczego Kowalski jest taki zadowolony?*
'Why is Kowalski so pleased?'

B: *Syn mu zdał na studia!*
'His (DAT) son has passed the entrance exam to the university!'

– though it is worth noting that the person in question cannot be any related person, but must be a central member of the sphere of empathy – i.e. a child, grandchild, parent, lover, spouse, possibly a sibling or a grandparent.

Wierzbicka also claims that example (522) is of doubtful acceptability, which supposedly shows that "the dative can't be used unless the action produces a specifiable change of state" (404). Again, this is not true. Although the sentence is somewhat odd when the verb is *męczyć* 'to tire, torment', I feel it is perfectly acceptable with *torturować* 'to torture' and (523), where the directly affected participant is the target person's child, is fully acceptable with both verbs.

(522)   ?*Torturowali/Męczyli mu żonę.*   (Wierzbicka 1988: 405)
'They tortured/tormented his (DAT) wife.'

(523)   *Torturowali/Męczyli mu dziecko.*
'They tortured/tormented his (DAT) child.'

It is worth noting that dative sentences of this kind usually work better if the directly involved person is the target person's child or lover rather than spouse, suggesting that children are more central to the sphere of empathy than are spouses (cf. section 2.3.3).

Another doubtful distinction made by Wierzbicka is that between the dative in sentences expressing 'causing to have', 'causing not to have', and 'coming not to have'. Wierzbicka observes that although one can use the dative to refer to a person who is *given* something, one cannot, she tells us, use it to name the individual who simply comes to have something – in other words, Polish doesn't seem to have a dative of 'spontaneous acquisition', although it does have a dative of 'spontaneous loss'. To support her claim, she cites the following ungrammatical sentences:

(524)   **Przybłąkał   nam   się   pies.*   (Wierzbicka 1988:394)
came wandering us:DAT INTR dog:NOM
'A dog has "adopted" us.'

(525)   *List   mu   przyszedł.   (Wierzbicka 1988: 395)
        letter:NOM him:DAT came
        'He got a letter.'

Again, this statement is inaccurate at the purely descriptive level: we have already seen examples of fully acceptable dative constructions describing spontaneous acquisition (see section 2.2.1), two of which are repeated here for convenience.

(526)   Napatoczył nam   się   bardzo śmieszny szczeniak.
        turned up us:DAT INTR very funny   puppy:NOM
        'We were adopted by this funny little puppy.'

(527)   Wpadła mi   w ręce   bardzo ciekawa   książka.
        fell into me:DAT in hands:ACC very   interesting book:NOM
        'I [accidentally] came across a very interesting book./I chanced upon a very interesting book.'

So why are (524) and (525) unacceptable? The verbs *przybłąkać się* 'to come wandering' and *przyjść* 'to come walking' profile movement, not acquisition; their semantic representations do not evoke the personal sphere, and consequently, there is nothing in the sentence to motivate the use of the dative. Dative nominals can occur with both of these verbs, but they need a supporting context: the verb itself does not license their occurrence. This is made clear by examples (528) and (529), where the relevant part of the personal sphere is explicitly specified: the speaker's home in (528), the forest ranger's district in (529). (Notice that in the case of the latter, the reference to the relevant aspect of the personal sphere doesn't even occur in the same sentence as the dative: it was introduced into the discourse several sentences earlier by another speaker.) It is not very difficult to envisage how one might be affected if a crowd of children descends upon one; and a forest ranger may be assumed to take a professional interest in the animals that are to be found in his district, especially if they are unusual. Naturally, both of these facts provide further motivation for the occurrence of the dative.[101]

(528)   Przyszła mi   do domu   cała   czereda   dzieci.
        came   me:DAT to house:GEN whole   crowd:NOM   children:GEN
        'A whole crowd of kids came to my house.'

(529)   A: *Jakie zwierzęta ma pan u siebie w leśnictwie?*
        A: 'What sorts of animals do you have in your district?'
        Leśniczy: *Sarny, dziki, lisy. Czasami trafi się borsuk albo wilk. Raz przybłąkał mi się nawet niedźwiedź.*
        Forest ranger: 'Deer, boar, foxes. Occasionally you will chance upon a badger or a wolf. Once even a bear came my way.' (lit., 'Once came wandering to me (DAT) even a bear.')

Another aspect of Wierzbicka's analysis which needs refinement is its treatment of the contrast between the nominative and the dative when the verb allows both. She claims that the difference between expressions such as *przypomniałam sobie* 'I remembered' (lit. 'I recalled something to myself') and *przypomniało mi się* 'I remembered (lit. 'something recalled itself to me') is one of volitionality: the former designates a voluntary action and the latter a non-voluntary one. This is not entirely satisfactory: although the most prototypical use of *przypomniałam sobie* is to describe a situation in which the experiencer was consciously trying to recall something, the expression is actually neutral with respect to volitionality and *could* be used to describe spontaneous recall – cf. example (530a) below, where Ola presumably *did not want* the painful memory to come back. In the same vein, *przypomniało mi się* could be used to describe a situation in which the experiencer wanted very much to remember something, but couldn't, until the memory popped into his/her sphere of awareness quite unexpectedly (530b). In chapter 3, I described the contrast as one of construal: the nominative construal, by portraying the experiencer as an active, agent-like participant, invokes connotations of effort, volitionality, and control; the dative, with its highlighting of the sphere of awareness, portrays the experience as an autonomous process which, once initiated, proceeds independently of the experiencer's efforts or control. (See the discussion in section 3.7 for more details.)

(530) a. *Ola   przypomniała sobie,   jak bardzo jej ojciec*
Ola:NOM recalled   REFL:DAT how much   her father:NOM
cierpiał przed śmiercią.
suffered before death:INST
'Ola remembered how much her father had suffered before he died.'

(530) b. *Wreszcie przypomniało mi   się   jego nazwisko.*
at last   recalled   me:DAT INTR his   name:NOM
'I finally remembered his name./His name finally came back to me.'

Failure to allow for the role of construal in determining the form of a sentence also leads Wierzbicka to a less than satisfactory account of the use of the dative with verbs of communication. She maintains that Polish (in contrast to, for example, French) does not have a 'dative of addressee', but a dative of 'entertained audience' (531) and of a 'person caused to know' (532).

(531)   *Kasia przeczytała Jasiowi książkę.*   (Wierzbicka 1988: 397)
'Kasia read the book for Jaś (DAT).'

(532)   *Powiedziała mu prawdę.*   (Wierzbicka 1988: 398)
'She told him (DAT) the truth.'

This distinction allows her to account for the ungrammaticality of (533), where the referent of the dative pronoun is an addressee, but one who does not obtain new information as a result of the act of communication.

(533)   *Dobra robota, to cię nauczy, krzyknął mu pasażer.
        (Wierzbicka 1988: 398)
        'Well done, that will teach you, the passenger shouted to him (DAT).'

However, such a formulation leads her to a rather clumsy explanation of why (534) *is* acceptable: she claims that, like (532), it describes an act of 'causing to know', but the message is implied rather than explicitly stated, since a greeting implies good wishes.

(534)   Powiedziała mu dzień dobry.   (Wierzbicka 1988: 399)
        'She said hello to him (DAT).'

Her analysis runs into even more serious problems when she has to account for the unacceptability of (535): she is forced to introduce a distinction between 'knowing that' and 'knowing about', and to stipulate that "in Polish, one can only use the dative to refer to a person caused to KNOW THAT, but not to refer to a person caused to KNOW ABOUT" (400).

(535)   *Uczyła mu geografii.   (Wierzbicka 1988: 400).
        'She taught him (DAT) geography.'

However, sentences with what I have called 'verbs of making manifest' (536) *are* grammatical, in spite of the fact that they take dative addressees and describe attempts to make the target person 'know about' something. Moreover, 'verbs of causing to know that' can also take accusative complements (537). Hence, Wierzbicka's analysis makes incorrect predictions.

(536)   Wytłumaczyła mu geografię.
        'She explained geography to him (DAT).'

(537)   Dyrektor poinformował nas, że zamierza zwolnić organizatorów strajku.
        'The director informed us (ACC) that he intends to fire the organizers of the strike.'

I argued in section 4.2 that sentences such as (531), (532), (534) and (536) describe processes whereby an utterance or message enters the target person's sphere of awareness; the TP typically comes to know something as a result, but this effect is implicated rather than explicitly stated. This provides for a natural explanation of the grammaticality of (534) and the ungrammaticality of (535) (where the verb profiles the addressee's learning as well as the teacher's efforts), and also of the contrast between dative and accusative verbs of communication. (533) is ungrammatical because manner-of-speaking verbs such as *krzyczeć* 'to scream' profile only the production of sounds (which don't even have to be speech sounds); hence, they do not evoke the sphere of awareness, and do not normally take dative complements. One can *krzyczeć* in the middle of the wilderness without even hoping to be heard; on the other hand, *powiedzieć* 'to say, tell' clearly implies the presence of an addressee (though the addressee may be the same person as the speaker: *Powiedziała sobie, że nigdy więcej tego nie zrobi* 'She told herself that she would never do it again.').

Thirdly, Wierzbicka's analysis does not account for the role that inference and knowledge of the world play in the interpretation of sentences with datives. This may be illustrated with example (538), which, she argues, indicates that the dative has another special sense: it is used to refer to "a person whose body part is being looked at or investigated" (412).

(538)   *Adam patrzył Ewie na nogi.*   (Wierzbicka 1988: 412)
        'Adam was looking at Ewa's (DAT) legs.'

What she does not point out is that the sentence becomes much less felicitous if another part of the body is substituted for *nogi* 'legs':

(539)   ?? *Adam patrzył Ewie na łokieć/na stopy/na nos.*
        'Adam was looking at Ewa's (DAT) elbow/feet/nose.'

I observed in section 2.1 that the acceptability of (538) is due largely to its sexual overtones, which are absent in (539). Thus, what makes (538) interpretable is *shared knowledge* about which parts of the body are 'sexy', what behaviors may be considered as having a sexual significance, etc. – which, it is worth noting, is culture-specific: not all men share the typical Western male's fascination with women's legs. A sentence such as *Adam patrzył Ewie na nos* 'Adam looked at Ewa's (DAT) nose' might be appropriate if Ewa's nose was of the Cyrano type, and he was ostentatiously staring at it; given this contextual information, it would be fairly easy for the addressee to envisage how and why she may have been affected.

Wierzbicka goes on to say that this particular use can be extended to cover situations involving the inspection of a person's clothes (540), but not to possessions not worn on the body; thus, she claims, (541) is ungrammatical.

(540)   *Matka zajrzała Jasiowi do kieszeni.*   (Wierzbicka 1988: 412)
        'Mother looked into Jaś's (DAT) pocket.'

(541)   (*) *Matka zajrzała Jasiowi do szuflady.*   (Wierzbicka 1988: 412)
        'Mother looked into Jaś's (DAT) drawer.'

However, (541) is perfectly acceptable if, for example, Jaś kept personal articles in the drawer (see the discussion in 2.1), and (540) does not necessarily imply that Jaś was wearing the garment with the pocket when the mother looked into it.

What all these examples illustrate is that it is impossible to account for the distribution of the dative in purely semantic (as opposed to semanto-pragmatic) terms. The next four sentences will provide another telling illustration of the same point.

(542) Piotr położył Pawłowi rękę na ramieniu. (Wierzbicka 1988: 409)
       'Piotr put his hand on Paweł's (DAT) shoulder.'

(543) *Piotr dotknął Pawłowi ramienia. (Wierzbicka 1988: 409)
       'Piotr touched Paweł's (DAT) shoulder.'

(544) Ewa dotknęła Adamowi czoła. (Wierzbicka 1988: 414)
       'Ewa touched Adam's (DAT) forehead.'

(545) *Ewa dotknęła Adama w czoło. (Wierzbicka 1988: 414)
       'Ewa touched Adam (ACC) on the forehead.'

Wierzbicka claims on page 409 that the difference in acceptability between the first two of these sentences is due to the fact that (542), but not (543), "explicitly refers to an object or body part coming into contact with a part of a person's body". Then, on page 414, she maintains that "verbs which signal contact with a body part without explicitly referring to emotions don't allow the affected person to be treated as the primary object of the action (and to be referred to in the accusative)"; this is supposed to explain the grammaticality of (544) and the ungrammaticality of (545).

There are two serious errors in this formulation. First, the ungrammaticality of (545) has nothing to do with the use of the accusative case, as illustrated by the full acceptability of (546); it is due to the fact that it is impossible to specify the active zone of *dotknąć* 'to touch' (i.e. the part of the body directly involved) by means of a prepositional phrase with *w* 'in': in other words, *dotknąć* does not collocate with *w czoło* 'on the forehead'.

(546) Ewa dotknęła Adama.
       'Ewa touched Adam (ACC).'

Secondly, and more importantly, if (544) is acceptable because it overtly signals emotional affectedness as well as contact with a body part, why is (543) unacceptable?

Before embarking on an explanation of this obvious contradiction, I would like to point out that although there is a difference in the acceptability of these two sentences, it is not as clear-cut as the starred-unstarred dichotomy suggests. The use of the dative with *dotknąć* 'to touch' is a very unprototypical usage. The verb merely indicates that a trajector came into contact with a landmark; it does not indicate that the landmark underwent any change as a result. Consequently, the target person is affected in exactly the same way as the part of his body that came into contact with the trajector. Since there is no reason to distinguish between the target person's affectedness and the patient's affectedness, the most natural construal is to use the accusative to indicate that the whole person is the patient of the action (recall that there is a preference for assigning participant status to humans over inanimate entities and to wholes rather than to parts). The use of the dative is possible, but extremely unprototypical, and being far removed from the prototype, it is extremely sensitive to various pragmatic factors. What we have, therefore, are subtle gradations of acceptability rather than a clear cut-off point beyond which everything is ungrammatical. For example, (547) is better than (543), because, like (538), it is open to a sexual interpretation, which is not very likely in (543), given that mainstream Polish culture is heterosexual and that the shoulder, for most people, is not a sexually interesting part of the body. By varying the sex of the participants and the body part involved, we obtain intermediate degrees of acceptability (548-549).

(547)   ? *Piotr dotknął Ewie uda.*
        'Piotr touched Ewa's (DAT) thigh.'

(548)   ?? *Ewa dotknęła Krysi uda.*
        'Ewa touched Krysia's (DAT) thigh.'

(549)   ?? *Piotr dotknął Ewie policzka.*
        'Piotr touched Ewa's (DAT) cheek.'

What, then, makes (544) a fairly acceptable sentence? A clue to the answer is provided by the fact that it seems to be acceptable only on the interpretation that Ewa touched Adam's forehead to determine whether he had a fever. Hence, the sentence describes an action which involves more than just touching: it is an act of caring for a sick person. The motivation for the use of the dative in (544) is thus exactly the same as in (550).

(550) a. *Ewa zmierzyła Adamowi temperaturę.*
          'Ewa took Adam's (DAT) temperature.

(550) b. *Ewa opatrzyła Adamowi ranę.*
          'Ewa dressed Adam's (DAT) wound.'

(550) c. *Ewa zmieniła Adamowi opatrunek.*
          'Ewa changed the dressing on Adam's (DAT) wound.'

(550) d. *Ewa pobrała Adamowi krew.*
          'Ewa took a blood sample from Adam (DAT).'

To summarize: Wierzbicka's account, though very insightful, does not adequately account for all the data. By restricting her analysis to sentence meaning only, she misses out the important role that contextual information and encyclopedic knowledge play in the interpretation of dative constructions. She makes a number of unnecessary distinctions (thirty-one uses is rather excessive – and the paper doesn't even address the problem of "governed" and "ethic" datives!), and she makes no attempt to show the relationships between the various uses. Moreover, she focuses entirely on "objective" motivation, and doesn't allow for the role of construal. This leads to problematic explanations of the contrast between nominative and dative experiencers when a verb allows both, and as far as I can see precludes any explanation of the special implications of sentences with "ethic" datives; it also makes it impossible to explain the difference between dative and accusative addressees.

7.1.2. Miller

Localistic approaches to grammar have a natural affinity to cognitive analyses: both seek to explain form in terms of semantic structure, and both claim that semantic structure is best represented by appealing to spatial concepts (cf. the role of image schemata and spatial metaphors in cognitive grammar).[102] I will discuss a cognitive approach to case expressed entirely in image-schematic terms in the next section; in this section, I will deal with non-cognitive localistic approaches, and specifically, with Miller's (1974) analysis of the Russian dative, which will provide a good illustration of the strengths and weaknesses of such approaches.

Miller proposes a generative-semantics-style framework in which superficial case endings are derived from underlying locative and directional constructions; surface representations, he maintains, differ from deep structure because they also convey information about surface syntax (e.g. surface syntactic functions such as S, O, and IO). He proposes the following semantic characterizations of the Russian cases:

> The accusative signifies movement to an object, to a position inside, on, underneath, behind, above an object; the dative signifies movement towards or up to an object, but not into one of the positions just mentioned...; the genitive signifies location at an object, movement from an object or movement as far as an object; the instrumental signifies 'within the borders of' – this allows for what Kuryłowicz calls the instrument of 'traversed space' and for the sociative instrumental; the propositional signifies 'place where'. The nominative, I believe (along with Fillmore), is the one case ending which has only a Satzfunktion, since its role is to indicate which noun in the sentence is the topic. (247)

His whole case is based on a localist analysis of the verb *dat'* 'to give', which, he argues, can be represented as movement of an object from the giver to the receiver. Stative verbs which take dative complements are derived from underlying directional sentences. Thus, he claims that the three sentences in (551) have the same underlying structure (and, hence, by implication, that they are synonymous), the last sentence being the most faithful reflection of the semantic structure and the first sentence its least faithful reflection. He also points out that the first sentence, but not the other two, could mean that Petr tried and succeeded in recalling the song. This leads him to conclude that (551a) is ambiguous, and propose a different underlying structure for the agentive (one with a superordinate causative predicate).

(551) a. *Petr vspomnil ètu pesnju.* (Miller 1974: 250-251)
'Petr (NOM) remembered this song (ACC).'

(551) b. *Petru   vspomnialas'   èta pesnja.*
Petr:DAT remembered itself this song:NOM
'Petr remembered this song.'

(551) c. *Petru   prišla na pamjat' èta pesnja.*
Petr:DAT came to memory this song:NOM
'Petr remembered this song.'

A cognitive account of the same data would differ in several respects. First, it is not true that (551a-551c) are synonymous. Although they may describe the same situation, they construe it differently, and hence differ in meaning. The first sentence is not ambiguous, but vague: although a nominative noun is prototypically agentive, it can also refer to a participant who plays other roles, as long as the latter is the most prominent entity in the situations described by the sentence. (551b) and (551c) also differ in meaning: in (551c), *èta pesnja* 'this song' plays a more active role than in (551b), since it is construed as having independent existence outside of Peter's sphere of awareness and being capable of moving around on its own.

Miller's analysis cannot account for the subtle differences in meaning between these sentences. It also cannot account for their syntactic form – and he is disarmingly frank about it: all he has to say about "the processes by which one is to proceed from the deep semantic structures which have been postulated to the surface structures" is that "at the moment these processes are unknown" (258). Furthermore, his analysis does not provide a satisfactory account of the semantic differences between the cases. For example, the localistic definitions quoted above do not distinguish between the dative and the accusative – or, for that matter, between these two and the genitive – which he tacitly acknowledges in his account of the semantic contrast between (552a) and (552b).

(552) a. *Petr nenavidit Borisa.* (Miller 1974: 252)
'Petr (NOM) hates Boris (ACC).'

(552) b. *Boris nenavisten Petru.*
'Petr (DAT) hates Boris (NOM).'

The first, he maintains, describes a situation in which "hate passes from Peter to Boris"; the second, a situation in which something ("hatefulness") passes from Boris to Peter. Then he adds, "the occurrence of a dative case inflexion or an accusative case inflexion is not significant for present purposes, since they are both directional" (253).

Miller's treatment of synonymy is likewise rather cavalier. He acknowledges that in earlier work he assumed that the three sentences in (553) were paraphrases, and then comments that "this assumption is clearly incorrect in the light of the preceding remarks about direction and the dative case" (253) – as if synonymy was something one could *assume*! What this comment amounts to is a statement that whether or not two sentences are synonymous is not a fact of language, but something that is predicted by the theory.

(553) a. *Petr   ponimaet   teoriju.*   (Miller 1974: 253)
Petr:NOM understands theory:ACC
'Petr understands the theory.'

(553) b. *Petru   ponjatna   teorija.*
Petr:DAT understandable theory:NOM
'Petr understands the theory.'

(553) c. *U Petra   ponimanie   teorii.*
at Petr:GEN understanding:NOM theory:GEN
'Petr understands the theory.'

I argued earlier (section 2.2.11; see also 7.1.5 below) why the characterization of the Polish dative as an allative case is inadequate. Such an analysis is somewhat more convincing in the case of Russian, which allows allative uses which are impossible in Polish. Still, there are clearly non-allative verbs in Russian which govern the dative – e.g. all the stative verbs for which Miller postulates an allative analysis. It is possible that they should be analyzed as involving subjective motion,[103] but such a claim should be based on language data rather than decreed by the linguist.

7.1.3. Smith

This and the next two sections are devoted to a comparison of the approach proposed here with other cognitive treatments of case. I will begin with Michael Smith's (1985, 1987, 1989, 1992) study of the contrast between the accusative and the dative in German. As mentioned in the preceding section, his description is expressed entirely in image-schematic terms. He proposes the path-goal schema (figure 16) as the basic meaning of the accusative case. The two elements of this schema, i.e. the directional nature of the path and the fact that it reaches the goal, motivate extensions of the basic sense: directionality is the prototype for the more abstract notion of asymmetry inherent in transitive events (an action is conceptualized as movement along an abstract chain from the head to the tail), and the fact that the path reaches the goal makes it possible to extend the category to convey the notion of completeness.

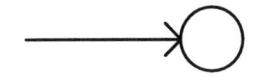

Figure 16. The ACC schema

The German dative, according to Smith, is associated with three image schemata: 'movement from source', 'container-content', and 'link'. However, these do not cover all the uses of the case, so he proposes a more general meaning which subsumes all dative usages, namely, "any situation ... in which the ACC configuration is lacking" (1992: 395). Experiencers, he argues, can be subsumed under the link schema since they are a "kind of conduit for the flow of energy in a prototypical transitive clause" (407), i.e. they are both affected by the action *and* are actual or potential actors in their own right. He proposes a special variant of the link schema (figure 17) as a representation of the semantic structure of 'experiencer', arguing that it reflects the two-sided nature of experiencers and the causal connection between the agent's action and the experiencer's reaction.

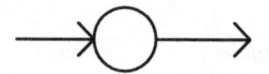

Figure 17. Smith's experiencer schema

Smith's analysis is certainly interesting, but nevertheless it presents certain problems. His treatment of the dative makes it a wastebasket category: anything that isn't accusative is dative. Since the definition of the accusative that he proposes ("tail of an action chain or action chain analogue", i.e. Langacker's definition of direct object) is very abstract, the distinction between the two cases gets lost in clouds of abstraction. Secondly, his analysis of experiencers is not very convincing. I don't see why energy should be seen as flowing "through" the dative participant. If experiencers are to be defined relative to their position on the action chain/action chain analogue, then surely Rudzka-Ostyn's (1992) treatment of them as endpoints is intuitively more plausible.

In spite of its weaknesses, Smith's approach is certainly worth pursuing. Perhaps the greatest merit of his analysis is the fact that it employs the same conceptual apparatus to deal with the contrast between the accusative and the dative in both the clausal and the prepositional realm. He argues very convincingly that a preposition governs a particular case because it is semantically compatible with that case; when a preposition co-occurs with more than one case, the combinations differ in meaning in ways that are predictable from the meanings of the cases.

7.1.4. Janda

Janda 1993 is the first book-length study of the semantics of case in Slavic languages conducted in a cognitive framework. Janda provides detailed descriptions of the Czech dative and the Russian instrumental, and brief discussions of the Russian dative and the Czech instrumental for the sake of comparison. The following discussion will concentrate on her analysis of the Czech dative.

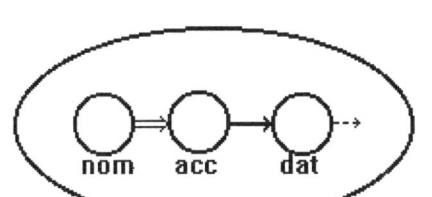

Figure 18. Janda's schema 1

Like Smith, Janda defines case categories in image-schematic terms, but she also provides, for each schema, a "prose" description equivalent to the pictorial representation. She proposes two basic schemas ("paradigmatic variants") for the dative category, each with a number of syntagmatic variants (i.e. similar meanings which occur in different construction types: for example, the dative in sentences such as *Umarła mu matka* 'His (DAT) mother died' is a syntagmatic variant of the dative in the more prototypical three-argument construction *Bandyci zabili mu matkę* 'The bandits killed his (DAT) mother'). The dative prototype, she maintains, is the indirect object in sentences with verbs of giving and their synonyms, and is defined by the following scenario: "A nominative acts on an accusative to bring it to a dative. The dative retains independent status." (53) The corresponding pictorial representation is provided in Figure 18.

The other paradigmatic variant is the free dative, represented graphically in Figure 19. The scenario that she proposes for this sense is "[a] nominative acts on an accusative in a dative's sphere of control in a setting" (53).

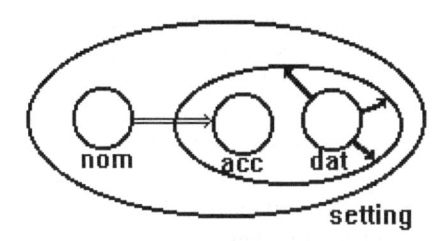

Figure 19. Janda's schema 2

Janda thus maintains the traditional distinction between "free" and "governed" datives, although it is not at all clear why she does so. I argued in Chapter 2 that the personal sphere also includes one's possessions; giving, therefore, is naturally construed as adding an item to another individual's personal sphere (specifically, the sphere of influence, or, in Janda's terminology, the sphere of control) and hence the sphere of influence is a salient aspect of the semantic description of verbs of giving. Thus, there is no need to assign a different schema to dative nominals occurring with verbs of giving. I have also shown that, at least in Polish, there is a continuum of "governedness", rather than two discrete classes of dative constructions – and Czech doesn't seem to differ from Polish in this respect.

Janda acknowledges that the two senses grade off into each other, and even states that "it appears that schema 1 is merely a degenerate version of schema 2, in which the personal sphere has been collapsed" (90). But then she goes on to say that "[t]he dative of the indirect object must be recognized as a potential agent of a further action, but the same cannot be said of the free dative. All that is required of the free dative is that is that it experience the action; it need not carry it any farther" (*ibid.*). She doesn't explain, however, why the potential to be the agent in another event is so important, and why only indirect-object datives have this property: surely (554), a sentence with a "free" dative, can be interpreted as indicating that Marek can now do something with the knife..

(554)   *Alicja naostrzyła Markowi nóż.*
        'Alicja sharpened the knife for Marek (DAT).'

Furthermore, Janda's semantic characterization of the dative is too general, as it will also accommodate nominative and accusative experiencers. The governed dative in two-argument constructions is defined as follows: "The nominative acts on a dative in a setting. The dative retains independent status" (55). This subsumes situations such as that described in (555), unless we postulate that the non-subject participant here does not enjoy independent status, which seems entirely arbitrary (Magda certainly is a "potential agent of a further action").

(555)   *Zachowanie Piotra rozzłościło Magdę.*
        'Piotr's behavior (NOM) annoyed Magda (ACC).'

Finally, Janda also does not seem to appreciate the crucial role that general knowledge and pragmatics play in motivating the use of the dative case. Although she acknowledges the existence of "pragmatic" uses of the dative ("ethic" and "emotional" datives, "dative of solidarity"), these are distant relatives of the closely intertwined "semantic" family. This leads her to some rather unsatisfactory claims. For example, she analyzes (556) as an instance of "intransitive taking" (66), presumably because the gas moves away from its original location. However, what is relevant for the dative participant in (556) is not the whereabouts of gas particles as such, but the fact that the house might blow up (or possibly the effect of the leak on the gas bill). To arrive at this interpretation, the listener must integrate semantic information from the sentence with knowledge about gas, explosions, gas meters, etc.

(556)   *Uniká nám   plyn   v bytè.*
        leaks us:DAT gas: NOM in apartment:LOC
        'We have a gas leak in the apartment.'

Janda also has nothing to say about the subtle interplay of linguistic and non-linguistic knowledge of the type that have been discussed in sections 2.1 and 7.1.1

above. Czech datives may very well be quite different from their Polish cousins, but surely, even for Czech, it is not enough to say that "all that is required is that the dative's sphere of control be affected in any way at all" (81).

Thus, although her analysis is very revealing in many respects, particularly the structuring of the network of senses that she proposes (prototype + paradigmatic variants + syntagmatic variants of the latter), her analysis suffers from two shortcomings: it does not show how the dative contrasts with other case categories (and hence she can get away with sweeping generalizations such as the one cited in the paragraph above), and it doesn't provide for a systematic integration of semantic, pragmatic, and non-linguistic knowledge.

7.1.5. Rudzka-Ostyn

Rudzka-Ostyn 1992 is the only cognitive study of the Polish dative that I know of. It is a very insightful analysis of the reflexive *sobie* (including the "ethic" or "expressive" uses of the type discussed in section 2.3), from which one can infer how she would treat the dative category as a whole.

It is encouraging to note that Rudzka-Ostyn's analysis and my own converge on a number of points, although we have worked independently of each other (I did not come across her paper until the present study was nearly complete). She also postulates a dative "domain of control" and hints at the existence of a "domain or responsibility/interest" in a footnote (p. 339). The dative category, she maintains, has prototype structure, and she repeatedly stresses the importance of construal:

> The prototypical construal highlights the experiencer as a recipient of a concrete object that enters his domain of control, here strongly associated with his actual or future location. As we move away from the prototype, the objects received become increasingly less concrete; spatial accessibility gives way to perceptual and cognitive accessibility. At a certain point, what is accessed is some unspecified effect that the actions might produce. The actions themselves change from volitional to accidental, but even when volitional, the dative referent is not necessarily their objective and intended endpoint. Many peripheral variants of *sobie* code referents that acquire this status only via the speaker's subjective construal of the situation. (362)

She explicitly states that the "expressive" *sobie* is meaningful, and either serves to "emphasize the limitation of the experience to the dative sphere of control" or to designate "the subjectively construed recipient of the effects of the given state or event" (358); in the latter case, the speaker "subjectively superimpose[s] the role of experiencer onto the nominative referent" (361).

However, Rudzka-Ostyn proposes a rather different semantic characterization of the dative which in my opinion is inadequate. She regards the use of the dative with verbs of giving as prototypical, and bases her definition on this prototype: "the referent of the dative/indirect object serves not only as the end-point of the transfer but also as an entity that can be affected by it, that can react, mentally or physically, to whatever enters its 'domain of control'" (336). Thus, according to Rudzka-Ostyn, the dative conflates two notions: that of "action's terminal" and "affectee". Other uses are extensions from the recipient prototype: for example the transfer can be metaphorical, the entity transferred may be an action rather than an object, etc.

Rudzka-Ostyn's insistence that the dative is essentially an allative case lands her in the same problems as other allative descriptions (for example Miller's). First of all, many uses of the dative simply do not fit the allative schema. Although the notion of movement towards the TP is certainly present in sentences containing verbs of transfer, it is not clear that it is contributed by the dative and not the verb. It is absent in sentences with verbs of creation and verbs of preparing for use. Rudzka-Ostyn acknowledges this and suggests that in this case "the concept of accessibility may suffice" (343); these uses, in her opinion, are metonymic extensions from the prototype. Moreover, the dative is also used when the verb profiles movement *away* from the TP, as in (557).

(557) *Ktoś ukradł Magdzie pieniądze.*
Someone:NOM stole Magda:DAT money:ACC
'Someone stole the money from Magda.'

According to Rudzka-Ostyn, in these sentences the patient of the action moves outside the TP's sphere of control, but the effects of the action are construed as moving towards the recipient. This is not an unreasonable proposal, but one would need some evidence before accepting it.

The allative analysis is even more problematic when the verb is stative, as in example (558) and (559), and for "ethic" datives, as exemplified in (560).

(558) *Magdzie było zimno.*
Magda:DAT it was cold
'Magda was cold.'

(559) *Człowiek (jest) człowiekowi wilkiem.*
man:NOM is man:DAT wolf:INST
'Man is a wolf to man.'

(560) *Czytam sobie książkę.*
I read REFL:DAT book:ACC
'I am (quietly) reading (my) book (and enjoying myself).'

Rudzka-Ostyn claims that the first two examples, the verb, though normally stative, acquires dynamic properties in the presence of the dative; this creates "an impression of transitivity" (356) and the dative participant is viewed as a subjective endpoint. Similarly, in sentences like (560) the dative participant is to be regarded as "a subjectively construed recipient of the effects of the given state or event" (358). It seems that all the motivation for this explanation is theory-internal:

having once assumed that the dative prototypically designates the recipient, she attempts to relate the non-central uses to this prototype – even when this amounts to trying to fit a round peg into a square hole.

Another problem with the Rudzka-Ostyn's analysis is that it does not provide a satisfactory account of the contrast between the accusative and the dative – although at least she is aware of the problem and does address it:

> It is this dual role of an action's terminal and an affectee (without being acted on) that distinguishes many dative variants from the accusative case. A typical referent of the accusative is also affected by the given action and often serves as its end-point but, unlike a dative referent, it is (1) acted upon, and (2) its ability to react the action's effects – even when objectively there – is disregarded. (336)

> A number of linguists have raised objections to the concept of affectedness [as a semantic characterization of the dative – ED], pointing out that the entities profiled by the direct objects/accusatives are also 'affected'. Although these are pertinent observations, one may still want to keep the concept, but specify that in the case of datives it often combines with that of recipient. In the case of accusatives, the same concept will combine with the notion of manipulation (at least in the prototypical instances) and that of direct involvement in the process instigated by the agent. (365)

These criteria will distinguish prototypical datives and prototypical accusatives, but they simply do not work for less central members of the two categories. The accusative case is often used to mark a "terminal" participant not manipulated by the agent, as in (561) and numerous examples in chapter 4; and it is fully compatible with predicates that indicate that the patient reacted in a specified way, as in (562-563). Conversely, the dative can be used to code a participant that is the direct recipient of the agent's action, and hence "acted on", as in (564).

(561)   *Piotr zawołał Adama.*
        'Piotr called (summoned) Adam (ACC).'

(562)   *Piotr zmusił Adama do wyjazdu.*
        'Piotr forced Adam (ACC) to leave.'

(563)   *Piotr nauczył Adama angielskiego.*
        'Piotr taught Adam (ACC) English.'

(564)   *Piotr   obciął Adamowi   włosy.*
        Piotr:NOM cut   Adam:DAT hair:ACC
        'Piotr cut Adam's hair.'

7.2. Schemas and prototypes

The primary purpose of this study was to show that *cases have meanings*. These can be defined either in terms of prototypes and extensions from the prototype, or as overarching schemas. The former approach is favored by Lakoff (1982, 1987), while Langacker (1987a) prefers the latter; however, as Langacker himself acknowledges (371ff), they are complementary rather than mutually exclusive.

The prototypical meanings of the cases are easier to establish, and can be found in any traditional description (Bartnicka-Dąbkowska, Jaworski & Sinielnikoff 1964, Benni et al 1923, Szober 1959): the nominative prototypically designates the agent of the action, the accusative is used to refer to the patient; the dative, to the person indirectly affected by a change in a person or object belonging to his personal sphere.[104]

I have shown in earlier work (Dąbrowska 1987 and 1994a) that cases form networks of senses, and explored the links between the various uses in some detail. I will not repeat the arguments here, but a few comments about the sources of prototype effects within the dative category are in order.

Dative nominals exhibit four types of prototype effects. The first is due to the fact that some participants are more likely to be thought of as possessing a personal sphere than others. The personal sphere is prototypically associated with humans; other kinds of participants (organizations, animals, aliens, etc.) are sometimes credited with one as well, but there is often doubt about whether they are really capable of experiencing the results of the process designated by the verb, and this leads to doubts about the acceptability of sentences with datives. Wierzbicka finds (565) odd because she thinks a dog will not feel pleased when improvements are made to its home. I find it perfectly natural, perhaps because, being the proud owner of a beautiful cat, I am quite willing to attribute human emotions to animals.

(565)   (?) *Pomalowałem budę   Reksowi.*   (Wierzbicka 1988: 402)
         I painted   kennel:ACC Rex:DAT
         'I painted Rex's kennel for him.'

The second source of prototype effects is a consequence of the fact that some regions of the personal sphere are cognitively more basic than others. Thus, the sphere of influence is more basic than the more abstract sphere of potency, which comprises actions and processes that one can influence or whose occurrence is contingent on one's will as well as the people and objects one has control over. The sphere of empathy and the sphere of awareness are likewise more abstract than the sphere of influence, and are at least partially understood in metaphorical terms, whereas the sphere of influence is more directly linked to our experience of objects.

Prototype effects of the third type result from the fact that some objects and people belonging to the sphere of influence and the sphere of empathy are more central within these spheres than others. Body parts are more central elements of the sphere of influence than the clothes one is wearing, which in turn are more central than other personal possessions, which are more central than non-personal possessions, objects one is holding, objects one is about to use, etc. Similarly, a child is usually considered more central in the sphere of empathy than a spouse, who is in turn more central than siblings, grandparents, and best friends; more distant relatives and other acquaintances occupy peripheral regions in the sphere of empathy, if they are included in it at all. We have also seen (cf. section 2.1) that both of these spheres have fuzzy boundaries, in that what is actually included depends on the speaker's conceptualization of the event.

The prototype structure of elements belonging to the personal sphere explains why sentences with datives differ in acceptability according to how central the patient of the action is in the sphere of empathy or the sphere of influence. One's hand is a more central element than one's shoe, which in turn is more central than the bumper of one's car; hence the gradience in acceptability exhibited by the sentences in (566). Similarly, one's daughter is central in one's sphere of empathy, while friends and acquaintances occupy the peripheries, and, as a consequence, (567a) is fully acceptable, (567b) is borderline, and (567c) is rather odd.

(566) a. *Pies   polizał mi   rękę.*
           dog:NOM licked   me:DAT hand:ACC
           'The dog licked my hand.'

(566) b. ? *Pies   polizał mi   but.*   (Wierzbicka 1988: 402)
           dog:NOM licked   me:DAT shoe:ACC
           'The dog licked my shoe.'

(566) c. ?? *Pies   polizał mi   zderzak.*
           dog:NOM licked   me:DAT bumper:ACC
           'The dog licked my [car's] bumper.'

(567) a. *Córka   wyjechała mu   do Ameryki.*
           daughter:NOM went away him:DAT to America:GEN
           'His daughter has gone away to America.'

(567) b. ? *Najlepszy przyjaciel   wyjechał   mu   do Ameryki*
           best   friend:NOM went away him:DAT to America:GEN
           'His best friend has gone away to America.'

(567) c. ?? *Kolega   wyjechał   mu   do Ameryki.*
           friend:NOM went away him:DAT to America:GEN
           'A friend of his has gone away to America.'

Finally, prototype effects also arise as a result of the fact that some events are more likely to indirectly affect the target person than others. Generally, change-of-state verbs yield more acceptable dative constructions than verbs which designate actions which do not result in any perceptible change in the patient, especially when the patient occupies a peripheral position in the personal sphere. Thus, if the verb in (566c) is replaced with one that indicates that the patient was permanently marred as a result of the action, the resulting sentence is perfectly acceptable (568). Again, intermediate degrees of acceptability can be obtained by manipulating the extent and durability of the change.

(568)   Pies   podrapał mi   zderzak.
dog:NOM scratched me:DAT bumper:ACC
'A dog has scratched my (car's) bumper.'

I would like to conclude the discussion of case prototypes with some observations about the *functionality* of prototype organization. To be a feasible communication tool, language must be flexible enough to describe an infinite variety of situations, both real and imagined, and it must provide a means of describing these situations quickly, i.e. in as few words as possible. To be learnable and usable, it must make do with a relatively small number of grammatical categories. The clustering of attributes in prototypes is an efficient way of meeting these conflicting demands, since it allows users to communicate a great deal of information about typical situations very quickly. Less typical situations are accommodated by extensions from the prototype.[105] Their untypical nature is usually clear from the context, but there are also linguistic ways of signaling this (e.g. passive morphology on the verb when the normally less prominent participant becomes subject, the presence of both nominative and dative marking in nominative-dative constructions, the lack of a nominal which controls verb agreement in impersonal constructions).

Category schemas are somewhat more difficult to define than prototypes, but the relevant characterizations can be formulated as follows: the nominative designates the most prominent entity in a relationship; the accusative designates the object acted on by the agent (or "the tail of an action chain or action chain analogue"); the dative designates the target person, i.e. the person affected by a process occurring in his personal sphere.

It will be clear from the characterization given above that the dative category is actually "larger" than the proposed superschema, since the latter does not subsume the allative uses. These, I argued in section 2.2.11, bear family resemblance to a number of other uses; however, I suggested that generalizing the schema to accommodate the allative sense would make it too general.[106] The proposed description captures the fact that the "pure" allatives are peripheral, highly constrained uses; and the level of generality at which it is expressed makes it possible to formulate significant generalizations about the dative.

It must be stressed, however, that although the target person superschema subsumes all the remaining uses of the dative, it does not follow that, once we have established this general meaning, our job of describing the semantics of the dative is done. 'Target person' is just one node in a large network of schemas of various degrees of generality; it cannot supplant the local schemas because it is not specific enough to predict the linguistic contexts in which the dative can occur or the particular meanings that it conveys in these contexts. For example, there is no reason (other than linguistic convention) why Polish should have the three variants of the "ethic dative" discussed in section 2.3 (to express empathy, self-determination, and to signal inclusion in the sphere of influence in imperatives), and only these three; and, moreover, there is no reason (other than linguistic convention) why these particular uses should be almost entirely restricted to personal pronouns. The conventions of Polish might well have been different: for example, one can imagine an ethic dative evoking the sphere of awareness in the same way that the established uses evoke the sphere of potency and the sphere of empathy, which would allow one to say

(569) Piotr   biegał mi   po   ogrodzie.
       Piotr-NOM ran   me:DAT all over garden:LOC

to mean 'I was aware that Piotr was running all over the garden' (rather than 'Piotr was running all over my garden'). The category superschema would not change if this new use were added to the inventory of local schemas – or, for that matter, if a few of the existing uses were lost. By the same token, the use of the dative as opposed to the nominative or the accusative with specific verbs conveys subtle shades of meaning, which, though compatible with the specifications of the abstract superschema, cannot be predicted from it: they are additional aspects of meaning which have become conventionally associated with particular uses. Local schemas are not simply contextual variants of the superschema: the linguistic knowledge embodied in them is not deducible from the latter, and they must be listed in the grammar alongside the more general formulations.

This is where the network model is superior to the abstractionist approach to case semantics briefly outlined in section 1.1.2. A general formulation such as Jakobson's [+DIRECTIONAL/ASCRIPTIVE, -QUANTIFYING, +MARGINAL/ PERIPHERAL] is simply too abstract to predict the full range of uses (cf. Taylor 1990). Since the network contains both global and local schemas, it can accommodate the unity as well as the diversity of the various uses. The global schemas play primarily an organizing role – they hold the category together – while the local schemas are used in assembling novel expressions (cf. Langacker 1988).

7.3. The status of semantic roles

In the introductory chapter I maintained that the case grammar approach to the semantics of case – that of beginning the analysis by postulating a set of primitives and attempting to fit the data into this framework – was fundamentally misguided. I argued that a much more promising approach is to begin by examining the range of uses associated with a particular "surface" case and exploring the relationships between them. However, I have used case grammar notions such as agent, patient, and experiencer throughout this study, and so some comments about the status of these constructs are in order.

I take it as self-evident that people are capable of perceiving relationships between objects in their environment, including the relationships between the various participants in a process. For example, having formed the concept of an activity such as driving, they are aware that it takes two to drive, and that the two participants (driver and vehicle) are involved in the action in rather different ways. Furthermore, they are able to conceive these relationships at various levels of abstraction: that is to say, they can think of a particular situation as 'Dr Pincombe driving his old red Trabant', 'driver maneuvering vehicle', or 'agent manipulating patient'.

Concepts traditionally referred to as semantic roles (case roles, theta roles, "deep" cases) form the highest level in this hierarchy of relationships that we extract from our experience of interactions in the world. These notions are not specifically linguistic, but rather pertain to the way we perceive and think about events in our environment. The various relationships differ in salience: some (such as agent and patient) are well-established concepts, while others (such as beneficiary or cause) are rather less prominent. Because of these differences, the set is essentially open-ended, and there may even be a fair amount of variation between individuals with regard to which schemas they extract, though one would expect basic concepts such as agent, patient, instrument and experiencer to be universal. Langacker compares these fairly abstract schemas (which he calls "role archetypes") to the highest peaks in a mountain range which "coexist with others that may be significant despite their lesser salience" (1991a: 237).

What then is the relationship between participant roles and case inflections? To answer this question, we must first observe that while the number of case categories available in any one language is fairly small, the number of relationships that speakers want to talk about is indefinitely large; moreover, the latter do not fall into a small number of neatly defined classes. Thus polysemy is inevitable if language is to be a viable communicative tool. Semantic role archetypes, I suggest, are simply salient local schemas. However, because of their salience, they enjoy a special status in the networks to which they belong: they function as cognitive reference points around which the other, less salient uses – the lower peaks in Langacker's mountain range – tend to cluster. Or, to coin a new metaphor, they are the seeds around which case categories grow, rather like crystals.

Thus we can see that from a strictly linguistic point of view, semantic roles are no more than glorified local schemas. This realization puts the whole issue of the inventory of semantic roles in a different perspective. Although the more salient relationships are more likely to be grammaticalized, different languages may well select different category centers (and hence have different inventories of morphological cases or their equivalents). It seems probable that the very fact that a particular language selects a particular semantic role as the center of a case category will render it more salient to its speakers, whatever its original status. In any case, it will certainly become introspectively more accessible,[107] and hence more likely to be chosen by the analyst as one of a small group of privileged relationships. It is no accident that the traditional inventories of "deep" cases did not include the target person role. The notion of "target person" is not as salient as that of agent or patient, and it is not grammaticalized in English: and since most of the inventories of deep cases were compiled by English-speaking linguists, it has been overlooked.

7.4. The importance of conventional imagery

Complementary to the major theme of this study – that cases have meanings – is the claim that the choice of a particular case form is semantically motivated. The form-meaning correlation is easy to establish for prototypical uses, but as we move away from the prototype, we encounter areas of overlap between cases. In these "disputed territories" the choice of case category will depend to a much greater degree on how the situation is organized for expressive purposes.

Sometimes the language allows the speaker to choose from a set of contrasting forms. The different forms correspond to different construals, i.e. different ways of viewing the situation – and hence to different meanings. We have seen in chapter 3 that the verb *chcieć* 'to want' can take either nominative or dative experiencers ('Janek wants to eat' can be expressed either as *Janek chce jeść* or as *Jankowi chce się jeść*) and that the two structures differ in meaning in ways predictable from the meanings of the cases. Similarly, the use of the "ethic" dative in *Nie płacz mi już* 'Now don't cry [my little one]' (see the discussion in 2.3.3) conveys nuances not present in the sentence without the dative.

In most cases, however, even when more than one conceptualization is in principle possible, the grammar requires a particular choice – in other words, it imposes a particular perspective on the situation. This, however, does not mean that grammar is "autonomous", or independent of semantics. For one thing, there are usually good reasons for choosing that particular perspective rather than another. Even more importantly, the grammatical choice reflects a conceptualization: there is an image behind the form. For example, sentences (570a-570b) construe similar situations in different ways. The verb in (570b), *smakować* 'to be tasty', I observed in section 3.5, profiles the taste qualities of food, and the dative places them in the TP's sphere of awareness. The verb in (570a), *lubić* 'to like', designates the experiencer's attitudes towards the food; hence, it is the experiencer rather than the object of experience that is the most prominent element of the conceptualization. We saw in section 3.5 that the differences in construal make *lubić* a more suitable lexical choice when one wants to say something about the experiencer's taste preferences, and *smakować* when one wishes to describe the taste sensations that a particular serving of food provokes in the person who eats it.

(570) a. *Magda   lubi lody   poziomkowe.*
Magda:NOM likes ice-cream:ACC wild strawberry
'Magda likes wild strawberry ice-cream.'

(570) b. *Magdzie   smakują   lody   poziomkowe.*
        Magda:DAT taste   ice-cream:NOM wild strawberry
        'Magda likes wild strawberry ice-cream.'

I have argued throughout this study that when grammatical distinctions cut across semantic classes, they nearly always serve to convey finer semantic distinctions within those classes. Thus, the contrast between the dative and the nominative helps to highlight differences between individuals who consciously appraise an object and those who merely follow a natural inclination, those who resolve to follow a particular course of action and those who allow themselves to be led by instinct, and so on. Similarly, the contrast between the dative and the accusative serves to accentuate the distinction between individuals who are merely lied to and those who are actually misled by an untruthful statement, or such fine nuances as the relevance of differences in the social status of the participants in the speech act designated by the verb.

I would like to conclude this section by anticipating a possible objection to the approach proposed here. Proponents of autonomous syntax would probably allege that the argument put forward in this study is circular: first it is claimed that form reflects meaning, and then, when possible counterexamples arise, semantic structures are postulated for them which match the proposed meanings. Since semantic structures are not readily accessible, my opponents might claim, the argument is difficult to falsify.

My response, of course, will be that the argument *is* falsifiable. It would be shown to be false if, for example, a verb allowed both nominative and dative experiencers, and the dative experiencer was more agentive than the nominative – i.e. if her involvement in the action was more volitional and/or she had more control over the process designated by the verb and/or she expended effort to sustain it. This, as we have seen in chapter 3, is never the case. Similarly, the analysis proposed here would also be shown to be incorrect if a verb which specifically asserted that the inactive human participant underwent a change of state as a result of the agent's action required a dative target. This likewise never happens. (We have seen in chapter 4 that many sentences with dative verbs strongly suggest that the target was transformed in some way, but this, I argued, is implicated rather than asserted.)

The argument, we might add, appears circular only if one *assumes* that grammar is autonomous. If, however, we look at the data with an unprejudiced eye, we will discover that in the vast majority of instances, the correlation between form and meaning is quite intimate. It is thus perfectly legitimate to begin the analysis by establishing the regular form-meaning correspondences, and then see if the results can be applied to the less clear instances. I hope I managed to convince the reader that they can indeed.

7.5. Motivation and predictability

One important point often made by cognitive linguists (e.g. Langacker 1987a, Lakoff 1987) is that motivation and arbitrariness is not an all-or-nothing affair. Language is not *fully* predictable. Given that *ukłonić się* 'to bow, greet' and *pozdrowić* 'to greet' are synonyms, we cannot predict that they will have the same syntactic properties (and in fact, as we have seen in section 4.2.7, they do not: *ukłonić się* takes dative objects and *pozdrowić* requires the accusative). On the other hand, true exceptions are extremely rare. Of all the verbs that have looked at in the preceding chapters, the nearest we have come to true exceptions were the verbs *zwymyślać* 'to abuse', *(ze)lżyć* 'to revile', and *wyzywać/wyzwać* 'to call [names]', which take accusative objects even though they designate the hurling of verbal insults rather than the effects these produce in the person at whom they are leveled. However, as we have seen in section 4.2.6, even in this case we can attest some residual motivation, and hence their object-selection properties are not entirely arbitrary. I suggested above that the overwhelming majority of the less-than-fully motivated usages arise in situations where although more than one construal is in principle possible, only one is exploited for linguistic purposes: in other words, in situations where the grammar imposes a particular choice of perspective. Such usages are certainly conventional, but they are not arbitrary, and if we accept the view that meaning embraces construal, then we must conclude that they are motivated semantically.

In this section, I will take another look at two such less-than-fully motivated constructions which were discussed in an earlier chapter. My purpose will be to review the motivation for the choice of construal that they require, and show that in both cases, there are good reasons for conventionalizing this particular choice.

The first of these structures is the subjectless construction with a dative experiencer, as in (571).

(571)   *Ani jest nudno/zimno/wygodnie.*
          'Ania (DAT) is bored/cold/comfortable.'

As noted in section 3.6, when the same predicates occur with a nominative NP, the sentence designates objective properties rather than subjective experience. Thus, the use of the dative conveys an important semantic distinction which would otherwise be lost, and although its use results in an a structure with very unusual grammatical properties – one which lacks a subject – the need to preserve an important semantic contrast overrides the general cognitive tendency to choose one prominent participant as the clausal trajector.

The second example involves structures with nominative-dative verbs such as *przypomnieć sobie* 'to remember' (lit., 'to remind oneself'), *wyobrazić sobie* 'to imagine' (lit., 'to present to oneself in the imagination'), *uświadomić sobie, uzmysłowić sobie uprzytomnić sobie, zdać sobie sprawę,* all meaning 'to realize' ('to make oneself realize'). The double case-marking in these constructions, I argued in section 3.7, reflects the dual role of experiencer (creator and perceiver of image). The fact that all of these verbs except *wyobrazić sobie* 'to imagine' have ditransitive counterparts provides additional support for this explanation.

An objection could be raised at this point. I have claimed in various places throughout chapter 3 that many other verbs fit both the nominative and the dative category, and yet they are not given a nominative-dative construal. For example, it is undeniable that verbs such as *rozumieć* 'to understand', *widzieć* 'to see', *wiedzieć* 'to know', *kochać* 'to love' strongly evoke sphere of awareness, but they do not occur in the construction with *sobie*. The reason for this is that, with these verbs, the experiencer cannot be seen as playing two distinct roles. Therefore, we are justified in maintaining that the formal contrast reflects a difference in the way these situations are conceptualized.

We might conclude the discussion in the last two sections by stating that linguistic form is "arbitrary" only to the extent that it is impossible to predict which of the myriads of possible relationships will actually be lexicalized (or grammaticalized) in any given language. However, given a specific construal of a situation, the properties of the corresponding linguistic structures fall out automatically. Moreover, although construal is to a certain extent conventional, the coding decisions "frozen" in the grammar are motivated semantically.

7.6. Final remarks

Most contemporary linguistic theories see case as a purely grammatical phenomenon. Case inflections, it is widely claimed, are meaningless endings which are either required in certain structural positions or governed by particular lexical items. Elaborate syntactic machinery is postulated in order to ensure that the endings appear where required, and when all else fails, diacritic features are called to the rescue. Little attention is paid to meaning, and even less to conceptualization: it is held to be purely coincidental that a particular verb should govern a particular case, or that a semantic contrast hinges on the choice of one case form rather than another.

I hope that the preceding pages of this monograph have provided ample evidence that a purely formal approach simply will not do the job: it cannot even specify the range of linguistic contexts in which the dative can occur, let alone provide an explanation of why a language should use the same form in such widely divergent grammatical contexts. In contrast, the approach proposed here accounts for both the meaning and the syntax of dative constructions, and elucidates the sometimes subtle relationship between the two. It allows a unified account of "free", "ethic", and "governed" datives, and of dative nominals in various structures (one-, two-, and three-argument constructions, as well as datives in constructions with semantically incorporated patients). It describes the interplay of linguistic and general knowledge in interpreting sentences with datives and shows how linguistic convention and the speaker's communicative intention co-determine the final shape of the utterance. Last but not least, it relates the semantic structure proposed as the meaning of the dative case to cultural concepts such as the notion of personal sphere and the craftsman and the mental arena models of the mind.

Notes

1. One of the most extreme versions of this approach is the treatment of case in Government and Binding theory. In GB, there are two strategies for assigning case, structural case assignment and inherent case assignment. Structural case assignment is the default strategy: the verb assigns the accusative case to the NP it governs, and INFL assigns nominative case to the subject NP. Inherent case is supposed to cover all the exceptions: some verbs and prepositions are subcategorized to occur with a particular case, and obligatorily assign that case. For example, *unikać* 'to avoid', obligatorily assigns GEN, *zazdrościć* 'to be jealous, to envy' assigns DAT and GEN, *zostać* 'to become' assigns INST, and so on.

    It is not my intention to indulge in a critique of the GB approach to case; suffice it to say that the whole theory is based almost entirely on data from minimally inflected languages such as English, and therefore encounters innumerable problems when confronted with a language that actually has case. As Brecht and Levine (1986) observe, even the relatively straightforward contrast between the accusative and the locative in prepositional phrases in Russian (*On xodil v park* 'He walked into the park (ACC)' vs. *On xodil v parke* 'He walked around in the park (LOC)', where the accusative coveys a directional meaning and the locative indicates that the process designated by the verb takes place within the boundaries of the object designated by the noun) is a problem for an approach that sees cases as meaningless labels attached to nouns. Blake (1994:63) points out another difficulty that this approach encounters: although the abstract case of GB theory and morphological case should not conflict, they sometimes do, even in English. From the perspective adopted in this study, the main problem with the GB approach is that it has nothing to say about the semantics of case and the relationships between a particular case, the constructions in which is occurs, and the lexical meaning of the governing verb. It is thus simply irrelevant for the present discussion. (See also section 5.5 and footnote 63.)

2. There are a number of critical evaluations of Jakobson's classic paper on case in Russian, and I shall not labor the point here (see e.g. Blake 1994, Chvany 1986, Smith 1987, van Schooneveld 1986, Wierzbicka 1980). Localist treatments of case include Anderson 1971 and 1987, Kempf 1978, Miller 1974, and Smith 1985, 1987, 1989 and 1992. See section 7.1.2 for a discussion.

3. See Janda 1986 for a similar discussion of the failure of these two approaches in defining another polysemous category – perfectivizing prefixes in Russian.

4. The proposed arrays of "deep" cases ranged in number from 3 to 30 (Tarvainen 1987).

5. For a more detailed discussion of the weaknesses of the case grammar approach, see Mellema 1974 and Dąbrowska 1987.

6. Cognitive linguistics maintains that grammar, morphology and the lexicon form a continuum of linguistic organization and that the same principles apply in all three areas.

7. Note that by recognizing the role of construal in human cognition, cognitive linguistics can offer notional definitions of grammatical categories. Thus, a noun designates a "thing", defined as "a region in some domain"; a verb designates a process, ("a relation with a positive temporal profile"). See Langacker 1987a: 183-274 for details.

8. These conventions are sometimes violated, however, as the following example from Pelletier (cited in Wierzbicka 1988: 507) illustrates:

    (i) [Mother termite about son] *Johnny is very choosy about his food. He will eat book, but he won't touch shelf.*

9. Passive clauses are thus "unnatural" in that what is objectively the most salient entity is not given trajector status. Subjectively, however, the passive subject *is* the more prominent participant: *Michael's teddy bear was stolen by the man next door* is only acceptable as an alternative to *The man next door stole Michael's teddy bear* when the speaker is more interested in what happened to the teddy bear than in what the man did. In other words, by choosing the passive construction the conceptualizer imposes a particular perspective on the event described. The choice of the patient as subject in the passive clause is not unlike other unusual trajector choices discussed earlier in this chapter – see examples (5) and (6)-(8).

10. However, prototypical subjects *are* heads of the profiled portion of the action chain. This generalization is easily captured in a cognitive account: the head is simply a local schema in the network of values of the grammatical category 'subject', probably one that is more deeply entrenched than the more abstract superschema.

11. Actually, even this more abstract characterization is not general enough to cover all direct objects. See Langacker 1987b, 1991a and 1991b for a discussion of other problem cases and an even more general formulation.

12. This is the position advocated in Taylor 1996. In Taylor's words, case markers are "morphemes which profile a highly schematic thing, construed

in terms of a relation with some other participant(s) in a situation" (1996: 107). The other option would be to assume that the profile of the case ending is relational. Since the composite expression – the noun stem plus affix combination – clearly has a nominal profile, this solution would require the additional assumption that the stem rather than the affix is the profile determinant. Thus case inflections would emerge as somewhat anomalous, since usually a morphologically complex expression inherits its profile from the affix, not the stem.Taylor (1996: 102ff) presents further arguments against this position.

13. This sense of the continuing relevance of a past action or event that the dative conveys is similar the meanings evoked by the perfect tenses in English. Therefore, the translations which follow make frequent use of the present perfect.

14. The term "personal sphere" is borrowed from Wierzbicka (1988), who in turn borrowed it from Bally. She uses it in a much narrower sense to refer to what I call here the "air bubble" around the body. Other linguists have used similar terms to refer to related concepts. Rudzka-Ostyn (1992) speaks of the *domain of control* and the *domain of responsibility/interest;* Janda (1993) of a *sphere of control,* Kuryłowicz (1964) of a *sphere of competence/interest,* and Langacker of the *recipient's dominion.* It will be useful to have a general term covering all these more specific notions, and since Wierzbicka's is the most neutral, I will use it in this wider sense. I will also use the expression "sphere of influence" to refer to a part of the personal sphere (see below).

15. I am using the term "evoke" in the frame-semantic sense (as in Fillmore 1975, 1978).

16. For a discussion of the role of the scope of predication, see Langacker 1987a.

17. This use of the dative contrasts with the use of the preposition *dla* 'for' with the genitive, which conveys the meaning 'for X's sake'. Thus, (70a) and (70b) differ in meaning from (i) and (ii) below:

(i) *Krystyna   odrobiła lekcje   dla Oli.*
   Krystyna:NOM did   homework:ACC for Ola:GEN
   'Krystyna did her homework for Ola/for Ola's sake.'

(ii) *Krystyna   otworzyła drzwi   dla Oli.*
    Krystyna:NOM opened   door:ACC for Ola:GEN
    'Krystyna opened the door for Ola's sake.'

Dla beneficiaries are different from dative beneficiaries in that the agent's action does not directly affect their potency: Krystyna's actions in (i)-(ii) neither enable Ola to carry on with her own plans nor free her from doing something she would otherwise have to do herself. See section 5.1 for further discussion.

18. *Kazać* 'to tell [to do something]' and *polecić* 'to direct', are also speech-act verbs, and imply the presence of an addressee. Since addressees are normally expressed by a dative nominal, this use is multiply motivated.

19. These usages are multiply motivated as well, since the dative NP is also the addressee of an act of communication – cf. note 18.

20. That is to say, these constructions do not contain a nominative NP which controls verb agreement, and are traditionally regarded as subjectless. It is possible, however, that they should be analyzed as having non-participant trajectors. See section 3.1.2 for a brief discussion.

21. See Lakoff 1987, Lakoff and Johnson 1980 and Sweetser 1984 and 1990 for a discussion of this metaphor.

22. The use of the dative with *podpowiadać* 'to prompt [another student in class with the correct answer]' is also partially motivated by the fact that it is a verb of helping as well as a verb of communication.

23. The process of replacing the dative by prepositional constructions has continued throughout the history of the language right up to the present day. See Buttler 1976.

24. That *przy-* is an allative prefix is evident from the following data:

    (i) *Magda   przybiegła   do domu.*
        Magda:NOM towards-ran to house:GEN
        'Magda came home running.'

    (ii) *Przybliżył   gazetę   do oczu.*
         towards-he drew closer newspaper:ACC to eyes:GEN
         'He brought the papers closer to his eyes.'

    (iii) *Do Krakowa   przybyło   wielu   rycerzy.*
          to Cracow:GEN towards-were many knights:GEN
          'Many knights came to Cracow.'

25. It is worth noting that formerly the group of "directional" mental predicates which governed the dative also included *cieszyć się* 'to be happy about something', *radować się* 'to rejoice about something', *zdumiewać się* 'to be surprised at something' (Buttler 1976:156). This provides further evidence

that the narrowing of the uses of the dative that has been observed over the centuries (cf. Pisarkowa 1984, Buttler 1976) can be attributed to the shifting of the category center away from the allative prototype (see below for further discussion).

26. For an explanation of the concepts of abstract motion and subjectivity, see Langacker 1983, 1986, 1987a, 1990a, 1991a, and 1991b.

27. However, Rudzka-Ostyn (1992), drawing on Langacker's (1987a, 1987b) notion of action chain, proposes a basically allative characterization of the Polish dative. In her account, stative predicates profile abstract motion. See section 7.1.5 for a discussion.

28. According to Kuryłowicz, "the dat. is genetically nothing else than an offshoot of the loc. with personal nouns. Persons are both physical objects and centers of a sphere of competence or interest" (1964: 190-191). In other words, it was the specialization of the dative to mark the center of the personal sphere that triggered the split in the first place, and hence the dative must have been primarily the exponent of this fairly abstract meaning from the very beginning, well before Indo-European split up into the major branches. The term "allative", then, must be interpreted as referring to a fairly abstract schema which subsumed goal, recipient and other well-established uses such as the dative of purpose as special cases.

29. That is to say, the purely allative use is severely restricted. As indicated earlier, a number of uses of the dative (e.g. 'recipient', 'beneficiary') can be subsumed under the allative schema, but these are also instantiations of the target person schema.

30. The semantic nuances associated by the ethic dative are virtually impossible to convey in another language. The reader should treat all the translations in this section as very rough approximations.

31. (145b) could also mean that the lipstick belongs to the speaker. Under this interpretation, the use of the dative is motivated by the fact that one's possessions belong to one's sphere of influence.

32. (157-159) would still be interpretable if presented out of context; to make sense out of them, however, one has to *assume* a very close emotional link between the speaker and the intended addressee.

33. I will use the term "target" to refer to any participant acted on by the agent or affected by the process designated by the verb – in other words, as a cover term for target person, patient, and theme.

34. See Langacker 1987a for a detailed discussion of the role of figure-ground organization in language.

35. This analysis was inspired by Van Oosten's (1977) and Lakoff's (1977) discussions of patient-subject constructions in English. Polish differs from English in that it allows explicit mention of the instigator of the process designated by the verb by means of a dative nominal – hence the label "dative patient-subject".

36. The semantic contribution of *się* is briefly discussed in the next subsection (3.1.2).

37. Constructions with *się,* then, are less transitive than transitives but more transitive than intransitives, and can be regarded as a kind of middle voice. It is worth noting in this connection that the account suggested here is quite similar to Manney's (1990) description of the Greek middle. Manney also argues that the contrast between active and middle is a contrast in the degree of transitivity, and suggests that "mental experience events are encoded by middle as opposed to active voice verbs if the conceptualized event instantiates a schema with either a defocused initial or terminal endpoint" (229).

38. For a discussion of the intermediate status of the experiencer role, see Rozwodowska 1989, Smith 1985, 1987: 345ff, 1992 and Janda 1993.

39. For a brief summary of the literature, see Schenker 1985.

40. In earlier work (Dąbrowska 1994b) I have referred to this model as the "homunculus model".

41. Recall the similarities in the distribution of dative nominals and locative/directional prepositional phrases (section 2.2.9, examples (100-102) and section 2.4 example (172)).

42. Note that the embedded clause in (213-215) can be replaced by a pronoun which is undeniably the subject:

   (i) *Michałowi   coś   się   śniło.*
   Michał:DAT something:NOM INTR it dreamed
   'Michał had a dream.'

   The trajector status of the locative expressions in (216-218) is rather more problematic, though the fact that they cannot be left out could perhaps be considered corroborating evidence. For a brief discussion of setting-subject constructions, see section 1.2.4.

43. Although some speakers accept (236b), most find it less acceptable than the (a) sentences. However, the negative counterpart of (236b) is perfectly acceptable (cf. (i); the objects are genitive rather than accusative because the verb is negated):

(i) *Magdzie nie chce się pracować/pisać wierszy/*
    Magda:DAT not it wants INTR work/ write poems:GEN/
    oglądać telewizji.
    watch television:GEN
    'Magda doesn't feel like working/writing poetry/watching television.'

Moreover, the dative construal also seems appropriate when the sentence expresses surprise:

(ii) *Że też ci się chce tak harować!*
     that EMPH you:DAT INTR it wants so slave away
     'What on earth are you slaving away like that for?'

(iii) *Że też ci się chce pisać te wierszydła!*
      that EMPH you:DAT INTR it wants write these horrible poems
      'Whatever makes you want to write these horrible poems!'

It is unclear why this should be so.

44. Some speakers also allow the dative with *zasmakować*; however, the nominative is the preferred option.

45. The (b) sentences also differ from their dative analogues in that the verb *być* is followed by an adjective rather than an adverb.

46. Freud's use of the terms *ego* and *id* is an interesting example of this identification with the rational aspect of the mind and dissociation from the irrational. I am not suggesting that the folk theory of mind incorporates psychoanalytic notions, but merely observing that in this as well as in many other instances, the expert theory appears to have been inspired by a folk theory.

47. The processes designated by these verbs also have externally ascertainable correlates (behaviors such as laughing or crying, certain characteristic gestures and facial expressions, etc.), which provides additional motivation for the use of the accusative.

48. *Donieść* 'to inform' (lit. 'to bring to'), *podać do wiadomości* 'to make known' (lit. 'to give to knowledge'), and *dać znać* 'to let know' (lit. 'to give

know') also take dative addressees, but this is primarily motivated by the grammatical properties of their basic transfer senses.

49. A non-contradictory interpretation of (296) is in principle possible, but it would involve assuming that the speaker had learned how to open the lock, forgot it, and now needs to be taught again.

50. Note that other verbs which designate an act of giving a name or title, such as *tytułować* 'to entitle, give a title', *chrzcić* 'to christen', and *mianować* 'to nominate' also govern the accusative case.

51. Perhaps it would have been more felicitous to say "inanimate" rather than "non-human". Whether or not one credits animals with a sphere of awareness depends, of course, on one's beliefs, but it seems safe to say that it is a prototypically human property.

52. An earlier version of this section appeared as "How to talk about bodily experience: The role of construal in determining the choice of case category" in Rosemary Hunt and Ursula Phillips (eds.), *Muza Donowa. A Celebration of Donald Pirie's Contribution to Polish Studies,* Astra Press, Nottingham, 1996.

53. This may be considered an instance of what Gazdar (1979: 56) calls scalar implicature: by not stating that the whole participant was affected, one conversationally implicates that the whole participant was not affected, just as saying *Some of the students passed the exam* implicates *Not all of the students passed the exam.*

54. It is, however, perfectly normal in English, which shows once again that the choice of construal is often determined by linguistic convention. The acceptability of the genitive in English is presumably due to the fact that the language lacks the dative alternative, and hence the special implications of the choice of the possessive construal do not arise (cf. note 53).

55. Notice that the default interpretation of *po-* in *Piotr podrapał Roberta* 'Piotr scratched Robert' is 'change of state', not 'limited duration'.

56. It would still be possible to use (333a) even if Kasia became completely naked as a result of the action – i.e. if she had been wearing nothing but the blouse. However, the verb itself does not specify that the passive participant became naked as a result of the action.

57. It could be argued that the semantic characterization of the verb *zaplombować* 'to fill (a cavity)', discussed in section 4.3.3, also specifies a default landmark (a cavity in a tooth). However, most people have many

teeth and only one (if that!) beard; therefore, the semantic description of *zaplombować* can only specify a range of possible landmarks rather than *the* landmark. Moreover, the prefix *za-* requires a landmark that can be covered/filled, and the filled object is definitely a tooth rather than the whole person. Therefore, the prefix also "votes" for accusative marking on *ząb* 'tooth'. See Dąbrowska (1996) for a discussion of how perfectivizing prefixes affect the combinatorial properties of verbs.

58. (357) differs from the sentences describing bodily sensations not only in that it has a true agent, but also in the case marking on the part of the body: it is accusative (*w bok*) rather than locative (*w boku*). This difference is due to the fact that (357) describes a process which involves the transmission of energy from the nominative to the accusative participant – a relationship which is clearly directional, whereas (347) describes a stative relationship. The contrast, therefore, is analogous to that between the locative and the directional prepositional phrase in *leżeć na stole* 'to be on the table (LOC)' and *wskoczyć na stół* 'to jump onto the table (ACC)'.

59. A simpler way of expressing these generalizations would be to say that the experiencer is accusative when the verb is transitive and dative when the verb is intransitive. This formulation, however, is deceptively simple, because transitivity itself is a matter of construal, and hence depends on linguistic convention (see Rice 1987). For example, a bodily process experienced as pain is given a transitive construal in Polish (*Boli mnie stopa* lit. 'My foot hurts me') and an intransitive one in English (*My foot hurts*).

60. For example, let us suppose that Dorota is Piotr's mother and Piotr has long hair which Dorota disapproves of, and she constantly tells him to have it cut. If, after months of constant nagging, Piotr finally gives in, one could, in principle, describe the event by uttering (372). In this usage, it is not just the hair, but also Piotr and the whole action which is construed as taking place in Dorota's personal sphere – her sphere of influence, to be exact.

61. Because the dative and the *dla* phrase differ in meaning, they can appear side by side in the same sentence:

    (i) *Dalila   obcięła włosy   Samsonowi   dla Filistynów.*
        Delilah:NOM cut   hair:ACC Samson:DAT for Philistines:GEN
        'Delilah cut Samson's hair for the Philistines.'

62. See Kalisz and Kubiński 1995 for a cognitive analysis of this contrast in Polish, and Smith 1987 for a discussion of an analogous distinction in German. Kalisz and Kubiński describe the contrast as one of perfectivity/imperfectivity: if the verb is perfective (in the Langackerian sense, not the traditional grammar sense) the preposition takes an accusative

object; if it is imperfective, the object is locative. However, this description is not fully adequate, since many perfective verbs require the locative:

(i) *Piotr   usiadł   na ławce.*
    Piotr:NOM sat down on bench:LOC
    'Piotr sat down on the bench.'

63. Of course such theories could be rescued by stipulating that there are two prepositions, na_1 and na_2, each of which governs just one case, and which happen to be homophonous. The problem with this is that there is not just one preposition which exhibits this contrast, but seven: *na* 'on', *w* 'in', *przed* 'in front of', *za* 'behind', *(po)nad* 'over, above', *pod* 'under', and *między* 'between', which makes the homophony solution rather less appealing.

64. In contemporary Polish *ku* + DAT has been nearly entirely replaced by the periphrastic expressions *w kierunku/w stronę* 'in the direction of'. Example (393) has a strongly archaic ring to it.

65. *Wbrew* does seem to require the hypothetical and the real course of events to be diametrically opposed: it is not enough for them to be merely different. For example, it would be odd to say

    (i) *Wbrew temu, co myślisz, Ania ma jedno dziecko.*
        'Contrary to what you think, Ania has got one child.'

    if the addressee thought she had at least three or four. Without any context, the best-sounding sentences with *wbrew* are those in which the main clause is negated, as in

    (ii) *Wbrew temu, co myślisz, Piotr nie ukradł tych pieniędzy.*
         'Contrary to what you think, Piotr didn't steal the money.'

    An affirmative version of the same sentence would presuppose that the addressee thinks that Piotr *didn't* steal the money, and would normally require contrastive stress on the main verb. An affirmative version with heavy stress on some other sentence element (for example on *Piotr*) would require a context in which only two individuals, say Piotr and Marek, could have stolen the money and the addressee believes that it was Marek who did it. In this context, saying that Piotr is the thief amounts to denying Marek's culpability.

66. For cognitivist work on *have*, see Brugman 1988, 1996, Carey 1994, 1996, Langacker 1993 and Taylor 1996: 341ff. For a cognitive treatment of 'external NP' constructions, see Cook 1989.

218 *Notes*

67. The verb *get* exhibits a very similar, though not identical, range of senses. However, with *get,* the situation is complicated by the fact that its profile also includes a schematic source of the possessed object. Moreover, *get* also has a whole family of 'become' senses (e.g. *He got angry*) which do not evoke the personal sphere at all.

68. The subject need not be human in sentences such as

    (i)   *The carpet has had a wash.*

    Such usages, however, are instantiations of a different construction, since the subject nominal is the *patient* rather than the agent of the action. Moreover, they are subject to a number of restrictions which are rather difficult to pin down. For example, it is not clear why the following sentences should be judged less felicitous than (i):

    (ii) ? *The carpet has had a dry.*
    (iii) ? *The fork has had a wash.*
    (iv) ? *The carpet had a wash last Tuesday.*

    The sentences appear to work best when the process is one in which it is normal for humans to participate as patients and when the patient is more or less human-sized. This would suggest that such usages are best treated as extensions of an established usage (i.e. the passive interpretation of sentences such as *John has had a wash*) only partially sanctioned by the *have a N* schema. See also note 72 for similar comments about the causative *have.*

69. Wierzbicka also mentions other differences between *have a fall* and *fall.* Although both presumably refer to unintentional actions, only the former must be initiated by the subject participant. If, as a result of Bill pushing him, Harry ends up with his face in the mud we can say that *Harry fell,* but not that *Harry had a fall.* The light verb construction also tends to play down the subject's responsibility for the event. If a horse throws off a rider and you want to comment on the rider's lack of skill, you might say *He fell off his horse;* if you were to express sympathy, however, you are more likely to say *He has had a fall* (see Wierzbicka 1988:336). This closely parallels the use of the dative to refer to "unlucky instigators" and other "innocent agents" (cf. the discussion of the dative patient-subject construction in Polish in section 3.1.1).

70. Wierzbicka does offer an explanation, but it is rather lame, to say the least. She suggests that *have* has two related functions: "in a sentence with two arguments, it converts a predication about the object into an (implicit) predication about the subject; in a sentence with one argument, it expands one simple (explicit) predication into a composite one; in both cases, it

implies something about the subject, over and above what is said explicitly" (Wierzbicka 1988: 346). In other words, she argues, *have* instructs the addressee to "look for a hidden predication about the subject" (347). In the case of the *have a* N construction, the hidden predication is that the subject experienced something. As we have seen, it is true that *Max had a swim* implies not only that Max swam, but also that he found, or was hoping to find, the swimming enjoyable. What Wierzbicka's account does not explain is why this "hidden predication" should have something to do with the subject participant's subjective experience and not, for example, with how fast he performed the action or his marital status.

71. Thus the semantic effect of adding *have* and converting the verb to a noun is similar to the effect of adding the reflexive dative pronoun *sobie* to an activity verb. (See section 2.3.4 for a discussion of this construction.) Wierzbicka notes the similarity, but is unable to explain why it should arise.

72. However, *have* causatives with inanimate subjects appear more acceptable when the verb is in the progressive form. Consider the following data:

(i) *The ice had the car skid.
(ii) ?The ice had the car skidding.
(iii) ??The cold had us running.
(iv) (?) The cold had us running upstairs to get our sweaters.
(v) (?) All that beer had Gordon running to the toilet.

I suspect that this usage is parasitic on the established construction: speakers accept some of these sentences because they resemble *have* causatives with human subjects; however, they are not fully sanctioned by the causative *have* schema, which requires a human subject. This would account for the extreme variability in acceptability judgements for these sentences. In an informal survey conducted among friends and colleagues, I obtained highly inconsistent judgements from different informants (the judgements given above represent the best consensus, and in some instances no more than an arithmetical average), and even from the same informants on different occasions; very few sentences were accepted without qualification. Moreover, it appears that in some instances at least my respondents personified the inanimate causer. For example, one speaker rejected (ii) but accepted (iv); when asked why, he explained that the latter is "OK because the cold can creep up on you". See also note 68 for similar observations about inanimate nouns in the light verb construction.

I have no ready explanation for why the sentences work with the progressive but not with the plain form of the verb: presumably it has something to do with the fact that the progressive requires that the causal influence and the process caused occur at the same time, and inanimate objects can normally exert causal influence only while they are in contact with the causee.

73. See also Chomsky 1965: 21-22 and Palmer 1987:164-165 for a discussion of the ambiguity of this construction.

74. Langacker notes these overtones of control or "potential for interaction", but claims that they are vestiges of the earlier concrete meaning of 'grasp, hold' which have not been entirely bleached out.

75. It should be stressed, however, that these differences are not as clear-cut as the main verb/auxiliary verb dichotomy might lead us to expect. It is well known that in some varieties of English (notably British English) the main verb *have* does not require *do* support in questions, negatives and emphatic sentences when it designates stative situations such as possession. However, *do* is necessary when *have* is used in a dynamic sense to describe experiences, achievements, etc. Compare:

(i) *Has she a book? No, she hasn't.*
(ii) **Had she a walk? *No, she hadn't.*

Moreover, only stative forms can be contracted. Thus, while (iii) is perfectly normal, "it would be very curious", according to Palmer (1987: 164), to say (iv).

(iii) *We've plenty of money.*
(iv) ? *We've a walk every day.*

However, this distinction is rather more fuzzy than Palmer makes it out to be. (iv) may be curious, but the contracted form is more acceptable in (v).

(v) (?) *We've a long walk every day before breakfast.*

76. Some of the special properties of *have to V* are presumably ascribable to the presence of *to*, which contributes the idea of futurity (cf. Brazil 1995) and possibly of a force pushing the trajector towards the action. Sweetser's (1984, 1990) analysis of obligation as a "compelling force driving a subject towards an act" (1990: 52) comes to mind here. However, it is clear that the construction is not fully compositional.

77. Langacker (1990, 1991a: 213ff) introduces the notions of *subjectivity* and *objectivity*, which

> ... pertain to the construal relation between a conceptualizer and the conception he entertains, i.e. between the subject and object of

conception.... With respect to this relation, an entity is said to be construed subjectively to the extent that its participation is confined to the subject role, and objectively when it is limited to the object role.... *Subjectification* is a semantic shift or extension in which an entity originally construed objectively comes to receive a more subjective construal. (1991a: 215).

The type of subjectification relevant here involves "reorienting" some facet of the profiled relationship from the "objective axis" to the "subjective axis" – in other words, (part of) what was originally the relationship between the trajector and the landmark is now a relationship between the profile and the ground. See the sources cited earlier for an in-depth discussion.

78. For a discussion of event integration and the concomitant syntactic integration of the clauses describing them, see Givón 1993 (chapter 7).

79. Palmer notes, however, that the present perfect is perfectly acceptable if the discourse topic is "Brighton" and "plays":

   (i) *Brighton has been visited by Queen Victoria.*
   (i') *Even Queen Victoria has visited Brighton.*
   (ii) *A lot of plays have been written by Shakespeare.*
   (ii') *Shakespeare has written most of the best plays we know.*

   This can be attributed to the fact that the personal sphere of a backgrounded participant is less salient, which favors the fully subjectified interpretation of the perfect.

80. Actually, (444) seems better than (443), presumably because authors – particularly outstanding authors like Shakespeare – are conventionally considered immortal.

81. Palmer (1987: 52) notes that the auxiliary is often stressed when the perfect receives an experiential interpretation. This could be regarded as an indication that it still resembles the content verb in certain respects – in other words, that this particular use is intermediate between the content verb and the fully grammaticalized auxiliary.

82. For a discussion of the *uchi/soto* distinction in Japanese culture, see Lebra 1976, Hendry 1987, and Rosenberger 1992.

83. For a summary of the linguistic consequences of social group membership, see Loveday 1986a and 1986b.

84. The rules for the correct use of honorifics are actually much more complex than this, since there are a number of complicating factors, including social status and gender. However, group membership is a crucial factor in determining the choice of the appropriate form. See Loveday 1986a, 1986b for a discussion.

85. In a now classic description of Japanese particles, Kuno (1973) calls this use of *ga* the "exhaustive listing" *ga*. Since the "exhaustive listing" *ga* is used after the questioned element in *wh*-questions and to signal the new information in answers to *wh*-questions, and since in other discourse contexts it appears to have a function similar to the cleft construction in English (it is usually translated with a cleft), I can see no great harm in calling it a focus marker, even though it cannot be used to mark *any* focused constituent.

86. This is a pretty desperate move for someone who believes in autonomous syntax, since restrictions on topicalization also have purely syntactic repercussions. For example, there appears to be a very intimate link between restrictions on topicalization and restrictions on relativization (see Kuno 1973, McCawley 1976).

87. As it stands, this description will not cover all topics – for example, it will not cover what McCawley (1976) calls "range topics", such as *bukka-wa* 'prices' in (i):

   (i) *Bukka-wa Nyuu-yooku-ga takakatta.*
   'As for prices, New York was high.'

   However, given that *Nyuu-yooku* in this example metonymically stands for 'prices in New York', it is not difficult to see that this particular usage is a special case of condition (2), since the set of prices in New York is a subset of the set of all prices.

88. With *wakaru*, the object of experience (English) can also take the accusative particle *o*, which yields a normal transitive construction:

   (i) *Tanaka-san-wa eigo-o wakaru.*
   Tanaka-Mr-TOP English-ACC understands
   'Mr Tanaka understands English.'

   The preferred usage, however, is with *ga*, except when conscious effort is implied on the part of the experiencer, as in

(ii) *Jakku-wa Rinda-no   kimochi-o/*ga*
Jack-TOP Linda-GEN feeling-ACC/*NOM
wakar-oo   to   suru.
understand-VOL COMP do
'Jack tries to understand Linda's feelings.'

The distinction is similar to the contrast in Polish between the use of the nominative to refer to the experiencer with mental processes which are construed as agentive and the dative with more passive experiences. See chapter 3.

89. Like *wakaru*, verbs suffixed with *-tai* allow accusative objects, but the nominative is the preferred form in most situations. Consider, however, the following example, taken from Makino and Tsutsui (1986: 444):

    (i) [Situation: The speaker has run five miles.]
    Watashi-wa mizu-ga/*o   nomitai.
    I-TOP   water-NOM/*ACC want to drink
    'I want to drink some water.'

    (ii) [Situation: The speaker has been told by the doctor to drink as much water as possible. He has just downed five pints and can have no more.]
    Watashi-wa mizu-o/?ga   nomitai   ga...
    I-TOP   water-ACC/? want to drink but
    'I want to drink some water but...'

    The variant with *o* is extremely awkward in the first situation, while in the second situation *o* is actually the preferred form. In other words, accusative coding of the object of experience is preferred when the situation involves conscious resolve, while the nominative is more appropriate when the sentence describes a physiological state. The parallels with the use of the dative and the nominative with the Polish *chcieć* 'to want' (section 3.4) are striking.

90. The other option – that of construing mental experience as an action – is rarely resorted to in Japanese, which tends to background the agent even in descriptions of prototypical physical causation (see Ikegami 1984, 1989, 1991). However, see notes 88 and 89 above.

91. It is quite common to construe knowing a language (or any other ability) as having control over an abstract object – hence expressions such as *to master a language, his command of English,* or the Polish *opanować angielski,* which literally means 'to capture (take possession of) English'.

92. For a brief overview of the generativist literature on passives, see Tsujimura 1996.

93. Wierzbicka (1988: 276) cites examples of indirect passives such as

   (i) *Kuruma-wa ressha-ni baa-o hikkakerareta.*
   car-TOP train-DAT bar-ACC pulled off:PASS
   'The train pulled the bumper bar off the car; the car was affected.'

   in which the external NP is inanimate. Such usages, however, are quite exceptional. They seem to work best with nouns referring to complex objects (such as cars) which are often personified (note the ungrammaticality of (ii) below). This suggests that they are best treated as extensions rather than instantiations of the indirect-passive construction.

   (ii) **Teeburu-wa haha-ni hyoomen-o fukareta.*
   table-TOP mother-DAT surface-ACC wiped:PASS
   'Mother wiped the top of the table; the table was affected.'
   (Wierzbicka 1988: 275)

94. Note that English *have* constructions also have semi-locative meanings (cf. the discussion of example (439) above). It was observed in Chapter 2 that Polish datives exhibit certain structural parallels with locative constructions as well.

95. An alternative explanation – not necessarily incompatible with Goldberg's – might be the inherent iconicity of the ditransitive construction: the fact that the patient NP appears immediately beside the recipient NP can be taken to iconically represent the fact that the patient is in the recipient's personal sphere (cf. section 1.2.2).

96. On patterns of polysemy, see Lakoff 1987; on metaphor, see Lakoff and Johnson 1980.

97. In this connection, note the parallels between locatives and personal sphere constructions in Polish (section 2.2.9) and the locative use of *have* in English (see note 94).

98. It seems that these two construals of the agent – as the source of energy for the action or as the center of sphere of potency – are what Ikegami (1984, 1989, 1991) has in mind when he contrasts Japanese, which he calls a *become*-language, with English and other European languages, which he calls *do*-languages. English habitually sees actions as the transfer of energy from an agent to a patient, and tends to impose the action-chain construal even when the event to be described does not involve an agentive participant

(for example by allowing expressions such as *This heat is killing me*). Japanese, in contrast, tends to background the agent even when objectively present. This is most easily accomplished by simply not mentioning the agent: thus where an English speaker would say *X did Y*, the Japanese will often say *Y happened*. However, as Ikegami points out, there are also a number of grammatical constructions which have evolved to this very end. Perhaps the most interesting of these, from our point of view, is the locative construal of the agent in honorific language, where it is particularly important to avoid mentioning the person honored. Thus to describe the annual rice-planting ritual, one might say

(i) *Tennoheika-ni-wa mizukara ine-no nae-o*
emperor-in-TOP personally rice-GEN young plant-ACC
o-ue-ni narimashita.
HON-plant-DAT became: POLITE
'The emperor planted young rice plants.' (Ikegami 1991a: 316)

which literally means something like 'In the emperor, the planting of young rice plants occurred'.

The preceding discussion demonstrates, I hope, that Ikegami's distinction is too hard-and-fast: both construals are possible in both languages, as witnessed by the use of *kara* to mark agents in Japanese and agentive *have* constructions in English. However, English and Japanese do appear to favor different construals: the Japanese have a clear predilection for conceptualizing actions as events unfolding spontaneously in the agent's personal sphere, while speakers of English prefer to see the agent as the source of the activity.

99. The construal underpinning Japanese causative constructions, then, features a personal sphere within a personal sphere: the action is located in the causee's sphere of potency, and the causee, in turn, is within the causer's sphere of potency.

100. In English as well as in many other languages, institution nouns tend to pattern syntactically more like human nouns than like inanimate nouns: for example, they can occur in the "first object" position of the ditransitive constructions (*He gave the museum one of his best paintings*), and they freely take the Saxon genitive (*the museum's collection;* cf. *Hamilton's collection, ??this room's collection*). This, however, is not the case in Japanese. One cannot say in Japanese *The heat made her tired* or *His stupidity infuriates me;* one must say instead something like *Being hot, she is tired* and *I am infuriated as a result of his stupidity*. Because of this tendency to avoid personification, institution nouns are conventionally construed as inanimate objects, not as virtual humans, and occur in grammatical contexts characteristic for non-human nouns.

101. Of course one may very well be affected by the arrival of a letter. However, the verb *przyjść* profiles only the arrival itself, not its possible consequences: it does not even imply that the letter reached its addressee. For example, it would be appropriate to say

  (i) *Do Piotra   przyszedł list.*
      to Piotr:GEN came   letter:NOM
      'A letter has come for Piotr.'

  if the letter arrived at Piotr's apartment while he was away on holiday. If one wanted to state that Piotr actually received the letter (i.e., the fact that it entered Piotr's personal sphere) one would say

  (ii) *Piotr dostał list.*
      'Piotr (NOM) got a letter (ACC).'

  It should also be stressed that the usage exemplified in (i) is rather idiomatic and not very representative of the verb *przyjść*, which normally means 'to arrive on foot'.

102. For a discussion of other localistic treatments of case, as well as the parallels between the traditional localists and localist trends in the cognitive paradigm, see Cienki 1995.

103. This is the analysis that Rudzka-Ostyn (1992) proposes for the corresponding Polish data (see section 7.1.5).

104. Rudzka-Ostyn (1992) and Wierzbicka (1988) suggest that 'recipient' is the prototypical meaning of the dative, and the other values are extensions thereof. My characterization of the prototype is slightly broader (it subsumes the recipient as a special case), but the difference between their definitions and my own is one of focus rather than of substance.

105. This aspect of prototype organization is discussed more fully in Lakoff 1987 and Rosch 1975, and also in my own paper on the linguistic categorization of spatial relations (Dąbrowska 1992). For similar comments about the functionality of prototype organization, see Rosch 1977 and Geeraerts 1988.

106. This state of affairs is quite typical: as Taylor observes, "the overwhelming majority of linguistic signs – lexical items, morphophonemic categories, grammatical constructions ... – exhibit a semantic and/or formal polyvalence which precludes the extraction of a single, overarching schema" (1990: 528).

107. See Geeraerts 1988 for a discussion of the relationship between prototypicality and accessibility to introspection.

Bibliography

Alfonso, Anthony
   1971   "On the 'adversative' passive in Japanese", *Association of Teachers of Japanese, Journal-Newsletter* 8.

Anderson, John
   1971   *A Grammar of case: Towards a localistic theory.* Cambridge: Cambridge University Press.
   1987   "Case grammar and the localist hypothesis", in: René Dirven & Günter Radden (eds.), 103-121.

Bach, Emmon & Robert T. Harms (eds.)
   1968   *Universals in linguistic theory.* New York: Holt, Rinehalt and Winston, Inc.

Bartnicka-Dąbkowska, Barbara, Michał Jaworski & Roxana Sinielnikoff
   1964   *Gramatyka opisowa języka polskiego z ćwiczeniami.* Vol. 2, *Fleksja. Składnia.* Warszawa: Państwowe Zakłady Wydawnictw Szkolnych.

Benni, Tytus, Jan Łoś, Kazimierz Nitsch, Janusz Rozwodowski & Henryk Ułaszyn
   1923   *Gramatyka języka polskiego.* Kraków: Polska Akademia Umiejętności.

Blake, Barry J.
   1994   *Case.* Cambridge: Cambridge University Press.

Brazil, David
   1995   *A Grammar of speech.* Oxford: Oxford University Press.

Brecht, Richard D. & Catherine V. Chvany (eds.)
   1974   *Slavic transformational syntax.* Ann Arbor: University of Michigan.

Brecht, Richard D. & James S. Levine
   1986   "Case and meaning", in: Richard D. Brecht & James S. Levine (eds.), 17-34

Brecht, Richard D. & James S. Levine (eds.)
   1986   *Case in Slavic.* Columbus, Ohio: Slavica Publishers.

Brückner, Aleksander
   1957   *Słownik etymologiczny języka polskiego.* Warszawa: Wiedza Powszechna.

Brugman, Claudia
   1988   The syntax and semantics of have and its complements. [Unpublished Ph.D. dissertation, University of California, Berkeley.]
   1996   "Mental spaces, constructional meaning, and pragmatic ambiguity", in: Gilles Fauconnier & Eve Sweetser (eds.), 29-56.

Buttler, Danuta
1976 *Innowacje składniowe współczesnej polszczyzny.* Warszawa: PWN.

Carey, Kathleen
1994 Pragmatics, Subjectivity and the Grammaticalization of the English Perfect. [Unpublished Ph.D. dissertation, University of California, San Diego.]
1996 "From resultativity to current relevance: Evidence from the history of English and modern Castilian Spanish", in: Adele E. Goldberg (ed.), 31-48.

Cienki, Alan
1995 "Nineteenth and twentieth century theories of case: A comparison of localist and cognitive approaches", *Historiographia Linguistica* XXII, 1/2: 123-162.

Chomsky, Noam
1965 *Aspects of the theory of syntax.* Cambridge, Mass.: MIT Press.

Chvany, Catherine V.
1986 "Jakobson's fourth and fifth dimensions: On reconciling the cube model of case meanings with the two-dimensional matrices for case forms", in: Richard D. Brecht & James S. Levine (eds.), 107-129.

Cole, Peter & Jerrold M. Sadock (eds.)
1977 *Syntax and semantics, Volume 8: Grammatical relations.* New York: Academic Press.

Comrie, Bernard
1976 "The syntax of causative constructions: Cross-linguistic similarities and differences", in: Masayoshi Shibatani (ed.) 1976b, 261-312.
1985 "Causative verb formation and other verb-deriving morphology", in: Timothy Shopen (ed.), 309-348.

Comrie, Bernard & Greville G. Corbett (eds.)
1993 *The Slavonic languages.* London: Routledge.

Cook, Haruko Minegashi
1989 *Schematic values of the Japanese nominal particles* wa *and* ga. Duisburg: L.A.U.D.

Corrigan, Roberta, Fred Eckman & Michael Noonan (eds.)
1989 *Linguistic categorization.* Amsterdam: John Benjamins.

Dąbrowska, Ewa
1987 The semantics of case [Unpublished M.A. Thesis, University of Gdańsk.]
1992 "Potoczność w służbie semantyki -- językowy model relacji przestrzennych w pionie", *Język a kultura.* Vol. 5, *Potoczność w języku i kulturze.* Wrocław: Wydawnictwo Centralnego Programu Badań Podstawowych 08.05 "Polska

kultura narodowa, jej tendencje rozwojowe i percepcja", 61-79.
1994a "Radial categories in grammar: The Polish instrumental case", *Linguistica Silesiana* 15: 83-94.
1994b "Nominative and dative experiencers: Two folk theories of the mind", *Linguistics* 32: 1029-1054.
1996 "The temporal structuring of events. A study of Polish perfectivizing prefixes", in: René Dirven & Martin Pütz (eds.)

Dirven, René & Martin Pütz (eds.)
1996 *The construal of space in language and thought.* Berlin: Mouton de Gruyter.

Dirven, René & Günter Radden (eds.)
1987 *Concepts of case.* Tübingen: Gunter Narr Verlag.

Doroszewski, Witold
1973 *Słownik poprawnej polszczyzny.* Warszawa: PWN.

Farmer, Ann Kathleen
1984 *Modularity in syntax: A study of Japanese and English.* Cambridge, Massachusetts: MIT Press.

Farmer, Ann Kathleen & Chisato Kitagawa (eds.)
1981 *Proceedings of the Arizona Conference on Japanese Linguistics. Coyote papers.* Vol. 2. Tucson: Department of Linguistics, University of Arizona.

Fauconnier, Giles & Eve Sweetser (eds.)
1996 *Spaces, worlds and grammar.* Chicago: Chicago University Press.

Fawcett, Robin P., M. A. K. Halliday, Sydney Lamb & Adam Makkai (eds.)
1984 *The semiotics of culture and language.* Vol. 1, *Language as a social semiotic.* London: Frances Pinter.

Fillmore, Charles
1968 "The case for case", in: Emmon Bach & Robert T. Harms (eds.), 1-88.
1975 "An alternative to checklist theories of meaning", *Proceedings of the annual meeting of the Berkeley Linguistic Society,* 1: 123-131.
1977 "The case for case reopened" in: Peter Cole & Jerrold M. Sadock (eds.), 3-26.
1978 "On the organization of semantic information in the lexicon." *Papers from the Parasession on the Lexicon, Chicago Linguistic Society,* 1-11.

Fillmore, Charles & Beryl T. Atkins
1992 "Toward a frame-based lexicon: The semantics of RISK and its neighbors", in: Adrienne Lehrer & Eva Feder Kittay (eds.), 75-85.

Gazdar, Gerald
  1979 *Pragmatics: Implicature, presupposition and logical form.* New York: Academic Press.
Geeraerts, Dirk
  1988 "Where does prototypicality come from?" in: Brygida Rudzka-Ostyn (ed.), 207-229.
Givón, Talmy
  1993 *English grammar. A function-based introduction.* Vols. 1-2. Amsterdam: John Benjamins.
Goldberg, Adele E.
  1992 "The inherent semantics of argument structure: The case of the English ditransitive construction", *Cognitive Linguistics* 3-1: 37-74.
Goldberg, Adele E. (ed.)
  1996 *Conceptual Structure, Discourse and Language.* Stanford: CSLI Publications.
Górska, Elżbieta (ed.)
  1993 *Images from the cognitive scene.* Kraków: Universitas.
Gropen, Jess, Steven Pinker, Michelle Hollander, Richard Goldberg & Ronald Wilson
  1989 "The learnability and acquisition of the dative alternations in English", *Language* 65: 203-257.
Gunji, Takao
  1987 *Japanese phrase structure grammar: A unification-based approach.* Dordrecht: Reidel.
Haiman, John (ed.)
  1985 *Iconicity in syntax.* (Typological studies in language 6.) Amsterdam: John Benjamins.
Hall, Edward Twitchell
  1959 *The silent language.* New York: Doubleday.
  1977 *Beyond culture.* Garden City: Anchor.
Hendry, Joy
  1987 *Understanding Japanese society.* London: Croom Helm.
Ikegami, Yoshihiko
  1984 "How universal is a localist hypothesis? A linguistic contribution to the study of 'semantic styles' of language", in: Robin P. Fawcett, M. A. K. Halliday, Sydney Lamb & Adam Makkai (eds.), 49-79.
  1989 *What we see when we see 'flying cranes': 'Motion' or 'transition'.* Duisburg: L.A.U.D.
  1991 "'Do-language' and 'become-language': Two contrasting types of linguistic representation" in: Yoshihiko Ikegami (ed.), 285-326.

Ikegami, Yoshihiko (ed.)
1991b   *The empire of signs. Semiotic essays on Japanese culture.* Amsterdam: John Benjamins.

Inoue, Kazuko
1969   *A study of Japanese syntax.* The Hague: Mouton.

Jackendoff, Ray
1993   *Patterns in the mind. Language and human nature.* New York: Harvester Wheatsheaf.

Jäkel, Olaf
1985   "The metaphorical concept of mind: 'Mental activity is manipulation'", in: John R. Taylor & Robert E. MacLaury (eds.), 197-299.

Jakobson, Roman
1958   "Morfologiceske nabljudenija nad slavjanskim skloneniem", in: *American contributions to the Fourth International Congress of Slavists.* The Hague: Gravenhage, 127-156.
[1971]   [reprinted in: *Selected writings II: Words and language* (Second edition). The Hague: Mouton, 154-183].

Janda, Laura A.
1986   *A semantic analysis of the Russian verbal prefixes za-, pere, do-, and ot-.* München: Verlag Otto Sagner.
1993   *A geography of case semantics: The Czech dative and the Russian instrumental.* Berlin: Mouton de Gruyter.

Kalisz, Roman & Wojciech Kubiński
1995   "Prepositions, cases and domains", in: Henryk Kardela & Gunner Person (eds.), 53-65.

Kardela, Henryk & Gunner Person (eds.)
1995   *New trends in semantics and lexicography.* Umeä: University of Umeä Press.

Kempf, Zdzisław
1978   *Próba teorii przypadków.* Vol. 1. Opole: TPN.

Kitagawa, Chisato
1982   "Topic constructions in Japanese", *Lingua* 57: 175-214.

Kumashiro, Toshiyuki
1993   "How the goal can be the source: The semantics of the Japanese dative marker *ni*", *LACUS Forum* 20: 401-417.

Kuno, Susumu
1973   *The structure of the Japanese language.* Cambridge, Massachusetts: MIT Press.

Kuryłowicz, Jerzy
1964   *The inflectional categories of Indoeuropean.* Heidelberg: Winter.

Lakoff, George
1977   "Linguistic gestalts", *Chicago Linguistic Society* 13: 236-286.

1982 *Categories and cognitive models.* (Cognitive Science Report No. 2.) Berkeley: Institute for Cognitive Studies, University of California.
1987 *Women, fire, and dangerous things.* Chicago: Chicago University Press.

Lakoff, George & Mark Johnson
1980 *Metaphors we live by.* Chicago: Chicago University Press.

Langacker, Ronald
1984 "Active zones", *Proceedings of the annual meeting of the Berkeley Linguistics Society* 10: 172-88.
1985 "Observations and speculations on subjectivity", in: John Haiman (ed.), 109-150.
1986 "Abstract motion", *Proceedings of the Annual Meeting of the Berkeley Linguistics Society* 12: 455-471.
1987a *Foundations of cognitive grammar.* Vol. 1, *Theoretical prerequisites.* Stanford, California: Stanford University Press.
1987b *Transitivity, case, and grammatical Rrelations: A cognititve grammar prospectus.* Duisburg: L.A.U.D.
1987c "Grammatical ramifications of the setting/participant distinction", *Proceedings of the Annual Meeting of the Berkeley Linguistics Society* 13: 383-394.
1988 "An overview of cognitive grammar", in: Brygida Rudzka-Ostyn (ed.), 3-48.
1990a "Subjectification", *Cognitive Linguistics* 1: 5-38.
1990b "Settings, participants and grammatical relations", in: Savas L. Tsohatsidis (ed.), 213-238.
1991a *Foundations of cognitive grammar.* Vol. 2, *Descriptive application.* Stanford, California: Stanford University Press.
1991b *Concept, image and symbol. The cognitive basis of grammar.* Berlin: Mouton de Gruyter.
1993 "Reference-point constructions", *Cognitive Linguistics* 4: 1-38.
1995 "Possession and possessive constructions", in: John R. Taylor & Robert E. MacLaury (eds.), 53-79.

Lebra, Takie Sugiyama
1976 *Japanese patterns of behavior.* Honolulu: University of Hawai Press.

Lehrer, Adrienne & Eva Feder Kittay (eds.)
1992 *Frames, fields, and contrasts. New essays in semantic and lexical organization.* Hillsdale, New Jersey: Lawrence Erlbaum Associates.

Loveday, Leo
1986a "Japanese sociolinguistics: An introductory survey", *Journal of Pragmatics* 10: 287-326.
1986b *Explorations in Japanese sociolinguistics.* Amsterdam: John Benjamins.

Makino, Seiichi & Michio Tsutsui
1986   *A dictionary of basic Japanese grammar.* Tokyo: The Japan Times, Ltd.
Manney, Linda
1990   "Mental experience verbs in modern Greek: A cognitive explanation for active versus middle voice", *Proceedings of the annual meeting of the Berkeley Linguistics Society* 16: 229-240.
Martin, Samuel E.
1962   *A reference grammar of Japanese.* New Haven: Yale University Press.
McCawley, James D.
1976   "Relativization", in: Masayoshi Shibatani (ed.) 1976a, 295-306.
Mellema, Paul
1974   "A brief against case grammar", *Foundations of Language* 11: 39-76.
1974   "A localist account of the dative case in Russian", in: Richard D. Brecht & Catherine V. Chvany (eds.) 244-261.
Nilsen, Don Lee Fred
1972   *Toward a semantic specification of deep case.* The Hague: Mouton.
Oehrle, Richard T. & Hiroko Nishio
1981   "Adversity", in: Ann Kathleen Farmer and Chisato Kitagawa (eds.), 163-185.
Palmer, Frank R.
1987   *The English Verb.* (2nd edition.) London: Longman.
1994   *Grammatical roles and relations.* Cambridge: Cambridge University Press.
Ortony, Andrew (ed.)
1979   *Metaphor and thought.* Cambridge: Cambridge University Press.
Paprotté Wolf & René Dirven (eds.)
1985   *The ubiquity of metaphor. Metaphor in language and thought.* Amsterdam: John Benjamins.
Pasich-Piasecka, Agnieszka
1993   "Polysemy of the Polish verbal prefix *prze-*", in: Elżbieta Górska (ed.) 11-26.
Pisarkowa, Krystyna
1984   *Historia składni języka polskiego.* Wrocław: Ossolineum.
Polański, Kazimierz (ed.)
1980   *Słownik syntaktyczno-generatywny czasowników polskich.* Vol. I. Wrocław: Zakład Narodowy im. Ossolinskich.
1984   *Słownik syntaktyczno-generatywny czasowników polskich.* Vol. II. Wrocław: Zakład Narodowy im. Ossolinskich.

1988 *Słownik syntaktyczno-generatywny czasowników polskich.* Vol. III. Wrocław: Zakład Narodowy im. Ossolinskich.

Quirk, Randolf, Sidney Greenbaum, Geoffrey Leech & Jan Svartnik
1985 *A comprehensive grammar of the English language.* London: Longman.

Reddy, Michael
1979 "The conduit metaphor", in: Andrew Ortony (ed.), 284-324.

Rice, Sally
1987 Towards a cognitive model of transitivity. [Unpublished Ph.D. dissertation, University of California, San Diego.]

Rosch, Eleanor
1975 "Cognitive reference points", *Cognitive Psychology* 7: 532-47.
1977 "Human categorization", in: Neil Warren (ed.), 1-49.

Rosenberger, Nancy R. (ed.)
1992 *Japanese sense of self.* Cambridge: Cambridge University Press.

Rozwodowska, Bożena
1989 "Are thematic relations discrete?", in: Roberta Corrigan, Fred Eckman & Michael Noonan (eds.), 115-130.

Rudzka-Ostyn, Brygida
1985 "Metaphoric processes in word formation. The case of prefixed verbs", in: Wolf Paprotté & René Dirven (eds.), 209-241.
1992 "Case relations in cognitive grammar. Some reflexive uses of the Polish dative", *Leuvense Bijdragen* 81: 327-373.

Rudzka-Ostyn, Brygida, (ed.)
1988 *Topics in cognitive linguistics.* Amsterdam: John Benjamins.

Schenker, Alexander M.
1985 "W sprawie się raz jeszcze", *Język polski* 65: 9-23.
1986 "On the reflexive verbs in Russian", *International Journal of Slavic Linguistics and Poetics* XXXIII: 27-41.
1993 "Protoslavonic", in: Bernard Comrie & Greville G. Corbett (eds.), 60-121.

Searle, John R.
1969 [1984] *Speech acts.* Cambridge: Cambridge University Press.

Shibatani, Masayoshi (ed.)
1976a *Syntax and semantics.* Volume 5: *Japanese generative grammar.* New York: Academic Press.
1976b *Syntax and semantics.* Volume 6: *The grammar of causative constructions.* New York: Academic Press.

Shopen, Timothy (ed.)
1985 *Language typology and syntactic description.* Volume 3: *Grammatical categories and the lexicon.* Cambridge: Cambridge University Press.

Smith, Michael B.
1985 "Event chains, grammatical relations, and the semantics of case in German", *Chicago Linguistic Society* 21: 388-407.
1987 The semantics of dative and accusative in German: An investigation in cognitive grammar. [Unpublished PhD dissertation, University of California, San Diego.]
1989 *Cases as conceptual categories: Evidence from German.* Duisburg: L.A.U.D.
1992 "The role of image schemas in German grammar", *Leuvense Bijdragen* 81: 385-410.

Song, Nam Sun
1993 *Thematic relations and transitivity in English, Japanese and Korean.* Honolulu: Center for Korean Studies, University of Hawai'i.

Sweetser, Eve
1984 Semantic structure and semantic change: A cognitive linguistic study of modality, perception, speech acts and logical relations. [Unpublished Ph.D. Dissertation, University of California at Berkeley.]
1990 *From etymology to pragmatics. Metaphorical and cultural aspects of semantic structure.* Cambridge: Cambridge University Press.

Szober, Stanisław
1959 *Gramatyka języka polskiego.* Warszawa: PWN.

Szymczak, Mieczysław (ed.)
1981 *Słownik języka polskiego.* Vol. I. Warszawa: PWN.
1983 *Słownik języka polskiego.* Vol. II. Warszawa: PWN.
1984 *Słownik języka polskiego.* Vol. III. Warszawa: PWN.

Tarvainen, Kalevi
1987 "Semantic cases in the framework of dependency grammar", in: René Dirven & Günter Radden (eds.), 75-102.

Taylor, John R.
1990 "Schemas, prototypes, and models: in search of the unity of the sign", in: Savas L. Tsohatzidis (ed.), 521-34.
1996 *Possessives in English. An exploration in cognitive Grammar.* Oxford: Clarendon Press.

Taylor, John R. & Robert E. MacLaury (eds.)
1995 *Language and the cognitive construal of the world.* Berlin: Mouton de Gruyter.

Topolińska, Zuzanna
1984 *Gramatyka współczesnego języka polskiego. Składnia.* Warszawa: PWN.

Tsohatsidis, Savas L. (ed.)
1990 *Meanings and prototypes. Studies in linguistic categorization.* London: Routledge.

Tsujimura, Natsuko
   1996 *An introduction to Japanese linguistics.* Cambridge, Massachusetts: Blackwell Publishers.

Van Oosten, Jeanne
   1977 "Subjects and agenthood in English", *Chicago Linguistic Society* 13: 459-471.

Van Schooneveld, Cornelis H.
   1986 "Jakobson's case system and syntax", in: Richard D. Brecht & James S. Levine (eds.), 373-385.

Warren, Neil (ed.)
   1977 *Studies in cross-cultural psychology.* Vol. 1. London: Academic Press.

Wierzbicka, Anna
   1980 *The case for surface case.* Ann Arbor: Karoma.
   1988 *The semantics of grammar.* Amsterdam: John Benjamins.

Index

accusative, xi, 1, 3, 12, 14-15, 21, 51, 68, 71, 98-116, 118-121, 124-125, 127, 136, 155, 165, 167, 185, 187, 189, 190-194, 197-198, 200-201, 204-205, 208
action chain, 11-12, 74, 76, 114, 146, 175, 192, 200
active zone, 115-117, 121, 187
addressee, 17, 20, 23, 25, 48, 51, 54, 58-60, 63, 66-68, 99-106, 110, 127, 131, 147, 148, 154, 157, 162, 172, 176-177, 184, 186
affected subject construction, 147, 152-153
agent, 4, 9, 12-14, 16-17, 26, 31, 34-35, 37, 44, 59, 61-64, 66, 69, 71-76, 79-81, 84, 86-87, 89, 93-94, 98, 103, 104, 110, 111, 114, 119, 121, 123, 126-129, 137, 140, 145, 147, 165-168, 170-174, 177-180, 184, 194, 197-202
allative, 49-54, 64, 68, 129, 136, 138, 191, 196, 200
aspect, 106, 108, 118, 145, 152
auxiliary *have*, 150–153

base, 8, 148
benefactive, 127, 147, 155, 169, 178
  See also beneficiary
beneficiary, 35, 51, 54, 127–129, 145, 176, 202
billiard-ball model, 11

case grammar, 4, 14, 201
case in traditional grammar, 1-2, 24, 55, 61, 143, 198
cases,
  Polish, prototypical values of, 198
  Polish, schematic values of, 12, 200
  Polish, uses of, 1-3, 5, 12, 15
  See also nominative, accusative, genitive
causative, 146-148, 153, 165–167, 173-174, 176-179
conduit metaphor, 100
construal, 2, 7-15, 37, 44-45, 47, 74-76, 81, 92, 127, 129, 132, 160, 184, 188, 190, 193, 195-196, 203, 206
  conventionality of, 7–11, 91–92, 97, 115, 124, 140, 203, 205-206
  dative vs. accusative construal of bodily experience, 111, 114-115, 187
  possessive construal of bodily experience, 114-115
  nominative construal of mental experience, 77, 79ff, 184
  dative construal of mental experience, 79ff
  nominative-dative construal of mental experience, 93, 200, 206
  dative vs. accusative construal of addressee, 99ff
  of agent as center of sphere of potency, 178
  of agent as source of energy, 178
context, 133
  role in motivating the dative, 19, 21-23, 30, 59-60, 63, 66, 68, 85, 117, 128, 181-183, 186, 188
conventionalization of implicature, 170
conversational implicature, 53, 103, 129, 134, 169, 185, 204
craftsman model, 77, 79, 207
Czech, 192–195

238 *Index*

dative patient subject construction, 71–73, 174
"deep" case, 4, 14, 202
detransitivizer, 49, 52, 72, 73–76
ditransitive, 94, 95, 130, 176-177, 206

English, 10, 130, 143–153, 159, 166-167, 173–178, 202, 208
epistemic forces, 140
ethic dative, 55-61, 63, 173, 188-189, 194-196, 200-201, 203, 206
experiencer, 14-15, 41-43, 49, 68-70, 75, 77, 79-84, 86, 88-90, 93-97, 115, 119-125, 160-164, 172-173, 184, 192, 195, 201-206
extension, 5-7, 52, 122, 138, 141-142, 152, 178, 180, 191, 196, 198, 200
external NP construction, 154–176

figure, 8-9, 11, 13, 69
figure-worthiness, 13, 69, 80, 96
Fillmore, 2, 4, 8, 64, 189
folk model, 42, 77–79, 82, 97
frame, 8, 64
free dative, 14, 25, 30, 36, 60, 64-68, 193, 194, 206

ga (Japanese particle), 155, 157, 160, 162-165, 167, 176
GB theory (*see* Government-Binding theory)
genitive, xi, 1, 3, 12, 130, 131, 149, 189, 190
German, 191
Goldberg, 130, 176-177
government, 1-2, 25–37, 38–51, 60, 64-66, 68, 99-109, 113, 124, 135, 138, 140, 188, 191-194, 206, 208
Government-Binding theory, 75, 208
grammatical relations, 11–12
    See also subject, object

have a N, 145-146, 176

homonymy, 178
homunculus, 42, 78, 97, 124
    See also mental arena model
honorific, xi, 154, 170, 172, 174

iconicity, 129, 134, 152
idealized cognitive model (ICM), 8
Ikegami, 172
image schema, 5, 189, 192
imagery (*see* construal)
imperative, 56, 58-60, 63, 201
impersonal constructions, xi, 73-75, 200
implicature (*see* conversational implicature, conventionalization of implicature)
indirect participant, 170
invariant (*see* semantic invariant)

Jakobson, 3, 208
Janda, 118, 192-194, 208
Japanese, 10, 15, 154-179

Kitagawa, 156-158, 163
Kuno, 157-158, 162-163
Kuryłowicz, 189

Lakoff, 4, 5, 8, 42, 77, 79, 198, 205
landmark, 8-9, 49, 52, 54, 64, 118, 129, 130, 132, 134, 137, 138, 140, 145, 149, 151, 152, 167, 174, 187
Langacker, 4-8, 10-14, 115, 130, 138, 148-152, 198, 200-202, 205
light verb, 145, 153, 173
linking strategies, 19-20, 25, 66, 133, 135
localistic theories of case, 51, 189-190
locative constructions, 172

mental arena model, 77, 79, 97, 125, 207
metaphor, 5, 6, 12, 41, 45-46, 49-51, 77, 79, 82, 89, 100, 124, 142, 178, 189, 196-198

meteorological phenomena, 75–76
metonymy, 5
Miller, 3, 189, 190-191, 208

network model (*see* semantic network)
nominative, xii, 1, 12, 14-15, 26, 35, 37-38, 50, 60-61, 66, 68-75, 77, 79-88, 91-98, 124, 127, 155, 160, 162, 164-165, 167, 175, 184, 189, 190, 193-195, 198, 200-201, 203-206, 208

object, 1, 11-13, 49, 51, 67, 74, 100-102, 104-106, 124, 145, 155-156, 162-163, 165-167, 175-178, 192-195, 197, 205

Palmer, 147, 153, 173
participant role (*see* semantic role)
participant-setting distinction, 12–14
passive, 12, 71, 172-173, 177, 179, 200
  indirect (adversative) passive, 158, 165, 167–170, 173-174, 178-179
patient, 4, 12, 14, 17, 21-23, 64, 66, 71-75, 98, 101, 114-115, 120, 122, 129, 147, 167, 172, 177, 187, 196--202
perfective, xii, 103, 106, 108, 118
perfectivizing prefixes, 104, 118-119
personal sphere, 16-26, 41, 47, 51-54, 60, 62, 64-69, 73, 83, 89, 92, 99-100, 105, 110-111, 115, 119, 127-133, 135-138, 143, 145-159, 164, 166-168, 170, 172-179, 181, 183, 193-194, 198-200, 207
polysemy, 5, 7, 77, 118, 138, 141-142, 173, 177-178, 202, 208
potency (*see* sphere of potency)
prepositional constructions, 49, 51, 54, 127–142
private sphere, 40, 53, 68, 147
process, 8, 11, 13, 54, 148

profile, 8-9, 11, 30-31, 43, 49, 64, 65, 74, 76, 99, 101, 103-106, 110-111, 115-117, 121, 149, 167, 174, 183, 185
profile-active zone discrepancy, 115–118
Protoslavonic, 49, 52, 54, 136
prototype, 5-6, 23, 26, 37, 93, 99, 120, 126, 136, 170, 180, 188, 191, 193, 195-200, 203

recipient, 25-27, 48, 51, 53-54, 64, 127, 130, 176-178, 180, 195-197
Reddy, 42, 48, 82, 100
reference point construction, 149-151
Rudzka-Ostyn, 4, 118, 195-196
Russian, 3, 10, 189, 191-192, 208

schema, 5, 7, 49, 51-54, 64, 129, 138, 140, 142, 150-151, 153, 169-170, 174, 179, 191-194, 196, 200
schematization, 5, 7
scope of predication, 27, 32, 72, 106
self-determination, 36, 61, 63, 201
semantic extension (*see* extension)
semantic invariant, 3–5
semantic network, 5-7. 54, 138-140, 153, 170-172, 177-179, 195, 200-202
semantic role, 4, 201–203
  See also "deep" case, agent, patient, recipient, target person, experiencer, beneficiary, addressee
setting, 43-44, 75, 79, 134, 156, 158, 172, 193
  See also participant/setting distinction, setting subject construction
setting-subject construction, 12–14, 75
się (*see* detransitivizer)
Smith, 2, 191-193, 208
social status, 56, 108-109, 154, 204

sphere of awareness, 41–48, 53, 66, 68-69, 77, 79-82, 88, 90-91, 95-100, 103, 105-107, 109, 121, 124-126, 132, 134, 145, 147, 160, 164, 172, 184-185, 190, 198, 201, 203, 206
sphere of empathy, 60, 68, 155, 159, 182, 198-199, 201
sphere of influence (*see* sphere of potency)
sphere of potency, 36-38, 68, 73, 137, 140, 151, 164-166, 172, 175, 178, 198, 201
subject, 1, 11-13, 34-35, 50, 66, 69-72, 74, 76- 82, 87-88, 91-94, 96, 125, 145-147, 151-152, 155-156, 158-159, 161-168, 172, 174-175, 200, 205, 208
   See also affected subject construction, setting subject construction, dative patient subject construction
subjectification, 151
subjectless constructions, 43, 75, 76, 81, 92, 205
superschema, 7, 54, 136, 138-139, 142, 170, 172, 200-201
Sweetser, 142
Szober, 2, 55, 198

target person, definition, 16ff
thing, 8, 11, 146, 149, 151-152, 174
topic, 155–164, 172–173, 189
   See also external NP construction
trajector, 8-13, 39-40, 52, 54, 69, 72, 74, 80-81, 89, 92, 95-96, 128, 130, 140, 149, 152, 167, 174-175, 187, 205
transitive construction, 64, 71-73, 161, 163, 176, 192
transitivity, 72-75, 88, 129, 162-163, 167, 175, 191, 194, 196
unlucky agent construction (*see* dative patient subject construction)

wa (Japanese topic particle), 155–164
   See also topic, external NP construction
Wierzbicka, 16, 21-24, 145-146, 180-189